The Great Lakes
Water Wars

The Great Lakes
Water Wars

~

Peter Annin

ISLANDPRESS

Washington • Covelo • London

© 2006 Peter Annin

All rights reserved under International and Pan-American Copyright Conventions. No part of this book may be reproduced in any form or by any means without permission in writing from the publisher: Island Press, 1718 Connecticut Avenue, NW, Suite 300, Washington, DC 20009.

ISLAND PRESS is a trademark of The Center for Resource Economics.

Library of Congress Cataloging-in-Publication data.
Annin, Peter.
  The Great Lakes water wars / Peter Annin.
    p. cm.
  ISBN 1-55963-087-6 (cloth : alk. paper)
    1. Water resources development—Great Lakes. 2. Water-supply—Great Lakes. I. Title.
  HD1695.G69A56 2006
  333.91′630977—dc22   2006009620

British Cataloguing-in-Publication data available.
Printed on recycled, acid-free paper
Text design by Joyce C. Weston
Manufactured in the United States of America
10 9 8 7 6 5 4

But wherever the truth may lie, this much is crystal-clear: our bigger-and-better society is now like a hypochondriac, so obsessed with its own economic health as to have lost the capacity to remain healthy. The whole world is so greedy for more bathtubs that it has lost the stability necessary to build them, or even to turn off the tap. Nothing could be more salutary at this stage than a little healthy contempt for a plethora of material blessings.

—Aldo Leopold, *A Sand County Almanac*

To Meri, Nick, and Reid

~

Contents

Author's Note

WHAT IS A WAR? This book does not allege that warships will once again ply the lower Great Lakes as they did during the War of 1812. Rather, it argues that the Great Lakes region is entering an era of unparalleled water tension. During the last half century, water quality has been the chief environmental obsession in the Great Lakes, including the "biological pollution" caused by exotic invasive species like the sea lamprey and zebra mussel. While water quality and exotics will continue to be serious and pressing regional concerns, increasing attention will focus on water quantity and availability. Water scarcity throughout the world—and even in parts of the Great Lakes region—will put mounting pressure on one of the most abundant freshwater ecosystems on earth. One could argue that the era of Great Lakes water tension has already begun. The question is, are the forty million Canadians and Americans who live in the Great Lakes Basin prepared for it? The Great Lakes governors and premiers have recently unveiled a plan designed to protect the waters of the Great Lakes from diversions and overuse. But water is an emotional issue in the region, and the proposal has caused confusion in many quarters. Much of the debate has been marked by more heat than light, and the discourse about this latest Great Lakes water-management plan is bound to drag on for years.

That plan—and the colorful history that brought it about, as well as the uncertainty of the region's water future—is the focus of this book. Though water issues are sometimes vexing, the public is obligated to understand them because water is the foundation of the ecosystem that keeps humans alive. An abundance of freshwater is the hallmark of the Great Lakes Basin. The lakes are the region's most important and precious natural resource—they define the area's economy, culture, and environment. This book—and its associated website, www.greatlakeswaterwars.com—is designed to help the general public bring the regional water debate into focus. It attempts to engage the citizen in one of the most important environmental issues of our time: the effort to protect the globally significant waters of the Great Lakes for the next one hundred years and beyond.

> *Peter Annin*
> *Madison, Wisconsin*
> *January, 2006*

Prologue

TODAY I STAND on the shores of Lake Superior and I see an intimidating, mercurial freshwater ocean. I see a lake the Ojibwa called Gitchee Gumee—"Big Sea"—and revered like no other. I see a lake whose average annual temperature is just 40 degrees Fahrenheit. Forty degrees. A shipwrecked person floating in such water would be dead in just a few hours. I see a lake whose violent temper sank the *Edmund Fitzgerald*, a 729-foot freighter that disappeared in 1975 in hurricane-force winds and twenty-five-foot waves, sending twenty-nine humbled men to a watery grave. I see a lake so large that she creates her own weather—often changing without warning, catching even the most seasoned sailor off-guard. I see a lake that is no place for charlatans—where there are old sailors and there are brazen sailors, but there are no old, brazen sailors.

Today I stand on the shores of Lake Superior and I see a unique, fragile, cold-water ecosystem. I see the largest surface area of delicious freshwater in the world. I see a lake so deep (more than 1,300 feet) that her steepest underwater canyon is the lowest spot on the North American continent. I see a lake so large that she could swallow all four of the other Great Lakes and still have room to spare. I see the mother of all lakes, the headwaters of a great basin that holds one-fifth of all the fresh surface water on the planet. I see a five-lake ecosystem that contains enough water to cover the Lower 48—every American acre south of the Canadian border—with 9.5 feet of crystal clear Great Lakes water. I see an ecosystem that quenches the thirst of billions of creatures and some forty million people in eight U.S. states and two Canadian provinces.

Today I stand on the shores of Lake Superior and I see a naïve innocent, a voluptuous bounty on the verge of violation. I see

Photo 0.1. *The shore of Lake Superior (Photo by Peter Scott Eide)*

millions of angry, parched people from far-flung venues who view "undeveloped water" as a wasted opportunity. I see dryland farmers clamoring with sharp spigots, claiming they can't feed the world without more irrigation. I see thousands of massive supertankers lining up on behalf of millions of thirsty Asians. I see endless Romanesque canals carrying water to manicured lawns in a burgeoning, unsustainable Sunbelt. I see anxious scientists who worry about the transformations that climate change could bring. I see Great Lakes politicians destructively bickering among themselves, ultimately threatening the lakes they hope to save. I see urban voters—with no connection to land, water, or wildlife—who elect their dilettante peers to public office, affecting water policy everywhere. I see countless people inexplicably bypassing cold, refreshing water from the tap, so they can spend more money on water in a bottle. I see subsidized farmers who waste water on inefficient irrigation by growing surplus crops that the nation doesn't need. I see international entrepreneurs rubbing their hands with the thought of getting rich from something that comes out of the ground for free. I see wasteful water practices throughout the Great Lakes Basin that historians will look back upon with scorn. I see water—clear, cold, luscious water—that most see the value in taking, and few see the value in leaving. I see millions upon millions of Great Lakes residents who underestimate the struggle that awaits them.

Today, when I stand on the shores of Lake Superior, I don't see a lake. I see a sprawling deep blue battleground that stretches from Duluth, Minnesota, to Trois Rivières, Québec—and I wonder, who will win the war?

PART I

Hope and Hopelessness

~

Chapter 1

To Have and Have Not

I T HAS BEEN SAID that if the twentieth century was the century of oil, then the twenty-first century will be the century of water.[1] While it's true that roughly three-quarters of the earth's surface is made up of water, all that blue space on the grade-school globe can be deceiving: 97 percent of the world's water is seawater—loaded with salt and unfit for drinking. The rest is drinkable, but two-thirds of that is locked up in the polar ice caps and unavailable. That means less than 1 percent of all the surface water on earth is accessible, potable freshwater.[2] Every day much of world is reminded of just what a precious resource freshwater can be. More than a billion people—one-sixth of the world's population— do not have access to clean drinking water, and 2.1 million people die annually because of unsafe drinking-water conditions.[3] By 2025, two-thirds of the world's population is expected to face water shortages—the vast majority of them in the developing world. Much of the world's population growth is occurring in areas where water is far from abundant. Global per capita water use has actually risen over time: during the last seventy years, as the world's population has tripled, water use has increased sixfold.[4] During the next one hundred years the world will be increasingly divided into two groups: the water "haves" and the water "have-nots," and most of the have-nots will be in the world's poorest countries. "At the beginning of the twenty-first Century, the Earth . . . is facing a serious water crisis," warned the United Nations in its 2003 report on world water development. "All the signs suggest that it is getting worse and will continue to do so unless corrective action is taken."[5]

Great Lakes Basin

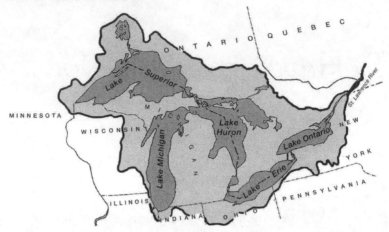

Fig. 1.1. *Precipitation that falls inside the Basin boundary eventually finds its way to the Great Lakes. Precipitation outside the Basin boundary ends up in the Mississippi River or other watersheds.*

As water scarcity becomes a divisive political issue throughout the world, inevitably there will be a rise in water tension. As this political friction grows, unprecedented domestic and international pressure will be directed at water-rich regions, leading to severe political, economic, social, and environmental stress. This is an enormously important issue for areas like the Great Lakes Basin (fig. 1.1). The Great Lakes hold 18 percent of all the fresh surface water on earth—more than half of that in Lake Superior alone. During this era of increased water scarcity, some water-stressed communities in wealthy countries will be forced to consider serious conservation measures for the first time. People elsewhere will demand that water-rich regions "share" their resource with the rest of the world. Increased pleas for humanitarian water assistance are expected as well. All of these factors are bound to contribute to heightened global water anxiety. "In an increasingly large number of places scarcity of water resources is a problem—where populations and economic demand are really coming up against limited natural supplies," says Peter Gleick, a global water expert at the Pacific Institute in Oakland, California. "I don't like the term 'water wars' . . .

But water is increasingly a factor in conflict, and there's a long history of violence over water, and I think it's going to get worse."[6]

Just how much fighting there has been over water is a matter of wide debate. But every two years, in his report on the world's water, Mr. Gleick updates what is perhaps the most comprehensive water conflict chronology ever compiled. The latest version of the chronology goes on and on for seventeen pages, listing scores of incidents between 3000 BC and the early part of the twenty-first century in which water was either used as a military tool, targeted by military opponents, or otherwise became a source of tension. Among the incidents on Mr. Gleick's list: (1) a series of bombings in California between 1907 and 1913 designed to prevent the diversion of water from the Owens Valley to Los Angeles; (2) the mobilization of the Arizona National Guard in 1935 during a dispute with California over water in the Colorado River; (3) an incident in August 2000 in which six people died after officials in China's southern Guangdong Province blew up a ditch to prevent a neighboring county from diverting water; and (4) violent riots that broke out in 2002 over controversial water allocations from India's Cauvery River.[7]

Asia has become one of the most volatile global water hot spots, a continent that holds 60 percent of the world's population but only 36 percent of the world's water and where many rivers and aquifers are already oversubscribed.[8] The Aral Sea, in the Central Asian nations of Uzbekistan and Kazakhstan, is one of the most overtapped water systems in the world and is now one-fourth its original size. "This is a serious problem in a lot of different places, many of them in Asia where you have the biggest disparity in population and available water," says Sandra Postel, director of the Global Water Policy Project in Amherst, Massachusetts. "That's translating into a fair amount of rivers running dry during long stretches of the year." China has responded to its significant water woes by embarking on a massive scheme known as the South-North Water Transfer Project, which plans to move 44 billion cubic meters of water per year via three different canals—spanning more than seven hundred miles each—from the Yangtze River Basin to water-hungry sections of northern China.[9]

Massive water-transfer projects are nothing new of course; the Romans turned them into an art form. So has California. But one of the most unique methods of water transportation to emerge has been the giant five-million-gallon bags that are towed through the sea to transport freshwater from places like Turkey to Cyprus.[10] Other proposals to transfer freshwater in giant bags along the west coast of North America have been met with controversy.[11] But scarcity drives up price, and it's the growing preciousness of clean, reliable freshwater that is ramping up its value to the point where these kinds of speculative adventures can even be considered.

The bottled water sector has been leading the charge in the entrepreneurial water world for years, thanks to healthy growth rates since the early 1990s. Bottled-water sales reached $100 billion globally in 2004 even though bottled water generally costs one thousand times more than high-quality tap water and is often less regulated.[12] Nestlé has long been a dominant player in the bottled-water industry, but PepsiCo and Coca-Cola have also aggressively entered the fray, thanks to profit margins that can far exceed those for soft drinks. Bottled water is a controversial issue in some parts of the Great Lakes region where there is growing concern about the localized effect that groundwater withdrawals can have on the levels and temperatures of cold-water lakes, springs, and streams. But since the Great Lakes Basin imports roughly fourteen times more bottled water than it exports, the controversy appears to have had little effect on sales.[13]

What's remarkable is that bottled-water sales have seen some of their strongest growth rates in the developing world, where demand for clean water is greatest but where the population can least afford the added expense.[14] Large multinational corporations have also increased their presence in the municipal water supply business, a move that has become controversial in the developing world because water supplies provided by for-profit corporations have sometimes resulted in rates that are beyond the reach of many customers.[15] The developing world isn't the only place that private water companies have run into trouble. In the late 1990s, Atlanta asked the United Water company to take over the city's water service in a much-publicized twenty-year deal.[16] Yet by 2003, Atlanta and United Water parted ways after a rocky four-year marriage. The divorce came after the company said it was losing $10 million per year in attempting to provide Atlanta's water service. Meanwhile, Atlanta's residents had grown tired of United Water's record, which included "boil only" alerts and brown water coming from household taps.[17]

The growing role of international corporations in the delivery of bottled, bulk, and municipal water has spawned a heated debate about whether water is an economic good or something that is held in the public trust and that people have a human right to access. There is concern among some experts that international trade regimes like the North American Free Trade Agreement and World Trade Organization protocols could interpret water as a "good." The divergent views on this issue regularly flare up at global water gatherings like the World Water Forum, a triennial event that is one of the largest gatherings of water aficionados of all stripes in the world. Many international legal experts say that the debate about whether water is a public resource or a private good remains unresolved.

While water scarcity is a serious problem in the developing world, it's a growing concern in North America as well. In fact, the Great Lakes Basin is literally surrounded on three sides by a wide variety of water scarcity and conflict. To the west, off and on for nearly one hundred years, farmers in Montana have been arguing with their colleagues in Alberta over water rights to the Milk and St. Mary rivers. Farther west, in the Klamath River Basin of southern Oregon and northern California, farmers squared off with the federal government in 2001 after an endangered species issue curtailed their water access and threatened their livelihoods.[18] Meanwhile, in southern California, the federal government was forced to all but wrest Colorado River water away from regional farmers so their water could be piecemealed out to sprawling metropolitan areas in southern California.[19] In south-central Arizona, an overdrawn aquifer has created a cone of depression near the town of Eloy; the soil has slumped more than twelve feet, creating mile-long cracks that have split the interstate and sliced deep into the earth.[20] To the south, in the Rio Grande Valley of Texas, Mexicans and Americans are arguing over the particulars of a 1944 treaty that sets strict limits on each nation's water rights.[21] Meanwhile, to the southeast, in the Apalachicola River Basin, the states of Alabama, Georgia, and Florida have been suing each other in federal court since the early 1990s over water issues that affect millions from Atlanta to the Gulf of Mexico.[22] Farther to the north, the U.S. Supreme Court intervened in a dispute between Virginia and Maryland in 2003 over water in the storied Potomac River.[23] And in Massachusetts, the overtapped Ipswich River outside Boston has been known to run dry, when overwithdrawals of the regional groundwater supply rob the waterway of its crucial base flow.[24]

In virtually all of these areas, population is rising, which means that water tensions will only get worse, and serious water shortages will be exacerbated by the drought cycle. "The United States is heading toward a water scarcity crisis," predicts Robert Glennon, a law professor at the University of Arizona and author of *Water Follies*, an influential book about groundwater in the United States. "Our current water use practices are unsustainable, and environmental factors threaten a water supply heavily burdened by increased demand."[25] One of the most sobering prognostications comes from the U.S. Department of the Interior. In 2003 the department published a map entitled "Potential Water Supply Crises by 2025" (fig. 1.2). The map shows only the western half of the continental U.S. and highlights a large number of areas where the department predicts the likelihood of future water conflict as either "highly likely," "substantial," or "moderate." Virtually every state on the map except South Dakota has some sort of a water trouble spot, with the most serious areas of concern being in Arizona, Texas, California, New Mexico, Colorado, Utah, and Nevada. Yet people continue to move to these arid parts of the country in droves, seemingly oblivious to the fact that sooner or later, something will have to change.

Potential Water Supply Crises by 2025

(Areas where existing supplies are not adequate to meet water demands for people, for farms, and for the environment).

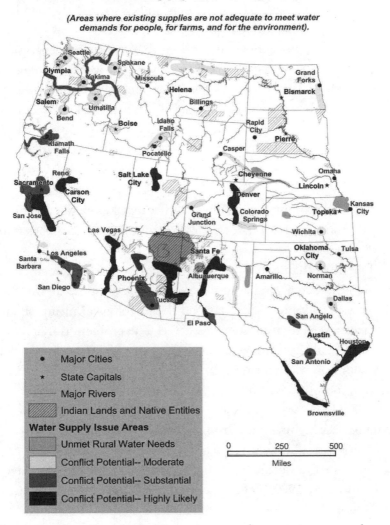

Fig. 1.2. *The western United States is expected to experience several water crises in the future. (U.S. Department of the Interior, May 2003)*

The most egregious example of this trend is in Las Vegas—the American city that more than any other represents a water mirage. Americans have some of the highest per capita water use in the world, and Las Vegas residents use more than twice as much as the average American.[26] In 2004 an ABC News report noted that five thousand people have been moving to Las Vegas every month. The city is building scores of new schools and has hired thousands of new teachers to handle the influx of students. Las Vegas has been churning out so many new subdivisions that the police department must issue new road maps to its officers every few weeks. "Unless we begin making plans, people in Las Vegas are going to be spending almost as much on their water as they will be on the land on which their house is built," warns Patrick Shea, former director of the U.S. Bureau of Land Management.[27] The ABC report featured an intriguing statement from Hal Rothman, author of *Neon Metropolis: How Las Vegas Started the Twenty-First Century*. "Water is a commodity," Mr. Rothman proclaimed. "It's a lot like oil. We use oil to heat Boston, but that oil doesn't come from Boston. It comes from Saudi Arabia."[28]

Talk like that makes residents nervous in the Great Lakes region—the Saudi Arabia of water. Why? Because it implies that people can continue to live beyond their ecological means simply by importing water from someplace else. The problem is that water is not like oil. Ecosystems don't depend on oil for their survival; they count on water for that. If all the oil on earth disappeared tomorrow, the world would be a very different place, but it would survive. If all the water on earth disappeared, however, life would come to a screeching halt. Truth be told, the boom in Las Vegas—and in a lot of other southwestern cities—has come at a severe ecological cost: the decimation of the once-mighty Colorado River. Since the early 1900s, southwestern officials have treated the Colorado more like a workhorse than an ecosystem. "To some conservationists, the Colorado River is the preeminent symbol of everything mankind has done wrong," wrote Marc Reisner back in 1986 in his seminal book *Cadillac Desert*. "Even as hydrologists amuse themselves by speculating about how many times each molecule of water has passed through pairs of kidneys—[the Colorado] is still unable to satisfy all the demands on it . . . [and though there are] plans to import water from as far away as Alaska—the twenty million people in the Colorado Basin will probably find themselves facing chronic shortages, if not some kind of catastrophe, before any of these grandiose schemes is built."[29]

Outside the American Southwest, there is very little sympathy for the unsustainable water problems faced by that region. Great Lakes Canadians are perhaps the least sympathetic of all. "Knowledgeable Canadians understand that there is no water shortage in the U.S.," says Ralph Pentland, a Canadian water expert. The problem, Mr. Pentland says, is not a shortage of good water, but a shortage of good water management. "If you look at the Colorado Basin . . . they have problems caused by eight decades of subsidization of dumb projects, plus a water law that doesn't make sense."

For decades, Canadians and Americans in the Great Lakes Basin have feared that the thirsty will come calling. The issue has always been, will the Great Lakes be ready for them? The topic is complicated by a wide debate within water circles about how much diversionary pressure the Great Lakes could realistically face as global water stress mounts. "I think the era of big, federal, subsidized water projects is over," declares Daniel Injerd, head of the Lake Michigan Management Section at the Illinois Department of Natural Resources. "I don't see a significant threat out there for Great Lakes water, probably not in my lifetime." Mr. Injerd's point is that diverting water over long distances is very, very expensive— so expensive that it's difficult to do without huge federal subsidies. So Mr. Injerd and many other water experts argue that an environmentally conscious America would never tolerate an enormously subsidized, multibillion-dollar diversion plan that ships water from one end of the nation to the other. His analysis is consistent with that of the International Joint Commission (IJC). The IJC was created by the Boundary Waters Treaty of 1909 to help resolve water disputes between Canada and the United States. In a report released in 2000, the IJC acknowledged the diversion anxiety in the Great Lakes region, but after extensive study it declared that "the era of major diversions and water transfers in the United States and Canada has ended."[30]

~

DESPITE THESE ASSURANCES, regional residents on both sides of the border remain worried about outsiders taking Great Lakes water. These fears are driven, in part, by a general lack of faith that government institutions will protect the environment. But such worries can also be attributed to the almost spiritual connection that millions of people have with the Great Lakes (for many Native Americans in the United States, and First Nations people in Canada, it *is* a spiritual connection). In other parts of North America, mountains, oceans and old-growth forests serve as the ecological talismans of the people. But for Canadians and Americans living in the Great Lakes region, nothing defines their relationship with the environment more than an abundance of freshwater— especially their sacred "Sweet Water Seas."

And there are those who take issue with the IJC's position on the threat of Great Lakes diversions. These observers argue that the diversion threat is not gone, but merely lies dormant. One need only follow the population and water-scarcity trend lines into the future, they say, and where the two lines intersect sometime later in the twenty-first century, water will become valuable enough to make a whole slew of wild diversion schemes a political reality again. "I don't think the era of water diversions is over by any means," argues Noah Hall, a professor at Wayne State University Law School in Michigan who spent years with the National Wildlife Federation. "To me it's not even a question, it's an inevitability. You look at what's happening to water supplies in almost every other part of the country—it used to be just the Southwest and California, but now you are seeing it in the Southeast, and the Northeast—the economics are fluid. It's a simple supply-and-demand model."

Water experts from outside the Great Lakes region are not prepared to write off the diversion threat either. "Never say never," says Sandra Postel. "Climate change is a huge wild card in this entire thing. If there's evidence that the agricultural heartland in this country is starting to dry up and needs irrigation, well, then I think that changes the whole dynamic." Other experts say that future diversion schemes will have to meet a strict economic litmus test— something that was often not required of the large-scale diversions of the past. "There'll be increased calls for new projects to move water from one place to another," predicts Peter Gleick. "But you don't have to move water very far before really expensive desalination starts to look economic. Water conservation and efficiency is far more cost-effective right now than most sources of new supply." Does that mean he thinks that the threat of diversions is a nonissue for the Great Lakes? "No, I *do* think it's an issue," he says. "I think the issue of large-scale, long-distance diversions is not a big worry. I would be much more concerned about some big city a hundred miles south of the Basin . . . And once you breach boundaries you're in potentially a lot of trouble."

For many water managers in the Great Lakes region this debate is purely academic—they say the Great Lakes don't have any water to spare. Yes, the lakes represent one of the largest collections of fresh surface water on earth—6 quadrillion gallons, or 5,439 cubic miles worth.[31] But less than 1 percent of that water is considered renewable, that is, recharged by rain, snowfall, and groundwater every year. The other 99 percent was deposited by glaciers during the last ice age (fig. 1.3). Think of it like a giant water bank account that earns less than 1 percent interest per year. If you start pulling water from the principal, you may need another ice age to get it back. "The Great Lakes are . . . more than just a resource to be consumed; they are also home to a great diversity of plants, animals, and other biota," said the IJC in its 2000 report. "If all interests in the Basin are considered, there is never a 'surplus' of water in the Great Lakes system; every drop of water has several potential uses."[32]

In many ways the glaciers defined the shape of the Great Lakes Basin. They advanced and receded repeatedly over thousands of years, scraping, eroding, rescraping, re-eroding the landscape, sanding down hills, and creating huge cavities in the softer areas of the Earth's surface. "We're talking a kilometer or so thick of ice going out in lobes and eroding through several of these basins," explains John Johnston, a post-doctoral fellow at the University of Waterloo in Ontario. The last glacier receded roughly ten thousand years ago, and as it melted and as water levels settled, it left behind the

Great Lakes Water System

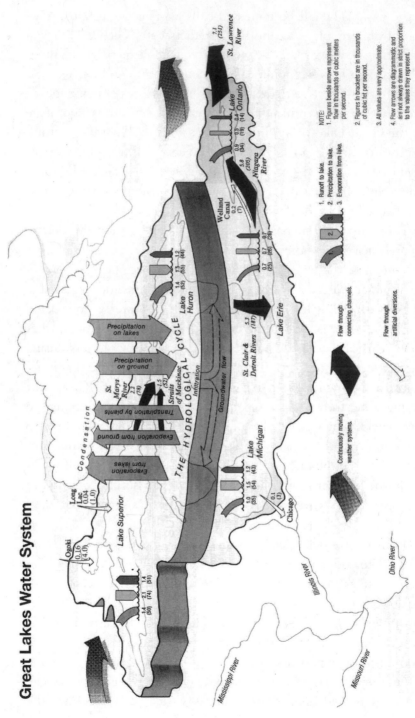

Fig 1.3. *Less than 1 percent of Great Lakes' water is renewed every year through precipitation and groundwater recharge.* (Based on the original from Fuller and Sheer, The Great Lakes: An Environmental Atlas and Resource Book and Brock University Cartography)

Great Lakes Profile

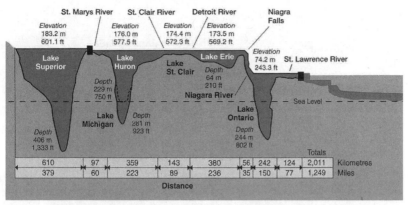

Fig. 1.4. *The Great Lakes are one ecosystem, but the individual lakes vary widely in depth and surface area. (Michigan Sea Grant Archives)*

geologic footprint of the contemporary Great Lakes Basin. The result is a large, water-rich ecosystem spanning more than 750 miles from one end to the other.[33]

While the Basin is considered to be one ecosystem, the individual lakes have unique characteristics that distinguish them from one another (fig. 1.4). Lake Superior is the largest, deepest, cleanest, and coldest lake in the system, with the least-populated shoreline—the lake is so large that it could swallow all the other lakes, plus three additional Lake Eries. Lake Michigan is the second largest lake by volume, though it comes in third in surface area. Its southern shoreline is one of the most heavily populated and industrialized in the region, home to roughly eight million people, or one-fifth of the population in the Basin. Lake Huron is the second largest lake by surface area, but the third largest by volume; and while much of the shoreline is heavily forested, it hosts more agriculture than Lake Superior, but less population than Lake Michigan. Lake Erie is the shallowest in the Basin, and the smallest by volume. With an average depth of just 62 feet, it's the warmest lake and for many years was by far the most heavily polluted. Lake Ontario, at the tail end of the system, is the smallest lake by surface

Lake Rankings

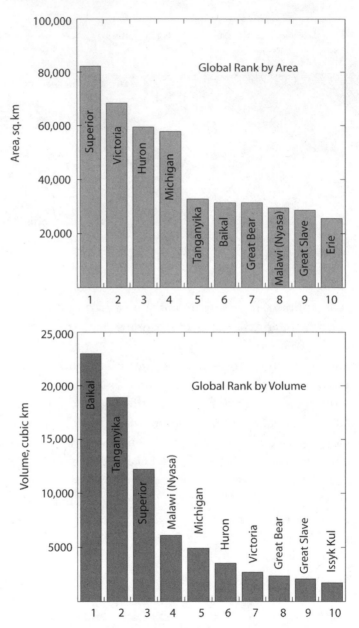

Fig. 1.5. *Four of the Great Lakes rank among the world's top ten by surface area. Three rank among the top ten by volume.* (Large Lakes Observatory, University of Minnesota–Duluth)

Water Use in the Great Lakes Basin

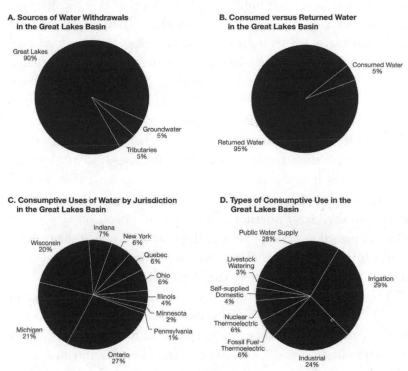

A. Sources of Water Withdrawals in the Great Lakes Basin

Great Lakes 90%
Groundwater 5%
Tributaries 5%

B. Consumed versus Returned Water in the Great Lakes Basin

Consumed Water 5%
Returned Water 95%

C. Consumptive Uses of Water by Jurisdiction in the Great Lakes Basin

Wisconsin 20%
Indiana 7%
New York 6%
Quebec 6%
Ohio 6%
Illinois 4%
Minnesota 2%
Pennsylvania 1%
Michigan 21%
Ontario 27%

D. Types of Consumptive Use in the Great Lakes Basin

Public Water Supply 28%
Irrigation 29%
Livestock Watering 3%
Self-supplied Domestic 4%
Nuclear Thermoelectric 6%
Fossil Fuel Thermoelectric 6%
Industrial 24%

Fig. 1.6. *Ontario consumes more water than any other Great Lakes jurisdiction, while agriculture consumes more water than any other sector. (International Joint Commission)*

arca, but it's deep—with a maximum depth of 802 feet it's deeper than Lake Huron.[34] Several of the Great Lakes rank among the largest in the world (fig. 1.5).

Great Lakes water nourishes millions of people in cities like Chicago, Cleveland, Detroit, Montréal, and Toronto, and it's the lifeblood of many industries, power plants, hydro facilities, and farms (fig. 1.6). Agriculture remains the greatest "consumer" of Great Lakes water, and it's the greatest consumer of water globally as well.[35] Great Lakes water also supports a vibrant multibillion-dollar regional tourism industry, a $4 billion fishery, and it floats the thousand-foot freighters that ply the lakes during the $3 billion Great Lakes shipping season. For every one-inch drop in Great

Lakes water levels, those thousand-foot freighters must shave 270 tons of cargo from their holds to ensure that they don't scrape bottom as they slip from one lake to another. That makes shipping more expensive, which influences the cost of everything from coal to steel—and the electric bills and automobiles that go with them.

While it's true that less than 1 percent of the water in the lakes is renewed every year, many industrialists argue that that statistic can be deceiving. While much of that 1 percent is being "used," they say it's not all being "consumed." When hydro plants cycle water through their turbines, they are using the water temporarily and returning it to the system. Water consumption (what is often called "consumptive use"), however, refers to water that is *not* returned to the lakes, whether lost through evaporation at a power plant or placed in a can of beer. "I think water is one of the region's competitive advantages. We don't have the sun of Arizona; we don't have the mountains of the West. We have water," says Jon Allan, director of environmental services at Consumers Energy in Michigan. "[But] we have to be very careful not to overregulate . . . to strike that balance for our water future but not do it in a way that really disadvantages us." According to Jim Nicholas, director of the U.S. Geological Survey's Water Science Center in Lansing, Michigan, the renewable supply in the Great Lakes Basin is equivalent to 161.6 billion gallons per day. Of that, he says, only 1.5 percent is actually being consumed, or lost from the system because of human use.

Some corporate officials cite those low consumption rates as proof that cities, farms, and industries in the Great Lakes Basin have not come close to using up all of the region's renewable water supply—suggesting that there's plenty of water left for humans to consume without affecting the ecosystem. This, however, is a conclusion that Mr. Nicholas is not willing to make. The problem with such claims, he says, is that they ignore the fact that the water in the Great Lakes region is already being used by the ecosystem, and it's not clear how increased water consumption might affect the region's unique water-dependent environment. "We have a lot more water than Arizona," he says. "[But] just having more water doesn't mean that there's more water available." Complicating matters, Mr. Nicholas says, the U.S. Geological Survey has backed away from reporting consumptive-use figures—nationally and in the Great Lakes region—in part because of concerns about how the data has been tabulated. As of 2006 the agency had no concrete figures on how much water is being consumed in the Basin, leaving the region in the frustrating position of not knowing how much additional consumptive use might be too much.

Since the 1980s officials have implemented a wide variety of policies to control Great Lakes water withdrawals and diversions. But most of those measures have proven awkward and dysfunctional. There is a growing belief in the Great Lakes region that the modern era of global water scarcity makes it imperative that officials develop a comprehensive, binding Great Lakes water-management regime. Encouraged by the IJC and the U.S. Congress, the region's governors and premiers spent more than six years crafting new water-management agreements. After scores of closed-door meetings, dozens of hearings, and thousands of public comments, on December 13, 2005, the Council of Great Lakes Governors—along with the premiers of Ontario and Québec—released the final version of its much-anticipated *Great Lakes–St. Lawrence River Basin Sustainable Water Resources Agreement* (the "International Agreement") and the companion *Great Lakes–St. Lawrence Basin Water Resources Compact* (the "Compact"). The agreement is a nonbinding international commitment between the eight Great Lakes states and two Canadian provinces to coordinate the sustainable management of the regional water supply. The Compact is designed to become a legally binding document that implements the terms of the International Agreement on the U.S. side of the border, which is where most of the regulatory weaknesses lie and the future demand for Great Lakes water is likely to be greatest.

Writing water law for the twenty-first century and beyond is a complicated venture, one that has left much of the public anxious about the process, the reasoning, and the road ahead. People are naturally resistant to change. The Compact has sparked confusion and fiery debates from Montréal to Duluth. The document faces an extraordinary uphill political battle: it must be passed by all eight legislatures in the Great Lakes states as well as by the U.S. Congress. The Compact-adoption process is expected to take years—possibly more than a decade—if it ever happens at all. Thousands and thousands of hours have been invested in drafting the document. Legal opinions have been solicited and resolicited in order to select the right wording and context. After years of negotiations and finessing, the Compact has left the hands of the lawyers and water managers and has entered the insecure realm of the politician, where it will be sniped at by a smattering of opponents.

As happens with any compromise document, there are those who feel the Compact goes too far, and there are those who feel it doesn't go far enough. Imperfect as it may be, if the Compact isn't adopted, and the current system of U.S. Great Lakes water laws is ruled unconstitutional, the Basin boundary will eventually be pierced (this issue is dealt with extensively in later chapters). And if the legal sanctity of that boundary fails, the Great Lakes will become more vulnerable to diversions and overexploitation. "Diversion is the hydra-headed monster in this story," warns former Wisconsin governor Tony Earl. "It's always been out there [and] keeps popping back to life . . . it never goes away." For decades the Great Lakes have been the target of a whole host of envious and sometimes far-fetched diversion proposals—fueling a regional paranoia that the lakes could go the way of the drained Aral Sea. The Aral Sea's demise is one of several water disasters that have prompted politicians and activists to push for stronger water regulations in the Great Lakes region (see chapter 2).

As potable freshwater becomes more precious, wild-eyed Great Lakes diversion schemes are likely to return, and water tensions and legal challenges are bound to follow. What's more, global warming could transform the lakes—and complicate the debate—in ways that are difficult to fathom. In short, the Great Lakes states and provinces are facing one of the most important moments in their collective history. Will they act as one regional voice to adopt a modern, binding water-management system that protects the

The Great Lakes Water Wars

world's most abundant freshwater reservoir? Or will the debate deteriorate into legislative constipation, divisiveness, conflict—and ultimately—failure? Can the Great Lakes states and provinces join together on behalf of one of the world's greatest resources? Or will the region—and the lakes themselves—die a death of a thousand cuts? This book tries to help answer those questions by revisiting a series of regional diversions and water-use controversies. These case studies help illustrate the weaknesses in the current Great Lakes water-management system. And they help explain why there is growing demand to implement new policies to protect the Great Lakes' globally significant and precious water resources. Nothing less than the regional culture, economy, and environment are at stake.

Chapter 2

The Aral Experiment

I N THE FAR NORTHWEST CORNER of arid Uzbekistan, in the sandy village of Muynak, stands a memorial to local soldiers who died in World War II. Here in the heart of Central Asia, once part of the sprawling Soviet empire, men boarded trains in the early 1940s for the Russian front to help their Soviet comrades beat back a threatening German invasion. Many of those soldiers, of course, did not return home alive. In Muynak, hundreds of names are listed at the base of the memorial's tilting obelisk. When it was built, the

Photo 2.1. *The Muynak war memorial. (Photo by Peter Annin)*

memorial was perched at the edge of the sapphire Aral Sea, once the fourth-largest inland body of water in the world. The monument made for a picturesque setting where relatives could pay their respects and leave a bouquet of flowers in the fresh sea air, while waterfowl flew overhead, shorebirds probed the water's edge, and cormorants dove for minnows in the shallows.

The war memorial at Muynak has since become a less inspiring place. The towering obelisk sits atop a dry thirty-foot cliff overlooking a sprawling scrub-brush desert that stretches for miles beyond the horizon. The cool sea breeze has been supplanted by a hot desert wind; the crashing waves have been replaced by aimless drifts of desert sand. At the base of the cliff, cattle wander among sparse vegetation, and off in the distance one can see the remnants of a ship graveyard, where Muynak's once-mighty fishing fleet was left to die after the waters of the Aral Sea faded away. At one time there were more than a hundred old fishing boats in this nautical cemetery—surreal rusting hulks beached awkwardly in the desert sand—but barely a dozen remain. Local officials had most of the boats dismantled for scrap, partly for money, and partly to remove these sad reminders that Muynak was once one of the most productive fishing villages in all of the Soviet Union.

Photo 2.2. *The ship graveyard at Muynak. (Photo by Peter Annin)*

The Aral Experiment

Photo 2.3. This rusting vessel is one of roughly a dozen that remain in Muynak's ship graveyard. (Photo by Peter Annin)

What happened to the Aral? In the 1950s, ambitious Soviet planners embarked on a massive water program designed to make the desert bloom. Engineers redirected much of the river flow that fed the sea, diverting the water to a massive complex of agricultural fields. The Soviets succeeded in their crusade; Central Asia became a booming marketplace—particularly for cotton. But this economic conquest had a severe ecological cost. In just a few decades, the water diversions left the Aral in ruins. Cut off from its freshwater feeder streams, the sea began shrinking. A generation later, the disastrous ecological effects of this grand plan have left thousands of Central Asians in shock. In less than half a century, water levels in the Aral have fallen by eighty vertical feet. The sea has lost 75 percent of its surface area and 90 percent of its volume.[1] The farmer's gain was the fisherman's loss—jobs dried up with the water, leaving chronic unemployment and social paralysis. The climate is different too. Like the North American Great Lakes, the old Aral moderated temperature extremes near the shoreline. Now Muynak's summers are hotter, winters colder, and regional precipitation patterns have changed.

In recent years, as Great Lakes officials have contemplated a new water-management system, the Aral Sea disaster has been invoked repeatedly by environmentalists and others as an ecological rallying cry—an example of what not to become. "Even the grandest of resources have dried-up or fallen to misuse," declared the environmental group Clean Wisconsin in a 2004 press release.[2] "Consider the vivid examples of the Aral Sea in Central Asia and the Colorado River in [the] Southwestern United States." Because many Great Lakes residents who refer to the Aral Sea know little about it, and because most have never been there, this chapter attempts to provide a firsthand look at the Aral Sea's desiccation. The purpose of this chapter is not to "prove" or "allege" that an Aral-like draining of the Great Lakes is in the offing, but rather to shed light on a place that is often referred to, but little understood. That way, as officials contemplate passage of the Great Lakes water Compact, regional citizens can decide for themselves whether there are any lessons to be learned from the Aral Sea's destruction.

~

STANDING IN THE MIDDLE of the seafloor in a place where the water was once forty-five feet deep, the magnitude of the disaster can be difficult to grasp—nothing but sand stretches off to the horizon in all directions. Photos cannot capture the true extent of this ecological calamity; it even challenges the bounds of the written word. The Aral has receded so far that it takes more than five hours of driving on the old seabed in a four-wheel-drive vehicle to get from Muynak, on the old south shore, to the edge of what's left of the shrunken Aral—a distance of more than sixty miles. Yes, there is still water in the Aral, but since 1960 the sea has shrunk to one-fourth its original surface area, and the water continues to fall by nearly two vertical feet per year. Islands have become peninsulas, peninsulas have become dry hills, and former sunken islands have emerged from the surface to split the old Aral into two water bodies—the "Large" Aral to the south and the "Small" Aral to the

Central Asia and the Aral Sea

Fig. 2.1. *Located in the heart of Central Asia, the Aral Sea straddles the boundary between Uzbekistan and Kazakhstan. (Randy Yeip of the Knight Center for Environmental Journalism at Michigan State University)*

north. It's expected that the Large Aral may split again. The sea's once slightly brackish waters have reached such high salinity levels that native fish species were extirpated long ago. The Large Aral is not dead yet, but it's in a death spiral that appears impossible to overcome (figs. 2.1 and 2.2).

The Aral Sea's demise is one of the greatest environmental crimes ever committed and a depressing example of water arrogance run amuck. It shows the damaging effects that shortsighted water policies can have on people, the economy, and the environment. To residents of the Great Lakes region, and of other water-rich parts of the world, the Aral Sea disaster serves as a reminder that the largest bodies of water on earth are vulnerable to overexploitation. "The Aral Sea is a dramatic example of what happens when you take abundant water for granted and suck, and suck, and suck and eventually it goes dry," says Noah Hall, a professor at Wayne State University. "It's everyone's worst nightmare." The Aral's woes show that if humans put their minds to it, a great body of water can be decimated in less than a generation. "The Aral Sea

The Great Lakes Water Wars

The Changing Profile of the Aral Sea

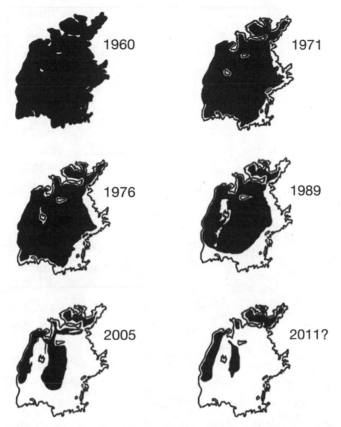

Fig. 2.2. *The Aral Sea has lost 90 percent of its volume and 75 percent of its surface area since 1960. (Philip Micklin, Department of Geography, Western Michigan University)*

is a biblical disaster," says Professor Nikolay Aladin, an Aral Sea expert with the Brackish Water Hydrobiology Lab in St. Petersburg. "It is really unbelievable what has happened here in just thirty to forty years."

It's hard to imagine that the Aral once hosted a thriving ecosystem chock-full of birds, fish, and other fauna. Much of the original shoreline was surrounded by thick reed beds teeming with life. "The coastal zone around the Aral Sea was a paradise for wildlife," explains Professor Ilia Joldasova, a fish biologist with the Uzbekistan Academy of Sciences. "A lot of people came to the Aral to fish and hunt. It was a tourist mecca. It was a thriving area—an oasis in the middle of the desert." What was remarkable about the Aral, she says, was not its biodiversity, but the productivity of the ecosystem, particularly along the south shore. "The southern bays were like a kindergarten for fish," she says. "In the spring, the bays held so many spawning fish that the water looked like it was boiling."

It's no surprise then that the fishing village of Muynak, also located on the sea's southern shore, was a thriving hub of commercial activity. All hours of the day and night, fishermen crowded the local wharves, transporting their catch to the Muynak cannery—one of the Soviet Union's largest. Uzabkay Irmuhanov, fifty-three, first started working at the cannery in the 1960s. Eventually he worked his way up to become chief mechanic at the facility, which once employed fifteen hundred people on three shifts, churning out sixteen million cans of fish per year. What didn't go into the cans was used for cattle and chicken feed. But as the sea shrank, Mr. Irmuhanov says, the output at the plant dropped at first to twelve million cans, and then six million cans. In order to keep the plant from closing, Soviet officials shipped in fish from as far away as the Baltic Sea and the Pacific Ocean to be processed here. But that proved to be unsustainable, and activity at the plant dwindled from three shifts down to one, and then none. "Officially it's not closed," he says with a straight face, gesturing to the plant over his shoulder. Great pains have been taken to mothball the cannery in a way that would allow Mr. Irmuhanov and his colleagues to restart the assembly line at a moment's notice. "If we got some fish, we could be processing again."

Kirbay Utaganov knows a thing or two about fish. An affable, friendly man with a deeply creased face that smiles easily behind thick glasses, Mr. Utaganov, seventy-five, spent decades working as a set-net fisherman on the Aral Sea. In his latter years he oversaw a crew of six as the captain of a boat called *854 Muynak*. When the Aral's waters began to recede he and his fellow fishermen became more and more alarmed. "I began to worry about how I would feed and clothe my children," he says. By the late 1970s Mr. Utaganov's catch dwindled to the point where he gave up on the Aral and went to Turkmenistan to work. Eventually he retired and became a pensioner, but he remains fond of gathering on a street corner near the fisherman's collective in Muynak, where he shares stories with many of his old fishing comrades. When asked if he thinks the sea will ever come back, he chuckles. "I don't think it's possible to bring the Aral back," he says. The errors of the past are too insurmountable. "Before, the water [seemed] unlimited, but now, if we want to or not, we need to conserve."

～

BACK IN THE 1950s, Joseph Stalin, the ruthless Soviet dictator, was the first leader to recognize the Aral as something other than a fish factory. Because the sea's waters were slightly brackish Stalin and his bureaucratic planners did not see opportunity in the sea itself, but in the freshwater rivers that fed it. The Amu Darya and Syr Darya rivers are like the twin Niles of Central Asia, and they played a key role in the grand Soviet vision to make the desert bloom. But reworking the hydrology of an entire region takes time, and Stalin, who died in 1953, didn't live long enough to see the transformation. It wasn't until 1960, under the reign of Soviet premier Nikita Khrushchev that large-scale diversions of the Amu Darya and Syr Darya rivers began and the irrigation era turned the Central Asian desert into a sea of green.

But as agricultural harvests ballooned, the Aral's water level dropped. At the sea's southern end, the broad delta of the Amu Darya began to dwindle, and within a few years the water level in the sea fell so far that the southern shore's spawning grounds dried up. This had devastating repercussions on the fishing industry. Professor Joldasova says that fishermen's catch rates at Muynak dropped from 25,000 metric tons per year in 1959 to 7,500 metric tons in 1968. By the mid 1970s, the sea's edge had receded so far from Muynak that local fishermen had to dig a canal connecting the fishing village to the receding water. As the water level fell, native fish (some of which resembled North American species like walleye, yellow perch, northern pike, and catfish) could no longer tolerate the accelerating salinity, and they died off. By the early 1980s, the annual Muynak fish harvest had fallen to just 3,500 metric tons. "Then, in 1983, the fishing industry collapsed," Professor Joldasova says. "And the government halted the catch." By that time, many fishermen had already left the region to work elsewhere. But some hung on to try and fish the lakes and reservoirs in the Amu Darya delta. But the delta's catch rates fluctuated wildly with the river's siphoned flow. "By the mid-1980s the amount of Amu Darya water reaching the Aral Sea fell to zero," Professor Joldasova says. And there was a time during the mid-1980s when the Amu Darya's water only made it as far as the city of Nukus, Uzbekistan, ninety miles upstream. The Muynak fishermen could no longer keep water in the canal, and their boats became stranded in what would eventually become the ship graveyard. By 1988 the water level had fallen so far that the sea separated into the Large Aral and the Small Aral with only a small stream connecting the two. In 1989 a dam was built that severed the stream, forever changing the face of one of the world's great water bodies.

After the breakup of the Soviet Union in 1991, international aid started to pour into the Aral Sea region almost as fast as word about the environmental disaster poured out. Much of that early money was wasted on misguided projects that have seen few lasting results, other than allegations of incompetence and graft. "All this money was spent on conferences and training and to rewrite the old projects and call them new projects," says Ubbiniyaz Ashirbekov, who heads up the Nukus office of the International Fund for Saving the Aral Sea. The flurry of funding and support from the international community has waned markedly from the early years, though some support continues. Regional squabbling and allegations of corruption left international organizations frustrated, while local leaders, in turn, have become disenchanted with the international community. "All these people promised to help us and we believed them," Mr. Ashirbekov says. "We were promised mountains of support, but now twelve years have passed and not even a hill has materialized."

The Aral Sea region was once managed as a geographic unit by Soviet bureaucrats in Moscow, but after the Soviet collapse, control transferred to five separate independent republics. During Soviet times it was easy to get the republics—Uzbekistan, Kazakhstan, Turkmenistan, Tajikistan, and Kyrgyzstan (they are often referred to as the "Five Stans")—to work together. That's because the Five Stans did what Moscow told them to do. But regional efforts to re-solve water issues have since become marked by national chauvin-ism and border disputes. "The World Bank went in there in 1992 [and said] 'we're going to use money to bring the five countries to-gether,'" remembers Michael Glantz, an Aral Sea expert at the Na-tional Center for Atmospheric Research in Boulder, Colorado. "After a couple years they abandoned that. They couldn't get them to work together."

Many of the Five Stans are poor nations, economically addicted to the irrigated agriculture that has led to the Aral Sea's demise. Changing to more efficient irrigation systems costs money. Taking crops out of production to conserve water costs money. Educating farmers on water efficiency costs money. These are expenses that the local republics are unwilling or unable to spare. "Significant water could be saved by changing water-use practices," says Jeff Ver-brugge, regional director for the Central Asia Free Exchange, which has tried to teach local farmers to conserve water. "The knowledge is improving," he says. "But I haven't seen the imple-mentation yet. But at least there's some listening going on."

Flood irrigation is by far the most common method used to water crops, and it's a highly inefficient means of water delivery. Not only does it waste water through extensive evaporation, but it also leads to salinized soils. As flood irrigation washes off the fields, it takes salts and other minerals with it. That, in turn, washes back into the river, so downstream irrigators end up watering their fields with salt deposits from upstream farms. This situation is repeated throughout the watershed, resulting in higher salinity farther down-stream. Throughout the lower Amu Darya drainage basin, salt is visible on the soil everywhere. Agricultural fields are tinged white between row crops, irrigation canals are rimmed like a margarita glass. Over time salt accumulates in the soil and groundwater, leading to declines in crop yields, and ultimately, to land that can't be farmed. Agricultural chemical use has dropped substantially from Soviet days, but regular chemical applications are still common. When farmers flush their fields, the cocktail of salt and pesticides is washed back into the river system, or down into the groundwater. In many parts of the Aral's watershed well water has extremely high salinity levels, and some believe that chemicals are a serious problem in the groundwater as well.

Many scientists and health workers argue that these agricultural practices, in combination with the receding waters, have led to serious health effects on the local population in places like Karakalpakstan, a semiautonomous republic in northwest Uzbekistan. Karakalpakstan borders the southern edge of the Large Aral and also encompasses the lower reaches of the Amu Darya River. Timothy Liddle is the project coordinator with Médecins Sans Frontières (Doctors Without Borders), an international aid organization with offices in Nukus, the regional Karakalpak capital. He says Karakalpak people suffer unusually high rates of birth defects, infant mortality, anemia, kidney disease, liver disease, and drug-resistant tuberculosis. "I'm very convinced that the health problems here in Karakalpakstan are related to the Aral Sea's decline," Mr. Liddle says. A report published by Médecins Sans Frontières (MSF) in 2002 said that Karakalpakstan is "threatened by complex chronic health problems linked directly to the [Aral Sea] environmental disaster, for which neither the causes nor measures to prevent them are clear. Potential health threats include salinization of drinking water, dust storms and the presence of agricultural chemical pollutants in the environment and the food chain."[3]

Chemical contamination that once was underwater is now whipped up by fierce winds—particularly in winter. The winds lift the soft, dry seabed—and the chemicals in it—forming contaminated dust storms that spread for hundreds of miles. One study estimated that forty-three million metric tons of regional salt and dust is blown into the air annually.[4] In the MSF study, conducted in co-operation with the Uzbek Ministry of Health and the World Health Organization (WHO), researchers detected dioxins and "dioxin-like" chemicals in Karakalpakstan food samples at levels almost three times higher than those recommended by the WHO.[5]

Although the work by MSF and others is compelling, not everyone agrees that the health problems in Karakalpakstan can be linked solely to the Aral Sea disaster. In its report, even MSF admitted, "Our understanding of these concerns is still limited." Sarah O'Hara is a professor of geography at the University of Nottingham in the United Kingdom who has done research on the health implications of dust in Central Asia. She says that while dust is definitely a concern, poor nutrition looms larger for many of the people who live in the lower Amu Darya and Syr Darya basins. The real cause of the regional cluster of ailments needs further study, she says. "The situation is extremely complicated." Professor Nick Aladin from St. Petersburg believes that chemical contamination was much worse during Soviet times, but now that local farmers can't afford to purchase as much fertilizer or pesticides, he has become skeptical of many of the contamination claims. "The idea that there's horrible chemical contamination in everything," he says, "is one of the myths of the Aral Sea."

~

CAN ANYTHING BE DONE to revive the Aral Sea ecosystem? Because of the sheer magnitude of the problem, local officials in Uzbekistan have practically given up all hope of restoring the Large Aral. The Amu Darya's delta is so far from the shrunken Aral's edge that it would be impossible to bring the sea back without spending billions and billions of dollars. "It would be good to restore all of the Aral Sea—give us the money and we will do it," says Ubbiniyaz Ashirbekov at the International Fund for Saving the Aral Sea. "Our pocket is empty." Instead, Mr. Ashirbekov and his colleagues have embarked on a less ambitious plan to reengineer the Amu Darya River delta near Muynak. They are in the process of constructing a series of delta-area shallow reservoirs (in addition to those that already exist) that will help bring at least some of the old fishing culture back to the region. Compared to the old Aral, the reservoirs are literally a drop in the bucket, but they have been embraced by the local population. Though there's not enough production to fire up the old cannery, area residents have taken to the reservoirs in canoes and small rowboats to pursue fish with spears and throw nets. Once again it's possible to make a little money as a fisherman. "These reservoirs have an economic and a social impact," says Professor Aladin, who endorses the reservoir program. "People here are so homesick for the sea that these reservoirs serve as a kind of compensation."

The reservoir expansion program has also brought wildlife back to the Amu Darya delta. The reservoirs are sprinkled with cormorants, gulls, terns, herons, waterfowl, and shorebirds, making them a vibrant contrast to the desert and old seabed that surround them. Another glimmer of hope, of a sort, can be found at the Small Aral Sea to the north. The Kazakhstan government has sealed off the Small Aral from the Large Aral by building a dam. Keeping the Small Aral separate has allowed the Kazakh government to use the diminished flows from the Syr Darya River to restore the Small Aral's water level. The dam has been met with mixed emotions in some sectors, because its seen as a sign that the Kazakh government has given up on the wider Aral ecosystem. "It is an extreme intervention," Professor O'Hara says. "It is helping to stabilize that part of the sea, but it is 'small.'" But Kazakh officials are seeing results. In recent years the Small Aral's salinity has dropped, species populations have rebounded, and water levels have risen. "The small sea will be saved by Kazakhstan," predicts Michael Glantz, "And the western part of the big sea will probably be saved only because it's so deep. But to save [the rest of the] big sea . . . that's not going to happen."

The limited successes in the Small Aral, and the reservoirs of the Amu Darya delta, seem diminutive in the face of the unmitigated disaster that surrounds them. The dry seabed of the old Aral is a bizarre and otherworldly place. Some areas are a flat, barren, brine-crunchy moonscape that stretches as far as the eye can see.

Photo 2.4. *The dry bed of the Aral Sea. In 1960 the water was perhaps forty five feet deep at this spot, which is now nearly sixty miles from the water's edge. (Photo by Peter Annin)*

Everywhere the land is tinted salty white. Standing in the middle of this great salt flat, it challenges the boundaries of the mind to imagine that a mere generation ago fish-filled waters were forty-five feet deep at this spot and fishing boats and other vessels sailed overhead. As a four-wheel-drive traverses this country, the old seabed's fine talc-like soil is easily stirred up by the tires. The dust rises like a great billowing sandstorm behind the rear bumper. Once airborne, the dust finds its way into everything—the hair, eyes, nose, and mouth.

But there are also incongruent oases in some isolated spots. In these areas, where the aquifer lies just below the surface, a new rich ecosystem has taken over. Lush fields of reeds and grasses stand more than six feet high, dwarfing human and vehicle alike. Honeybees pick over colorful wildflowers, and songbirds flit among the stems. Wildlife is abundant in this fertile cover. Pheasants and wild hares abound. So do foxes, jackals, wild boars—even wolves. Raptors, like harriers and eagles, are notably abundant. Though no surface water is visible here, these oases provide a fleeting glimpse of what the Aral ecosystem must have been like.

After hours and hours of dusty driving, finally, the blue hues of the Large Aral become visible off in the distance—a view that warrants stopping for a look. It's about this time that one begins to feel the microclimate that disappeared from Muynak decades ago. Out in the middle of the baking desert, the cooler air by the sea is a very welcome respite. When the vehicle finally reaches the water's edge, the sea smell is tangible. The breeze is cooler here; the briny whiteness of the soil even brighter. Boats are noticeably absent, and it seems eerily tranquil. A few wayward ducks fly over head, as do some herons. A handful of small gulls sits in the water fifty yards from shore. "They are here for the brine shrimp," says Professor Aladin. He adds that the shrimp are believed to have arrived in 2001, their eggs possibly transported by birds from the Caspian Sea three hundred miles to the west.

The sea is clear, cool, and extraordinarily salty. Like the Dead Sea in the Middle East, the high salinity of the Large Aral makes

Photo 2.5. *After hours and hours of dusty driving, the Aral Sea becomes visible off in the distance. (Photo by Peter Annin)*

The Great Lakes Water Wars

the water dense, increasing the buoyancy of things floating in it. It's possible for a grown person to float high in the water without a life-jacket—it would be very difficult to drown in such waters. After a dip in the Aral, there's no need for a towel. The evaporative powers of the desert slurp water droplets from the skin. After just a few tingling minutes, small clusters of salt stain the body at every spot where a drop once rested. It's hard to imagine anything surviving in such salty waters. And it's hard to imagine anyone ever allowing this wholesale ecological disaster to happen again.

~

WHAT LESSONS can Great Lakes residents learn from the Aral Sea's demise? Environmental advocates regularly point to the Aral Sea as a symbol of doom. Web sites and even peer-reviewed academic articles about the Great Lakes reference the Aral's desiccation. The suggestion from the environmental community is clear: if North Americans don't do a better job of managing water use, the Great Lakes too could become oversubscribed environmental disasters, leaving the regional ecology—and economy—in a shambles. But most scientists believe that an Aral-like disaster in the Great Lakes is extremely unlikely. Central Asia's desert climate contrasts sharply with that of the wet weather of the North American Great Lakes. In addition, they say it's hard to imagine that an Aral-like, industrial-scale diversion of water would ever be tolerated in the United States or Canada, where water regulations, and an environmentally conscious electorate, would rise up in revulsion to any such action.

That may be true, environmentalists say, but there's more than one way to drain a lake. Maybe the rapid decimation that occurred at the Aral Sea is not possible, but a slower, more methodical bleeding of the ecosystem is harder to rule out, particularly when factoring in the unpredictable concerns of climate change. A disaster is still a disaster, they say, whether it takes forty years or a century to occur. "It's not that we're ever going to lose the Great Lakes in their entirety," says Sarah Miller, coordinator with the Canadian

Environmental Law Association, "but we could severely compromise them in ways that we really don't understand today."

Professor Philip Micklin is one of the few Aral Sea experts who lives in the Great Lakes Basin. An emeritus professor of geography at Western Michigan University, he says the lessons of the Aral Sea are not complex. Like many other experts, he does not see a Great Lakes repeat of the Aral's desiccation. "The era of big, large-scale diversions is over," he declares. But he does believe that the Great Lakes are far from invincible, and those who think otherwise might pay closer attention to the Aral's history. Before the sea was drained, some Soviet scientists warned of environmental calamity, but they were ignored. "The big lesson is simple . . . Don't enter into activities that could have long-term damage unless you take a careful look at the potential consequences," he says. "And the problem is that once you make a commitment to give somebody water, you can't take it back, because they become dependent on it."

Professor Noah Hall would like to think that an Aral-like disaster could not be repeated in the Great Lakes region. But he is not as confident as Professor Micklin that the era of large-scale diversions is over. He is concerned that rising water use within the Great Lakes Basin, in combination with the threat of future diversions, could do harm—not necessarily on the scale of the Aral Sea, but enough to alter the ecosystem. "If something like what happened to the Aral Sea were to happen here," he says, "It's going to come as much from our own use of the water within the Basin . . . You'll have a death of five hundred cuts from diversions and five hundred cuts from in-Basin uses. You're not going to be able to point the finger at one or the other. You'll have to address both."

There are those, however, who stand on the shores of the Great Lakes and imply that the lakes are an endless bounty. Former Speaker of the U.S. House of Representatives Newt Gingrich attracted attention after making that suggestion in a Michigan speech during the fall of 2005. The idea that the Great Lakes could be drained was "nutty," he said, scolding those who might suggest otherwise.[6] While Congressman Gingrich was correct in suggesting that a wholesale draining of the Great Lakes is truly difficult to imagine, in the heavily populated Great Lakes Basin even a partial draining would be devastating to the region. Looking out over the massive expanse of clear Great Lakes waters, it's tempting to think that the Basin's resources are inexhaustible. But if nothing else, the Aral Sea's desiccation shows that large bodies of water like the Great Lakes are not indomitable. "People see how vast the Great Lakes are and mistake that vastness for invincibility," warns Cameron Davis, executive director at the Alliance for the Great Lakes in Chicago. But the Aral's experience shows that humans do have the power and the ability to destroy natural wonders like the Great Lakes, and long before that, irreparable harm would come to the regional ecosystem and economy. What's more, with the unpredictable advent of climate change (discussed in chapter 3) water managers in the Great Lakes region need to ensure that they don't inadvertently take steps today that could lead to irreparable harm tomorrow. Large lakes have limits. If care is not taken in their management, ecological and economic disaster will follow. The sad people of Muynak can testify to that as well as anyone on earth.

Chapter 3

Rising Temperatures, Falling Water?

ONTARIO'S WASAGA BEACH is one of the finest swimming destinations in all of North America. Nestled into the southeast corner of Lake Huron's expansive Georgian Bay, Wasaga boasts nine miles of white sand that slants out into Lake Huron's azure waters at such a gradual slope that a hundred yards from shore the water barely reaches a swimmer's waistline. A provincial park since 1962, Wasaga is just eighty miles from cosmopolitan Toronto, which helps explain why it is one of the most popular day-use tourist destinations in Canada. They come for the fun, and the sun, and to frolic in one of the most bountiful freshwater ecosystems on earth. "On a busy weekend we can have 60,000 to 120,000 people," says park superintendent Mark Shoreman. "We claim it's the world's longest freshwater beach."

But Wasaga is also an ideal place to witness the remarkable natural fluctuations that occur in Great Lakes water levels. Thanks to the faint tilt in the sand at Wasaga Beach, when Lake Huron's water level falls by one vertical foot, it can actually change the Wasaga Beach waterline by dozens of feet. In 1986, during historic high water levels on the Great Lakes, Wasaga's visitors only needed to amble a few yards from the tree line to reach the water's edge. But in 2000, when water levels approached historic lows, beachgoers were forced to walk 150 yards to the water, often dodging the large thickets of sedges and coastal meadow that had sprouted in the sand where water once stood.

Tourists find these widely varying lake levels to be alarming—something must be wrong, they assume. Nothing could be further from the truth. Vacillating lake levels are what experts refer to as "natural variability," and that variability plays a key role in the complex Great Lakes ecosystem. "Natural variability is an absolute necessity," says Douglas Wilcox, a wetlands expert with the U.S. Geological Survey's Great Lakes Science Center in Ann Arbor, Michigan. "The [Great Lakes] plant and animal communities are not only adapted to that variability, but they absolutely require that variability to provide habitat and food, and nesting/spawning [areas] to maintain their populations."

The interface between land and water is a rich and ecologically productive venue, and different creatures benefit at different water-level stages. During low water, long beaches and broad expanses of mudflats are created at the lakes' edges. These flats are actually seed banks that have been harboring the progeny of rare water-level-dependent plants for decades. When the waters recede, these areas are exposed to the air and the unique plants embark on a robust growth binge, creating all sorts of food, cover, and other habitat for a variety of important wetland species. In essence, these beaches and mudflats imitate a desert after a cloudburst—they bloom. That's precisely what happened in 2000, when lake levels dropped after a long period of high water. "It was incredible. It was just absolutely incredible," says Mr. Wilcox. "These sediments were exposed and just came back like gangbusters [with] the most diverse vegetation you can imagine." This is a cycle that has repeated itself for thousands of years in the Great Lakes Basin.

The extent of these lake-level fluctuations is impressive. It's not unusual for water levels in the Great Lakes to change by more than a foot from one year to the next. And the difference between the historic high and historic low water levels on some Great Lakes is more than 6 vertical feet.[1] Since water-level monitoring began in the mid-nineteenth century, record-keeping suggests that the lakes may operate roughly on a thirty-year cycle from high point to high point, with a dip falling approximately every fifteen years in between. Water fluctuations like that may be invigorating to the ecosystem, but they can cause headaches for humans who relish lake-level consistency. Docks can stand awkwardly high and dry one year, and then be under water a decade later.

What kind of effect will climate change have on these natural water-level fluctuations? That is one of the most intriguing and complex questions facing Great Lakes scientists and policymakers today. For example, when state and provincial officials gathered between 2001 and 2005 to craft their Great Lakes water-management system, climate change hovered in the background of the negotiating room. The problem is that nobody really knows how climate change will affect the Great Lakes ecosystem, but a number of the brightest minds in the region have expended significant time putting together some very authoritative projections.

Climate change—or global warming—is caused by the accumulation of excess carbon dioxide and other heat-trapping gases in the atmosphere. By confining that heat, these gases are gradually increasing temperatures on earth. The vast majority of scientists say that modern society—and the fossil fuel–powered automobiles and power plants that come with it—is at least partly to blame for the problem. Research shows that global temperatures are expected to increase by 2.52 to 10.44 degrees Fahrenheit by 2100 and that temperatures increased 1 degree Fahrenheit during the twentieth century.[2] While some prior studies have predicted that Great Lakes water levels will fall by 1.5 to 8 feet by century's end, those studies are considered out of date.[3] Research from 2003 suggests that some lake levels could rise by more than a foot during the next hundred years, or decline by 4.5 feet, depending on which assumptions are made and which scenarios are used.[4] These fluctuations would be in addition to the natural 6-foot variability that has already been recorded on some lakes since the mid-1800s. Which means that if the most pessimistic prognostications are borne out—or even just turn out to be half true—then water tensions in the Great Lakes region are bound to increase as everything from large-scale in-basin

Photos 3.1 and 3.2. *Water levels fluctuate widely—and naturally—on the Great Lakes, particularly on lakes Huron and Michigan. The top photo shows the U.S. Geological Survey's Hammond Bay Biological Station on Lake Huron during a period of high water in 1986. The second photo shows the same beach during a period of lower water levels in early 2006. (Top photo by USGS Hammond Bay Biological Station; bottom photo by Peter Annin)*

water consumption to tiny diversion proposals are met with greater scrutiny.

~

TO THE AVERAGE CITIZEN, it's hard to imagine that a temperature change of just a few degrees can have that much influence on an ecosystem. After all, most people can't tell the difference between, say, 55 and 60 degrees Fahrenheit when they are outdoors. But it's important to realize that during the last ice age more than ten thousand years ago—when the Great Lakes region was covered in a mile-thick sheet of glacial ice—the average global temperature was perhaps just 8 or 10 degrees Fahrenheit cooler than it is today. So when scientists warn that temperatures may rise a little more than 8 degrees Fahrenheit during the twenty-first century, essentially they are warning of a rapidly advancing ice age in reverse. "In the next hundred years we will have the same warming that has occurred since the last ice age, which ended roughly 10,000 years ago," predicts George Kling, a University of Michigan biology professor and the lead author of one Great Lakes climate report. "That's why people are so worried about a 6- to 10-degree Fahrenheit increase in temperature—because it is happening in only 100 years, and not in 10,000 or 20,000 years," he says. "We do not know which of the organisms on earth are going to be able to adapt to such a rapid temperature change."

Climate change will affect more than organisms, of course. As the water cycle in the region becomes more unpredictable, communities outside the Great Lakes Basin may find it ever more difficult to adapt to the challenges of global warming, resulting in even greater pressure to divert water outside the Great Lakes Basin. This could create a vicious cycle in which human demands for lake water rise just as climate change drops Great Lakes water levels to historic lows.

To understand the significance of these Great Lakes climate-change studies, one needs to grasp how the global climate research community works. By far the most influential climate change organization in the world is the Geneva-based IPCC—the

Intergovernmental Panel on Climate Change. Established in 1988 by the World Meteorological Organization and the United Nations Environment Programme, the IPCC doesn't conduct any of its own research, but rather serves as the lead monitor, sifter, and highlighter of the most important and salient peer-reviewed climate-change studies around the world. Then, every few years, after numerous committees of international scientists have reviewed the latest research, the IPCC publishes an "assessment" laying out its latest interpretation of where the global climate seems to be headed.[5]

The IPCC and other scientists depend heavily on climate-change models to conduct much of their work. Field observations play an important role as well. These models are extremely complicated computer programs—physics equations, really—that try to quantify and replicate all the key aspects of the earth's atmosphere on a computer. The models look at currents in the ocean, winds in the atmosphere, temperature changes—all of the various scientific principles that determine how our climate behaves. Over the years, approximately fifteen major models have been produced.[6] There is the Canadian Climate Centre Model, for example, or the Hadley Centre Model from the United Kingdom, and the National Center for Atmospheric Research Model in the United States. Each of these models has many similarities, but they also have their individual strengths and specialties. Scientists who monitor climate change are very familiar with the various models and how they parallel and differ from one another. The purpose of the models is to project what climate will do in the future. But to test a model's accuracy scientists will start back in, say, 1900 and run the model to see how closely it tracks actual changes in the atmosphere during the twentieth century. If the model closely replicates atmospheric changes during the past, then scientists gain confidence in the model's predictions for the future.

Scenarios play an important role in climate-change research as well. Scenarios are a series of different historical assumptions about the future that are plugged into the various climate-change models. For example, will China and India develop rapidly and burn enormous amounts of fossil fuels in the process, churning out mammoth amounts of heat-trapping gases? Or will they develop at a more gradual pace—or adopt more renewable fuels—that won't put such a burden on the climate? And while China and India are growing, will Western Europe, Japan, and the United States invest more heavily in renewable energy and hybrid and fuel-cell cars—all of which will reduce their emissions of greenhouse gases? And will the world's forests—which consume carbon dioxide and help reduce global warming—decline during the twenty-first century? Or will reforestation programs take off and help mitigate warming? It's with their scenarios that the scientists take out the crystal ball and attempt to predict the future. That's a very difficult job, of course, so scientists cover themselves by producing a large number of different scenarios and running them through the models. This allows researchers to come up with a range of potential climate-change prognostications. These various scenarios, and predictions, are then balanced by the IPCC in a peer-reviewed fashion, until an international scientific consensus is reached. The IPCC then releases the consensus or "assessment" to the public.

The most recent IPCC analysis as of this writing came out in 2001. It found that the 1990s were "very likely" the warmest decade on record and that 1998 was the warmest year in recorded history. (Research since this IPCC assessment found that the top five warmest years since the late 1800s have been 2005, 1998, 2002, 2003, and 2004.)[7] The IPCC also determined that the temperature spike during the twentieth century was larger than that experienced during any other hundred-year timeframe in the last thousand years.[8] The report added that these temperature changes have altered the global environment in several tangible ways: (1) sea levels have risen four to eight inches, (2) the period of ice cover in parts of the Northern Hemisphere has decreased by two weeks, (3) arctic sea ice has thinned by 40 percent, and (4) the Northern Hemisphere's growing season has increased by one to four days per decade since the 1960s.

More importantly, in the same report the IPCC predicted that things will get much worse in the twenty-first century. The speed with which the earth warms during the next century will likely have no precedent in the last ten thousand years, making the world a very different place.[9] The levels and predictability of global precipitation will change; glaciers will continue to retreat; sea levels will rise, posing new dangers to island and coastal communities; human health will be threatened by more disease; ecological productivity will be altered; and there will be an increased risk of extinction. Small temperature rises will increase global cereal crop production, but large temperature increases will bring declines. And most important for residents of the Great Lakes region, the IPCC predicted that tension over water will reach new heights. "Climate change," the report said, "will exacerbate water shortages in many water-scarce areas of the world."[10]

~

THOSE PROJECTIONS ARE FAR from comforting. But the IPCC is a global outfit, and its prognostications are for the entire planet. It's widely believed that climate change will affect different regions of the earth in different ways. How will the Great Lakes fare? It may seem counterintuitive, but scientists say that creating regional climate projections is even more difficult than crafting the global variety, because the closer one zeros in on a particular place, the harder it is to be specific about how climate will behave. "A lot of the basic understanding of climate change on the global scale is pretty well in hand," says Brent Lofgren, a Great Lakes climate-change expert with the National Oceanic and Atmospheric Administration (NOAA) in Ann Arbor, Michigan. "But a lot of the local impacts of climate change are more uncertain."

Two climate-change reports have been produced for the Great Lakes region since 2000. The first, released in October of that year, was a federal report called *Preparing for a Changing Climate*. This study is often referred to as the "Sousounis report," after its lead author Peter Sousounis, who was a University of Michigan professor at the time. The Sousounis report was conducted by climate experts in the Great Lakes states as part of a federal initiative to gauge how climate change will affect the United States. The study based its findings on two general circulation models: the Canadian Climate Centre Model and the United Kingdom's Hadley Centre Model.

The Sousounis report found that the Great Lakes region would be roughly 25 percent wetter by 2100 and that regional air temperatures could rise from 3.6 to 7.2 degrees Fahrenheit. But the report added that in many cases the increased wetness would be offset by more evaporation in a warmer world.[11] It predicted that economically important trees like the quaking aspen, yellow birch, red pine, and white pine will decline severely on the U.S. side of the Great Lakes Basin, which could bring roiling changes in the region's forest-products industry.[12] The report also cited alarming research about the decline of migratory bird species in the Great Lakes, the second most biologically diverse birding region in the Lower 48. "Particularly hard hit would be the wood warblers with large numbers of species projected to be extirpated from Michigan (61% lost), Minnesota (52% lost) and Wisconsin (67% lost)," the report said.[13] Finally, the report also foresaw a rise in violent weather, including floods, tornadoes, and blizzards. The region could expect a notable increase in heat waves and days above 90 degrees Fahrenheit, with traditional steady, soaking rains supplanted by raging downpours that increase erosion and runoff.[14]

Some of the report's most dramatic findings involved the Great Lakes themselves, particularly water levels. But the report came up with different results depending on which model it used. The Hadley model found that there would be little change in Great Lakes water levels—and even possibly a boost of more than one foot in some lakes. But the results from the Canadian model were more grim, showing potential lake-level drops of 0.7 to 2.4 feet by 2030 and of 2 to 5 feet by 2090.[15] If such lake-level declines were to occur, the report warned, "arguments for interbasin diversion of water into and out of the Great Lakes are also likely to intensify."[16] But with two models showing two very different predictions, the report's authors said policymakers need to be prepared for anything. "The different results from the two scenarios emphasize the necessity of having policies and water management plans that are robust enough to function over a wide range of water supplies, lake levels and flows," they said. "A drop in the levels of Lakes Michigan-Huron of about a meter in 30 years would severely change the nature of that immense body of water."[17]

To citizens living in and around the Great Lakes Basin, there's a big difference between a slight increase in lake levels and a drop of five feet. How do scientists expect the general public to interpret such widely varying results? "Every prediction contains some inherent uncertainty," says Peter Sousounis. "And what the two different modeling results show are some bounds on that uncertainty. It's the range." Okay, but it's still a big range. How does a scientist like Mr. Sousounis interpret that range? Does he see a rise in lake levels as being more likely, or a fall? "My perspective is that the results suggest that a decrease is more likely than an increase," he says. "If you were a betting person, for example, you wouldn't bet that the lake levels would rise . . . the results suggest that there is a higher probability than not that lake levels will fall by a significant amount."

The negative influence that lower water levels would have on the Great Lakes can't be overstated. Major declines could cripple the $3 billion Great Lakes shipping industry. The multibillion-dollar tourism industry would be affected as well. Michigan has more registered boats per capita than any other state in the nation, and the eight Great Lakes states are home to one-third of all registered boats in America. Retail sales of boating equipment in the region total more than $3 billion annually.[18] If boaters have problems getting to docks and marinas, it could result in millions of lost tourism revenue. Boating and shipping disruptions could increase demands for dredging, which would create another problem—what to do with the dredged material, much of which is contaminated owing to prior decades of Great Lakes pollution. Hydropower generation, especially in New York and Ontario, would also be hit hard. According to the International Joint Commission, low lake levels of the early 1960s resulted in hydropower losses on the Niagara and St. Lawrence rivers of 19 and 26 percent, respectively.[19] Those losses would certainly be even greater if climate change brings record low lake levels.

The Sousounis report pointed out that there would be some

benefits in the Great Lakes region from global warming, though not enough to offset the negatives. In some cases, lake-effect snow would be replaced by lake-effect rain. This would reduce snow-removal costs in many parts of the region, as well as snow-related traffic accidents (though any resulting savings would be offset by a decline in winter tourism like skiing and snowmobiling). Populations of game birds like bobwhite quail and ring-necked pheasants would likely increase, though duck hunting could decline. But the most significant benefits would come in the agricultural sector, as farmers would be able to take advantage of longer and warmer growing seasons that would likely bring greater yields.[20]

~

THE SOUSOUNIS REPORT was followed in April 2003 by another Great Lakes climate-change assessment that relied on updated modeling and new research. This second report, *Confronting Climate Change in the Great Lakes Region*, was produced by the Union of Concerned Scientists (UCS) and the Ecological Society of America, and it's commonly known as the "UCS report."[21] It emphasized that global warming has already started in the Great Lakes region. Winters are getting shorter, annual average temperatures are getting warmer, ice cover on lakes throughout the region is lessening, and the heavy rainstorms that experts have long said would be a hallmark of climate change are already on the rise.[22] The report predicted that by the end of the twenty-first century average winter temperatures in the region will be 5 to 12 degrees Fahrenheit warmer, summer temperatures will increase by 5 to 20 degrees Fahrenheit, and the regional growing season will expand by one to two months.

Like the Sousounis report, the UCS assessment also offered a range of options as to how climate change will affect Great Lakes water levels. The UCS report said water levels could either rise by 1.1 feet or drop by 4.5 feet during the next century.[23] Of the two scenarios, the UCS authors concurred with Mr. Sousounis, saying that a decline in lake levels was more likely. "Declines in both inland lakes and the Great Lakes are anticipated in the future," the authors wrote, adding that "water withdrawals from the Great Lakes are already the subject of contentious debate, and pressures for more water for irrigation, drinking and other human uses may intensify the conflicts as water shortages develop."[24]

The UCS report highlighted notable changes that are expected in precipitation as well. While more rain is likely to fall during the winter and spring, rainfall during the summer could plunge— possibly by as much as 50 percent.[25] This could increase water temperatures in fragile cold-water lakes and streams, reduce streamflow, and boost the importance of—and dependency on—irrigation for Great Lakes Basin agriculture. Evapotranspiration—a fancy word meaning water that evaporates from the earth's surface as well as water transmitted to the atmosphere by trees and other plants—is expected to increase, particularly in the winter and spring. That, in turn, could reduce soil moisture during key stages of the agricultural growing season. "Soil moisture is projected to increase as much as 80 percent during winter in some locales, but decrease regionally by up to 30 percent in summer and fall," the report said.[26]

Though many people expect climate change to be a gradual process, scientists warn that it doesn't always work that way. There are times when the climate cruises along on autopilot and then just hits a tipping point that brings on a whole new suite of changes. "It is possible that very abrupt and strong short-term changes in climate could occur as well," the UCS report warned. "An abrupt change is one that takes place so rapidly and unexpectedly within years to decades that human or natural systems have difficulty adapting."[27] The likelihood of an abrupt climate change is a matter of debate in the scientific community. But it has happened before, and many experts feel a burden to alert the public that it could occur again.[28] "One of the possible outcomes will be . . . an abrupt change," says Frank Quinn, a retired hydrologist from NOAA's Ann Arbor, Michigan, office. "That is very likely and that's really more the way the climate operates—where all of a sudden something triggers a change."[29]

The UCS report also highlighted the extremely important but unheralded role that ice cover plays in the ecology of the Great

Lakes. A century and a half of regional ice cover data shows that the fall freeze-up on regional lakes has already been pushed back by 1.5 days per decade, while the spring ice breakup has been occurring approximately two days sooner every ten years.[30] "Ice acts as a lid on the lakes to prevent evaporation during the winter, so if you don't have ice during the winter, you're going to get a lot more evaporation," says Katharine Hayhoe, from the University of Illinois Atmospheric Sciences Department, who contributed to the UCS report. "As temperatures rise because of climate change, you're going to get less ice cover during the winter."

One of the most important ecological functions that occurs in the lakes is something scientists refer to as "mixing." In the summer the Great Lakes stratify into different temperature layers as the sun heats the water near the surface and cooler waters stay near the bottom. In the winter, however, as the surface waters cool they sink and mix with the deep water. This extremely important biological event helps refresh and circulate lake water. Mixing infuses oxygen in the lower depths—oxygen that fish and other deep-water animals need to survive. Then as summer returns, the stratification cycle resumes, and the deeper lake sections rely on the oxygen they received during the winter mixing. But longer, hotter summers would extend the periods between winter mixings, potentially starving the deeper depths of oxygen. When sections of lakes or oceans run out of oxygen, these areas are referred to as "dead zones" because without oxygen few if any creatures can survive. The UCS report warned that climate change could increase Great Lakes summer dead zones, reducing productivity up and down the food chain. "Longer stratification periods and warmer bottom temperatures will increase oxygen depletion in the deep waters of the Great Lakes," the report said. "[This] will have negative impacts on most of the organisms in the lakes. Persistent dead zones can result in massive fish kills, damage to fisheries, toxic algal blooms, and foul-smelling, musty tasting drinking water."[31]

~

SCIENTISTS BELIEVE that documented ice-cover declines in the Great Lakes region are a key sign that climate change has already arrived. But what about the round of low lake levels that occurred in 2000? Was that also a climate-change hallmark? Probably not. "The big drop that we saw from 1998 through 2000 is something that I consider to be primarily attributable to natural variability," says NOAA's Brent Lofgren. "One of the points that I try to make to people is to not confuse global warming's effects with natural variability. Natural variability always has been, and always will be with us." So how will we know when lake-level fluctuations are caused by climate change rather than natural variability? "When we start to have consistently low levels," says Frank Quinn, the retired NOAA hydrologist, "When we start getting below what we would call our 'normal variability' on a consistent basis." If and when that time comes, it will have profound effects on the regional ecosystem—and the economy. The Great Lakes regional economy is a $2 trillion juggernaut. If the region were a country, it would have the third-largest economy in the world; only the U.S. and Japanese economies are larger.[32] Much of that economy is intimately tied to the region's water-rich resources, which means billions of dollars and an untold number of jobs.

In a 2000 report, the International Joint Commission cautioned policymakers not to assume that water-management regimes will remain the same under climate change. The IJC strongly discouraged the governments of the United States and Canada from taking any actions that might alter levels and flows in the Great Lakes—including major new in-basin consumptive uses and diversions. "The Commission believes that considerable caution should be exercised with respect to any factors potentially reducing water levels and outflows," the IJC report said. "For the 21st Century, there is a great deal of uncertainty regarding factors such as future consumptive uses, small-scale removals of water, and climate change . . . This—and the prospect of adverse cumulative impacts of new human interventions—suggests a need for great caution in dealing with those water use factors that are within the control of Basin managers."[33]

Dredging is one of the most common "human interventions" that has been used to assist the Great Lakes shipping industry. Why not just continue to dredge the Great Lakes' connecting channels deeper, if and when water levels drop in the future? That's been tried in the past, and the results weren't good. In 1917 a dredging project deepened a navigation channel in the St. Clair River north of Detroit, the main outflow from Lake Huron.[34] But, hydrologically speaking, dredging the channel was the equivalent of widening the drain in a bathtub, and the water levels in Lake Huron and Lake Michigan permanently dropped nearly sixteen inches—the single-largest manmade alteration of Great Lakes water levels.[35]

In addition, an engineering report released by W. F. Baird & Associates in 2005 alleged that forty years of erosion at the bottom of the same St. Clair River shipping channel has scoured out the bathtub drain even further. Engineers said that this erosion may have dropped Huron and Michigan lake levels by an additional foot or more—for a grand total of more than thirty inches.[36] That's an enormous amount of water. The Baird study estimated that the lost water was equivalent to one-fourth the volume of Lake Erie.[37] (The U.S. Army Corps of Engineers has raised questions about the Baird report—and the issue remains under further study.)[38] Whether or not this research is conclusive, there's no dispute that dredging on the river lowered lake levels by an alarming amount. This effect helps explain why any talk by the shipping industry or the Army Corps of Engineers to "improve," widen, or deepen the connecting channels between the Great Lakes is met with ferocious opposition.

~

BY NATURE—and training—scientists are reserved, careful, and conservative when making projections for the future. When scientists say that there are serious issues looming on the horizon, says Linda Mortsch, a climate-change researcher with Environment Canada in Waterloo, Ontario, policymakers should take heed. She believes that water availability is going to be the key issue for the public as climate change bears down on the Great Lakes. Consequently, she says that implementing a modern Great Lakes water-management system is imperative. "We have to think about how we're going to negotiate some of these hard decisions in terms of water use and allocation now," she says. "So we can have a rational, thoughtful discussion before we're in a crisis where emotions run high."

People can also channel their climate-change angst into creating a smaller greenhouse-gas footprint. They can conserve energy by installing low-energy fluorescent lightbulbs, purchasing a fuel-efficient vehicle, and supporting alternative-energy sources like solar power and wind. More importantly, scientists say, concerned citizens could convince the U.S. government to ratify the Kyoto Protocol—the international agreement designed to curb global greenhouse-gas emissions—or convince the government to otherwise commit to a substantial reduction in greenhouse gases (Canada has already ratified the Kyoto Protocol). "We lack leadership in dealing with these changes that we know are going to happen," says University of Michigan's Professor Kling. "There is an urgency about this that so many people downplay or just ignore that it's worrisome." What is particularly worrisome to scientists is that even if we were to cap greenhouse-gas emissions at current levels, the earth would continue to warm for decades to come.

~

SO WHAT DOES THIS ALL MEAN for the people at Ontario's Wasaga Beach? If the more optimistic lake-level scenarios hold true, not much. But if lake-level declines of 3 or even 4.5 feet are borne out, then a visit to Wasaga will be a very different experience indeed. During the first ten years of the park's history, visitors were actually permitted to drive their vehicles on the sand. But in the early 1970s, high water put a squeeze on the beach, pushing sunbathers and vehicles dangerously close together, so the park banned beach driving. With climate change threatening to drop Lake Huron several feet below the all-time lows, lake levels at Wasaga Beach could recede so far that visitors might be forced to walk hundreds of yards to the water.

Should a prolonged period of such low water occur, park superintendent Mark Shoreman says he won't be surprised if local residents and cottagers start talking about constructing small screen houses or other buildings closer to the water's edge. "At what point do you say that the shoreline is beyond shoreline and it's become land?" he asks rhetorically. Decades into the future, with the water potentially receding far away from washrooms and other facilities, might the park be forced to consider allowing vehicles back onto the beach—if for no other reason than to help seniors and other special-needs visitors with their "commute" to the water? "Transporting them to the water's edge?" he asks. "Who knows?" But if the worst climate-change projections come true, a long walk to the beach is likely to be the least of the region's concerns.

Chapter 4

Aversion to Diversion

I T WAS ONE OF THE BOLDEST engineering schemes ever con-
ceived on the face of the planet, and it called for replumbing
much of the natural hydrology of North America. It started in the
extreme Northwest—the wilds of Alaska—and marched methodi-
cally south through British Columbia before spanning across most
of the continent. The plan's western half envisioned harnessing
some of the largest and wildest rivers in Alaska, British Columbia,
and the Yukon Territory, including the Copper, Susitna, Tanana,
and Yukon. The Columbia and Fraser rivers would have been affected too.[1] The idea was to divert part of the flows of these raging
rivers into the mother of all reservoirs: the Rocky Mountain
Trench, a giant natural canyon stretching through most of British
Columbia.

Damming this canyon would create a surreal five-hundred-mile-
long inland sea, the waters of which could be sent to the rest of the
continent as needed along with up to seventy thousand megawatts
of surplus hydropower.[2] Of course, the plan called for much of this
diverted water to be sent to the American Southwest. The dry
Canadian prairies would get a cut too. The system's eastern branch
would send water into the Peace River Valley of Alberta and on
through Saskatchewan, Manitoba, and western Ontario until it
reached Lake Superior. This eastern arm of the system was referred
to as the Canadian–Great Lakes Canal or the Alberta–Great Lakes
Canal and would carry 40 million acre feet of water to Lake Superior annually.[3] That's enough water to raise the level of all five

Great Lakes, double the hydropower output at Niagara Falls, and still have water to spare for the Mississippi River watershed.[4]

Such was the vision of NAWAPA—the North American Water and Power Alliance—and it was estimated to cost anywhere between $100 billion and $300 billion (in 1960s dollars).[5] The project would have touched at least seven Canadian provinces or territories, thirty-three U.S. states, and a portion of northern Mexico (fig. 4.1).[6] Widely promoted in the 1960s by the Ralph M. Parsons Company of Pasadena, California, NAWAPA would later be viewed by environmentalists (as well as by most Alaskans and Canadians) as the hydrologic anti-Christ. Though it never came close to being built, it was the envy of several water engineers who were looking for a way to outdo the massive subsidized water projects that had been built in the 1930s, '40s, and '50s. These "welfare water" schemes came from a generation of men who believed that leaving water in its natural basin was somehow a missed economic opportunity. Water was meant to be moved and used where humans needed it most, rather than foolishly be permitted to flow into the sea. Behind their schemes lay a notable disregard for what these projects would do to the natural environment left behind by the displaced water. "NAWAPA, of course, is the granddaddy of them all—the most grandiose and the most ludicrous," says water expert Peter Gleick. "Some people have described it as a water engineer's wet dream—which is sort of a funny joke on all sorts of levels. It's a ridiculous idea. But it was the logical extension of a whole series of somewhat less ridiculous ideas, like . . . the massive plumbing projects that we built in the West."

NAWAPA seems bizarrely far-fetched today, but it had a number of influential supporters in the 1960s.[7] Though it merely envisioned the Great Lakes as a connecting channel in a much larger scheme, it struck a chord among regional residents who wondered how long it would take for someone to concoct a similar plan that just happened to send Great Lakes water in the opposite direction. NAWAPA helped inspire a generation of far-flung Great Lakes diversion schemes—none of which made any economic sense. "Diverting Great Lakes water is financially stupid," says Reg Gilbert,

The North American Water and Power Alliance Plan

Fig. 4.1. *The North American Water and Power Alliance (NAWAPA) was an unrealized scheme hatched during the 1960s to transport massive amounts of water throughout much of the continent. (By permission from Geographical, the magazine of the Royal Geographical Society)*

senior coordinator at Great Lakes United, in Buffalo, New York. "Even though it doesn't make sense, the fact that people keep thinking about it just shows you the magnetic attraction of the water body."

That history of desire has helped fuel the anti-diversion paranoia that remains rampant throughout the Great Lakes region. The anti-diversion movement hit its stride in the early 1980s when a string of diversion proposals prompted regional officials to push through a series of policies designed to keep Great Lakes water inside the Great Lakes Basin. Several of those measures continue to influence regional water policy, including the Great Lakes Charter of 1985 and the Water Resources Development Act of 1986. Each of these mechanisms heavily emphasized the legal sanctity of the Great Lakes Basin: the squiggly topographic line that rims the Great Lakes watershed like the edge of a soup bowl. Rain that falls inside that Basin line eventually finds its way to the Great Lakes, but rain that falls outside it ends up in the Mississippi, Atlantic, or Arctic watersheds. To the anti-diversion crowd, the edge of the Great Lakes Basin was the all-important line in the sand. Anyone residing outside that natural boundary or divide—even if they lived in a Great Lakes state or province—was not deserving of Great Lakes water.

~

THE GRAND CANAL was another water diversion scheme released in the 1960s and was sort of a NAWAPA of the East. While not quite as gargantuan, it was in the same league, with cost estimates between $100 billion and $200 billion (again, those are 1960s dollars).[8] The Great Recycling and Northern Development (GRAND) Canal was the brainchild of Canadian engineer Tom Kierans. Mr. Kierans was a student at McGill University in Montréal during the Great Depression, when he had to drop out because he lacked money. He took a train to British Columbia to pan for gold and en route passed through the drought-stricken Canadian prairie, which had become the northern edge of the Dust Bowl. A year later, Mr. Kierans returned with gold, but not enough. So he took a job in northern Ontario with a mining company. While working there he saw the large rivers flowing into James Bay on the southeast corner of Hudson Bay, and immediately he wondered about the possibility of shipping all that water out West. The result, years later, was the GRAND Canal plan that proposed building a massive berm across James Bay as a way to capture all the freshwater flowing into it. Mr. Kierans, who became a successful engineer in Canada, figured it would take about eight years of captured inflow to turn James Bay into a freshwater lake. When that was achieved, the water could be pumped south to the upper reaches of Lake Huron.

Once northern Lake Huron started receiving this enormous inflow of freshwater, Huron's natural water feed from Lake Superior would become superfluous. Mr. Kierans argued that most of the water that normally left the east end of Lake Superior via the St. Marys River could be pumped out of the west end to the Canadian prairies, allowing agricultural fields there to finally attain the bountiful production that Mother Nature's local rainfall never allowed. From the Canadian prairies, surplus water would be directed southward through Montana and Wyoming to the headwaters of the Colorado River system, where it would then tap into the already reworked hydrology of the American Southwest. James Bay water could be used to grow winter lettuce in Arizona and strawberries in California while greening up golf courses from Tucson to San Diego (fig. 4.2).

Mr. Kierans, who is now in his nineties, continues to tirelessly promote the GRAND Canal project. "We have got to realistically count on a billion people living on this continent by the end of this century," he says. "This is the most important project in the world today." According to Mr. Kierans, the beauty of his GRAND Canal plan—and what makes it superior to NAWAPA (which he argues was unrealistic) is that the GRAND Canal is not a diversion. Or so he claims. A diversion takes water from its natural basin and sends it somewhere else, he says, but the GRAND Canal plan waits until the freshwater reaches the sea and then sends it elsewhere,

The Grand Canal Proposed Distribution System

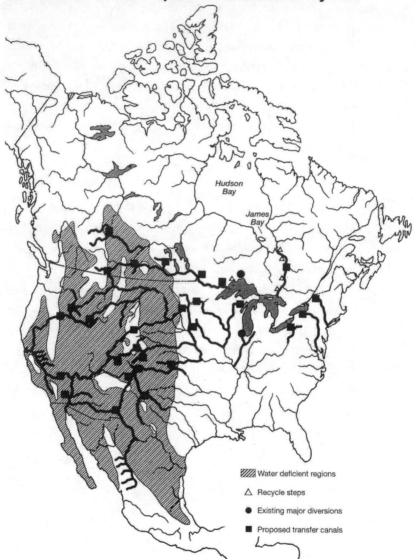

Fig. 4.2. *The GRAND Canal proposal envisioned capturing the freshwater inflows to James Bay and transporting them throughout North America. (© Tom Kierans)*

meaning that no freshwater ecosystem is ever robbed of its water. That's a "recycling" plan, not a diversion, he explains.

Semantics aside, Mr. Kierans's plan is unique for a number of reasons. Damming an expansive saltwater bay had not been proposed in North American before.[9] But what was truly unique about the GRAND Canal plan is that it came from a Canadian. Before Mr. Kierans stepped forward, the vast majority of North America's grandiose water plans had come from U.S. engineers—plans that were viewed by many Canadians as hegemonic schemes from bullying American watermongers. But this time, one of their own had drawn up an elaborate blueprint to send Canadian water south, and many of Mr. Kierans's compatriots found his ideas repugnant. "I was branded as a traitor in Canada for even suggesting this!" he complains. "People up here couldn't see the difference between 'diversion' and 'recycling' no matter what I said."

Like NAWAPA, the GRAND Canal has never come close to being built, but not every Canadian was opposed to it. Mr. Kierans managed to secure support for the GRAND Canal in very high places. Former Canadian prime minister Brian Mulroney viewed the plan "with enthusiasm,"[10] and Robert Bourassa, the former premier of Québec, was so bullish on the Canal that he devoted several pages to it in his 1985 book, *Power from the North*.[11]

The NAWAPA and GRAND Canal plans represent outlandish case studies that captured a lot of attention but never materialized. Over the years, however, many smaller diversion schemes have made it off the drawing board. In fact, the Great Lakes' diversion history dates back to the early 1800s. According to the International Joint Commission there have been at least four diversions *into* the Great Lakes since that time and at least four diversions out. There have also been six other "intra-Basin" diversions that artificially diverted water from one lake's basin to another. (Fig. 4.3 shows all of these diversions.) One of the first diversions came in 1825 when the Erie Canal opened in upstate New York, connecting Buffalo, on the shores of Lake Erie, with Albany, on the Hudson River, and allowing barges to travel all the way to New York City.[12] The largest and most controversial diversion out of the Basin took

Existing Diversions in the Great Lakes Basin

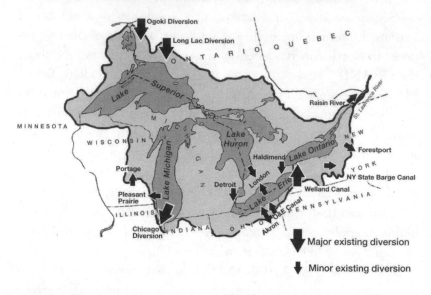

Existing Diversions in the Great Lakes Basin	Operational Date (original project)	Average Annual Flow	
		(cms)	(cfs)
Interbasin			
Long Lac (into Lake Superior basin)	1939	45	1,590
Ogoki (into Lake Superior basin)	1943	113	3,990
Chicago (out of Lake Michigan basin)	(1848)1900	91	3,200
Forestport (out of Lake Ontario basin)	1825	1.4	50
Portage Canal (into Lake Michigan basin)	1860	1	40
Ohio & Erie Canal (into Lake Erie basin)	1847	0.3	12
Pleasant Prairie (out of Lake Michigan basin	1990	0.1	5
Akron (out of and into Lake Erie basin)	1998	0.01	0.5
Intrabasin			
Welland Canal	(1829)1932	260	9,200
NY State Barge Canal (Erie Canal)	(1825)1918	20	700
Detroit	1975	4	145
London	1967	3	110
Raisin River	1968	0.7	25
Haldimand	1997	0.1	2

Fig. 4.3. There have been more than a dozen Great Lakes diversions since the 1800s—some more celebrated than others. (International Joint Commission)

place in 1900 when the state of Illinois reversed the Chicago River, diverting the river's highly polluted water away from Chicago's Lake Michigan water intake pipes and sending it down the Des Plaines and Illinois rivers toward St. Louis (see chapter 5). That diversion was later challenged in court by other Great Lakes states, resulting in a highly contentious Supreme Court case that dragged on for decades.

~

THE DIVERSION ISSUE erupted again in 1981 when a company announced plans to construct a 1,900-mile coal-slurry pipeline from Wyoming to the Great Lakes. Powder River Pipeline Inc. (PRPI) envisioned grinding coal and mixing it with water to create a slurry that would then be injected into a forty-two-inch pipe buried three feet underground. The pipeline would be able to ship as much as thirty-six million tons of coal per year to power plants in the Midwest. According to its proponents, the system would be cheaper and more efficient than shipping coal by rail. Published maps showed the pipeline forking as it reached the Great Lakes region, with one terminus near Duluth, Minnesota, on Lake Superior and a second ending north of Milwaukee on Lake Michigan.[13] The $2.8 billion project was the brainchild of energy industry entrepreneurs based in Oklahoma, Mississippi, and Montana.[14]

But the project got off to a rocky start. PRPI needed water to make the slurry and taking water from dry Western states and piping it to the wet Great Lakes was not the most popular idea. Nevertheless, the investors made headway in securing the necessary water near the Wyoming and Montana coal beds. PRPI was working these Western water leads late in 1981 when William Westhoff, the Mississippi executive charged with promoting the project, gave a speech at a coal export conference in Superior, Wisconsin. During the speech he made the mistake of saying "as an afterthought" that if Western water could not be secured for the project, PRPI was also considering installing a return waterline that would send Lake Superior water west where it could be used to create the slurry.[15]

That comment was picked up by the media and transmitted

throughout the Great Lakes Basin, provoking outrage. Mr. Westhoff was taken aback by the public reaction and he had to devote considerable time to damage control. "We have seen the headlines where the [Great Lakes] governors are going to get together and put a surtax on water going to the West," Mr. Westoff said in a meeting with Wisconsin officials a year later. "There was a headline that came out in one of the papers that said we would drain Lake Superior dry . . . We don't plan to use Lake Superior water, not now, never did, and I don't think we ever will. I would like to lay that to rest if we could."[16] The following year PRPI abandoned the project completely after essential federal eminent domain legislation—which would have permitted the pipeline to be built on railroad rights-of-way—failed to pass on Capitol Hill. Despite Mr. Westhoff's attempts to explain away his offhand remark, his project is still known in the Great Lakes region as the pipeline that planned to use Lake Superior water to transport coal slurry from Wyoming to Middle America.

In fairness to Mr. Westhoff, the Great Lakes governors were already on edge when he and his investors came along. The governors had been looking anxiously to the West—not to Wyoming or Montana—but toward the dry High Plains and the infamous Ogallala Aquifer that lies beneath them. Aquifers are reservoirs of water that, contrary to popular belief, are not large open underground lakes. Instead, the water is housed in cracks, crevices, and holes in underground rock formations or subterranean sand or gravel beds. The Ogallala is huge, stretching from South Dakota through Nebraska, Kansas, eastern Colorado, and Oklahoma to the base of the Texas panhandle; it underlies small sections of Wyoming and New Mexico too (fig. 4.4). Despite its enormous size, by the late 1970s the Ogallala had proven vulnerable. Thanks to irrigated agriculture on the arid plains, water levels in the aquifer had plummeted by more than one hundred feet in some areas, but rainfall replenished the water table at rates of just one to six inches per year.[17] Thousands of years ago the Ogallala slowly filled with water, and in less than a hundred years modern irrigated agriculture threatened to suck it dry. "A continuation of existing usage patterns is expected

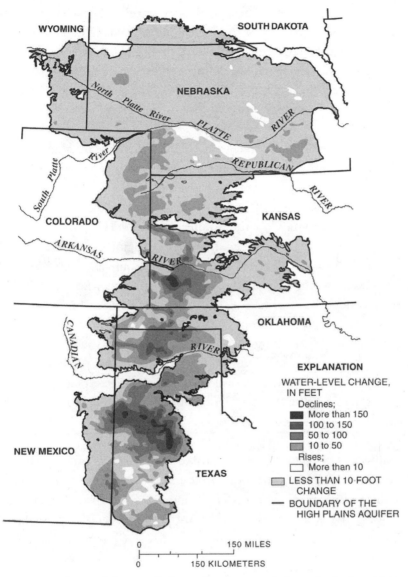

Fig. 4.4. *The Ogallala Aquifer has suffered severe declines. In the late 1970s the U.S. Army Corps of Engineers alarmed Great Lakes officials by studying the transport of water to the Ogallala region from "adjacent areas." (Courtesy of the U.S. Geological Survey)*

to result in depletion, or near depletion, of this sole major source of water in a large portion of the High Plains," said a federal report in 1982.[18] By the mid-1970s, 20 percent of all the irrigated land in the United States was using Ogallala Aquifer water. The High Plains had also become a major meat supplier, with 40 percent of all the beef cattle in America fattened there using locally grown irrigated grain.[19]

The status quo was clearly not sustainable, but High Plains farmers were counting on their congressmen to keep them afloat. In 1976 High Plains states pushed legislation through Congress asking the U.S. Army Corps of Engineers to conduct a highly controversial $6 million study on the aquifer's decline. The purpose of the study was to examine the economic and engineering feasibility of transporting water to the Ogallala region from "adjacent areas."[20] The *Six-State High Plains Ogallala Aquifer Regional Resources Study* sent a shock wave of alarm through many neighboring states and made Great Lakes governors furious. One of the eight Great Lakes states (Minnesota) is immediately "adjacent" to one of the Ogallala states (South Dakota). The governors had long worried that a federally subsidized water boondoggle might contemplate shipping Great Lakes water to the Southwest, but the High Plains were much closer and seemed much more threatening.

The Corps ended up interpreting the word "adjacent" quite literally, however, and did not consider studying the prospect of diverting water from any of the Great Lakes states. The controversial study zeroed in on four key diversion concepts that ranged from tapping the Missouri River in South Dakota, to diverting water from several streams in Arkansas and/or Texas.[21] The four scenarios varied widely in construction cost—and none of them was cheap— ranging from $3.6 billion to $27.8 billion (in 1977 dollars). A key operating expense was the enormous amount of electricity that would be required to move the water uphill to the High Plains. The Corps estimated that anywhere from sixteen to forty-nine pumping plants would have to be built to move the water. The unit cost of this water—even without the ultimate farmer delivery expense— rounded out to somewhere between $227 per acre foot to $569 per acre foot.[22] Those were (and are) unconscionably high water costs. As a point of comparison, nearly three decades of inflation later, Western agricultural water is considered expensive when it costs around $100 per acre foot.[23] At such high prices, taxpayers would be better off buying out many Ogallala farmers and turning their spreads back into bison range.[24]

Then the academic community got involved. The extraordinary cost figures unveiled by the Corps' study helped sink any realistic plans of diverting Great Lakes water to the Ogallala region. But to reinforce the point further, University of Michigan professor Jonathan Bulkley examined the additional cost of transferring Lake Superior water to the Missouri River, where—theoretically at least—the Lake Superior water could connect up with two of the Corps' hypothetical Ogallala diversion schemes. The idea was not to promote Great Lakes diversions, but to show how ridiculously expensive they would be. Professor Bulkley found that sending Lake Superior water to the Ogallala—not to mention anywhere farther to the southwest—would be laughably expensive. "Anybody that's thinking about pumping Great Lakes water to Arizona is out of their skull," he says.

According to his research, building a 611-mile canal capable of carrying water from Lake Superior to Yankton, South Dakota, at 10,000 cubic feet per second would cost $20 billion. Additionally, the water would have to be lifted uphill from Lake Superior to the higher elevations at Yankton, which would take a total of eighteen pumping stations requiring the electricity of seven 1,000-megawatt power plants. The power plants alone would cost an additional $7 billion (in 1982 dollars), not counting annual operating expenses. When Professor Bulkley's steep water cost calculations ($27 billion) were added to the extraordinary water cost estimates in the Corps' Ogallala study ($3.6 billion to $27.8 billion), shipping Great Lakes water west sounded more like fiction than science.

~

WHILE THOSE RESULTS WERE DAMNING, Great Lakes politicians were still rattled because federal officials had funded the

Ogallala diversion study in the first place. The idea that the U.S. government would spend millions of dollars investigating the bulk transfer of water from one basin to another fed right into the heart of Great Lakes residents' worst diversion nightmares. The coal-slurry pipeline proposal and the Ogallala study set off a period of deep insecurity in the Great Lakes region—a situation that only worsened when the U.S. Supreme Court announced its decision in *Sporhase v. Nebraska*, at about the same time.

The *Sporhase* case had its roots in a remote section of rural Nebraska, but resonated throughout the United States. It raised serious doubts about whether a state had the authority to prevent water from being diverted outside its borders. *Sporhase* began with a Nebraska law that prohibited groundwater from being exported to another state—if that other state refused to allow *its* water to be exported to Nebraska. A farmer with property on both sides of the Nebraska/Colorado border challenged the law as a violation of the interstate commerce clause in the U.S. Constitution. In 1982 the Supreme Court ruled in favor of the farmer, declaring groundwater to be an article of commerce and that Nebraska's reciprocity requirement was therefore a barrier to interstate trade under the commerce clause. The justices said that while the federal government gave states great leeway in setting water policy, infringing on interstate commerce crossed a constitutional line.[25]

For the Great Lakes governors, the ruling shattered hopes that they could pass legislation banning diversions of Great Lakes water outside their states' borders. "[*Sporhase* makes] it clear that water 'embargoes' enacted by the Great Lakes States, while serving an important purpose in signaling the region's basic opposition to diversion, will almost certainly be struck down if challenged," predicted a briefing paper prepared for the Great Lakes governors in the wake of the decision. "Once struck down, of course, the [Great Lakes] states would be left scrambling to design and implement defensible legislation."[26] As hard as it was for them to admit, having individual states pass an outright ban on Great Lakes diversions was not an option. The governors would have to come up with some other mechanism for protecting Great Lakes water.

~

THE COAL SLURRY/Ogallala/*Sporhase* convergence was interpreted ominously in the Great Lakes region as a pro-diversion triple whammy. Though the economics didn't make sense, water—in the West it is said—tends to flow uphill toward money, and Great Lakes politicians worried that none of their existing laws could stop diversions of Great Lakes water. The only thing that came close was the 1909 Boundary Waters Treaty between the United States and Canada, which was designed to help resolve border water disputes. But the Boundary Waters Treaty had two huge holes in it. First, it only seemed to apply when diversions were large enough to influence the "level or flow" of the Great Lakes. As an example, the proposed coal-slurry pipeline—at 17 cubic feet per second, or 11 million gallons of water per day—would have imperceptibly influenced Lake Superior levels.[27] But if a large number of similar-sized diversions were implemented, their cumulative effects could influence Great Lakes water levels. And yet those impacts would not be covered under the treaty. That meant the Boundary Waters Treaty did not protect the Great Lakes from the most likely diversion problem—death by a thousand straws. Second, because Lake Michigan is the only Great Lake that lies entirely within U.S. borders, it's technically not a "boundary" water and is presumed by many to be excluded from the treaty. This means that diversion proposals relating to Lake Michigan would not be covered.[28]

But there's nothing like a little adversity to captivate the attention of a handful of sleepy governors. The pro-diversion triple whammy helped rally politicians, bureaucrats, and activists from throughout the Great Lakes region. Things got rolling in January 1982 with the formation of the Council of Great Lakes Governors, which was designed to help coordinate regional responses to all sorts of Great Lakes issues, including the diversion threat.[29]

Later that year, Great Lakes governors and premiers met on Michigan's Mackinac Island and declared that no Great Lakes water could be diverted without clearance from all of the Great Lakes governors and premiers as well as from the federal governments in the United States and Canada. The declaration lacked the force of law, but sent a clear signal. In 1983, federal legislation was introduced in the United States to prevent diversions from the lakes without the consent of the Great Lakes states (though it didn't pass). Then the Great Lakes governors adopted a resolution supporting the federal legislation and encouraging Great Lakes governors to adopt anti-diversion laws in each of their states. (Even though those laws would likely be found unconstitutional, they could be used to slow down diversion proposals until a regional anti-diversion policy was implemented.) Then in late 1983, the Council of Great Lakes Governors appointed a special anti-diversion taskforce that was given one year to draw up an in-depth and authoritative study on Great Lakes diversions, including a recommended action plan.[30]

The taskforce was a mixture of lawyers and policymakers and included one representative from each Great Lake state and province. It was led by Peter McAvoy, an aide to Wisconsin governor Tony Earl, a Democrat. Mr. McAvoy says the team quickly decided not to pursue a legally binding regional water compact because it would be too complicated and would take too long to implement. In addition, federal officials told the team that the Great Lakes states and provinces didn't have the right under international law to pen a water treaty with one another. No one was interested in asking the federal governments to beef up the 1909 Boundary Waters Treaty—that would take forever. And given that the U.S. government had just conducted a water-diversion study that sent shudders through the region, the governors were not keen on getting Washington involved at all. They were much more interested in working with the provincial premiers in Ontario and Québec to implement a regional agreement on their own.

~

AFTER MONTHS OF DELIBERATIONS, in late 1984 the taskforce recommended creating what it called the Great Lakes Charter. A regional agreement meant to be signed by the governors and premiers, the Charter was designed to control Great Lakes diversions outside the Basin as well as consumptive uses inside it. The

Charter was the first in what would eventually become a string of water-regulatory systems that would follow in subsequent decades. It was a historic first step that had profound influence on future water management policy in the region. In many ways the Charter was a unique document. It declared that the waters of the Great Lakes were a precious natural resource "shared and held in trust" by the Great Lakes states and provinces. In *Sporhase* the Supreme Court may have ruled that water was an article of commerce, but in the Charter the governors and premiers were saying that under the public trust doctrine the people were the ultimate beneficiaries of that article of commerce.[31] Mr. McAvoy says the Charter tried to capture the idea that the water in the Great Lakes is "a shared resource. We don't own it . . . we share it with other states and provinces." The Charter proclaimed the waters of the Great Lakes to be "finite" and warned that future diversions out of the Basin— and consumptive uses within the Basin—could have an adverse impact on the environment, economy and welfare of the region.

The Charter had three main purposes: to "conserve [lake] levels and flows" in the face of an anticipated increase in demand; to protect the ecosystem; and to provide a "cooperative" mechanism to manage the water resources sustainably. It outlined five key principles: (1) that the lakes be managed as one hydrologic system; (2) that the signatory jurisdictions commit to a spirit of cooperation; (3) that new and increased diversions and consumptive uses were a "serious" concern; (4) that each state or province would provide "prior notice and consultation" to the others about any new "major" diversion or consumptive use proposals, *and* that each state or province would seek the "consent and concurrence" of all the other states and provinces before permitting a proposed withdrawal; and finally (5) that the governors and premiers agree to create a common database of information on water use in the Great Lakes Basin (how else would they know when the number of diversions and consumptive uses had gone too far?). In addition, they agreed to form a Water Resources Management Committee, which would rely on the new database to coordinate water policy within the Basin.[32]

One key question that came up during the Charter's drafting process involved the size of diversions that would be subjected to regional scrutiny. Should the governors and premiers hold a regional consultation every time someone proposed diverting a few gallons outside the Basin? Or should they leave control of small diversions up to the individual states and provinces and save the serious regional vetting for the bigger water withdrawals? The taskforce decided that small diversions and consumptive uses were not deserving of laborious regional review, and it set specific trigger levels that would invoke the Charter's principles.

The Charter committed all signatories to keeping track of every diversion or consumptive use in excess of 100,000 gallons per day. Once a diversion or consumptive use rose to the level of 2 million gallons per day (mgd), the Charter required signatories to "regulate" such water uses, presumably with a strict permitting system. If a state or province received a permit application to divert or consume more than 5 mgd of water per day, that's when the regional "prior notice" would be triggered, and all the other states and provinces would need to be notified before the withdrawal could be approved. After receiving this notice, if the other governors or premiers had concerns about the size, shape, or worthiness of the proposed water use, they could request a "consultation," which was more than just a conference call. "Consultation" meant a face-to-face meeting where the proposed withdrawal would be thoroughly examined, and concerns could be aired. According to the Charter, no governor or premier could approve a large-scale diversion or consumptive use without "the consent and concurrence of all affected Great Lakes States and Provinces."

"[The Charter] was designed to be a fence to prevent diversions and [to create] a process and a means to say no," says Richard Bartz, head of the Division of Water at the Ohio Department of Natural Resources, who was a key member of the taskforce. But it was also designed to focus new attention on large-scale consumptive use within the Basin, which was a forward-looking idea that forced the Great Lakes states and provinces to come to grips with the sustainability of their own water use.

The Charter had one significant drawback, however. It was a nonbinding agreement that any state or province could ignore without penalty. Why did the taskforce decide to go with a non-binding agreement? In part, because members wanted to adopt something fast, and water compacts and international treaties can take years. But they also drew up an alternative way to eventually make the principles of the Charter legally binding in every state and province: by having each governor and premier follow through on the Charter by passing a series of binding water standards into law. These standards would codify the nuts and bolts of the Charter within state and provincial statutes. Once each state and province adopted the legislative standards, the Charter would gain a binding force similar to that of a regional compact. As Peter McAvoy describes it, the governors and premiers were agreeing to "do everything that we can to ensure that . . . our laws will be amended, or added to, to reflect our commitment to seeing this thing through." That's how the taskforce envisioned the Charter getting its teeth without involving federal officials.

~

EVERYBODY LIKED THAT IDEA except for Michigan, which didn't want the legislative standards included in the Charter. Before one can understand Michigan's opposition, one needs to understand how the state differs from its neighbors on both sides of the border. Michigan is defined by the Great Lakes more than any other state or province because all but a smidgen of the state lies entirely within the Great Lakes Basin. No other Great Lakes state or province has such a large percentage of land in the watershed. Minnesota may be "the land of 10,000 lakes," but Michigan considers itself to be the "Great Lakes State," and it is the only state to touch four of the five Great Lakes (though the province of Ontario does too). Because Michigan is so defined by the lakes, no state arguably has more to lose from large-scale diversions of water from the Basin. Or at least that's the way Michiganders look at it. Great Lakes water diversions are an enormous political issue in the state.

Why, then, would a state that's worried about diversions be

opposed to including legislative standards in the Charter? In short, because Michigan thought the standards were too lax. Michigan residents are so fervently opposed to diversions that the only agreement that would pass muster in the state was an outright ban—no matter what the Supreme Court said in *Sporhase v. Nebraska*. The other states wouldn't agree to a diversion ban precisely because of the *Sporhase* decision—they assumed the Supreme Court would throw it out. But as Michigan's Charter negotiating team saw it, asking their governor to sign a nonbinding document that permitted diversions under 5 mgd was bad enough. Forcing him to push a bill through the Michigan legislature that made Great Lakes diversions legal would be political suicide. They realized that a ban on diversions was likely to be found unconstitutional, but try explaining that to the average voter. Michigan officials told the taskforce to take the legislative standards out of the Charter because such standards made it look like Michigan was approving diversions. So the standards were pulled from the Charter and handed out separately at the Charter-signing ceremony. The governors and premiers had a blueprint for the laws they were supposed to pass—it just wasn't integrated into the Charter itself.

Michigan may have held its ground on the legislative standards, but it gave in during another behind-the-scenes dispute. While the taskforce deliberations were underway, research showed that consumptive uses of water inside the Basin had the same effect on the Great Lakes ecosystem as diversions outside the Basin. Water taken permanently from the ecosystem was lost whether it was shipped to the Ogallala by pipeline or left the Basin in a bottle of juice. In addition, the Canadians pointed out that the majority of the consumptive use was on the U.S. side of the border. "It was interesting because that whole [taskforce] was set up to look at diversions," remembers Dick Bartz. "And Canada came to the table and said, 'We just got this report here and [most] of the in-Basin consumptive uses are from the U.S. side. If you want us to talk about diversions, then *we* want to talk about in-Basin consumptive uses, because the impact on the resource is exactly the same.'"

That didn't sit well with Michigan either. An agreement

curbing diversions was easy for Michigan to sign because it can use all the water it wants without its use ever being considered a diversion. Unlike the rest of the states and provinces, Michigan could ship water from one end of the state to the other and it would not break the rules. But a Charter that applied to diversions *and* consumptive uses would put Michigan under the same regulatory scrutiny as everyone else, and Michigan didn't like that idea. Diversions were the real threat to the lakes, Michigan argued, not consumptive uses. But the Canadians saw that argument as water hypocrisy—as did many other states—so Michigan eventually backed down. From that point onward, consumptive uses were lumped together on an equal footing with diversions in the Charter.

After months of negotiations, by January 1985 the Charter task-force had developed a document that was ready for the governors and premiers to sign. A ceremony was set for February 11, 1985, in Milwaukee. In a skyscraper boardroom overlooking Lake Michigan, the majority of the Great Lakes governors and premiers gathered, along with regional water officials and the media, to make the Charter official.[33] The politicians viewed the ceremony as an important milestone in Great Lakes water-management history. "Some of them delivered these really eloquent speeches," Peter McAvoy recalls. "They were quite moving. They did not just come and do this photo op."

Three years after the triple whammy, the governors and premiers had finally adopted a progressive water-management system. Officially the Charter was designed to "manage" large-scale diversions, but everyone in the room hoped the document could be used to ban them. In-Basin consumptive uses would now be vetted more than ever. Though the Charter was marked by political compromise, and held no standing in law, the good-faith agreement gave the governors and premiers a mechanism for resolving regional water disputes that were too small to trigger the Boundary Waters Treaty. And there was hope that the states and provinces would each pass legislation to make this good-faith agreement binding.

Great Lakes politicians were sending a signal to the rest of the continent—and even the world. Perhaps it was unconstitutional for individual states to ban interstate water transfers, but the governors and premiers were determined to make it difficult for someone to undertake long-range, large-scale diversions from the Great Lakes Basin. Wisconsin moved swiftly to pass laws adopting the Charter's standards. Other states followed later, but for years Michigan remained less than enthusiastic about the Charter's language. More than two decades after the Charter was signed, on February 28, 2006, Michigan finally adopted a comprehensive water-management law, making it the last Great Lakes state to recognize at least some of the Charter's language in its statutes. Meanwhile, in Canada, Québec approached the Charter with a laissez-faire attitude as well, taking some fifteen years to integrate Charter-like language into its water laws. And while Ontario was slow to reference the Charter in its statutes, provincial water laws already matched or exceeded the Charter in many areas.

～

THE INK on the Great Lakes Charter was barely dry when the diversion threat returned—and this time it was a lot closer to home than the Ogallala Aquifer. During 1985 and 1986, New York City was going through a serious drought. America's largest city was on a major water alert, and conservation measures were drummed into the heads of people from Staten Island to the Bronx. Officials were under serious pressure to come up with contingency plans for alternate water supplies and it wasn't long before people started mentioning the Great Lakes. Just seven months after the Charter-signing ceremony, New York State environment commissioner Henry Williams formed a thirteen-member panel to explore a wide variety of water options, and diverting water from Lake Ontario or Lake Erie was one of them. "It's inescapable that the abundant water supply in the Great Lakes will be included in any consideration of water allocation in New York State," he announced during September of 1985. "It's not to say it will happen, but it will be considered."[34]

The announcement provoked a bitter reaction in the Basin, as many of New York's Great Lakes neighbors saw it as an affront to the spirit of the Charter. The move raised serious regional questions about Governor Mario Cuomo's political credibility—a point that some New York journalists were happy to point out. "The raid on Great Lakes water may be sooner and closer to home than you think," wrote Paul MacClennan, environment reporter for *The Buffalo News*. "What a predicament that poses for the Cuomo administration. The governor on the one hand signed the Great Lakes Charter earlier this year and a basic premise of the eight state-two province agreement is to preserve the lakes' water . . . But Cuomo also has heavy political debts downstate and a continuing water shortage that threatens the New York City metropolitan area."[35] Like other diversion scares, the New York City option eventually faded away, but it continued to haunt Great Lakes residents, who wondered if New York might resurrect this diversion idea sometime in the future.

The scare from New York only reinforced the Charter's non-binding nature, and some Great Lakes leaders hungered for something more. A gentlemen's agreement was a great start, but these officials believed that a legally binding statute was still necessary to throw down a barrier against large-scale Great Lakes diversions—to New York City or anywhere else. Some officials looked to the U.S. Congress for help. They set their eyes on amending the federal Water Resources Development Act (WRDA, pronounced "WORD-uh") by inserting a special section—1109—that referred specifically to Great Lakes diversions. WRDA is federal legislation that is renewed periodically for major public-works projects, and frequently it is rife with pork and other special-interest legislation. Several Great Lakes states saw the 1986 version of WRDA as an opportunity to erect a stronger barrier to Great Lakes diversions, and they managed to slip in the wording without incident.

Section 1109 of WRDA was short (two pages) but powerful. It said that any proposal to divert water outside the Great Lakes Basin needed the unanimous approval of all eight Great Lakes governors. What's more, it covered diversions of all sizes—there was no longer a 5 mgd trigger. Anyone who wanted to divert a single drop of water outside the Great Lakes Basin would have to run the WRDA gauntlet first. While the Charter had targeted diversions *and* in-Basin consumptive uses, WRDA was strictly an anti-diversion document. WRDA went on to say that neither the Army Corps of Engineers nor any other federal agency could even study the feasibility of diverting water from the Great Lakes without the unanimous approval of all eight Great Lakes governors. WRDA was a dream come true to Michigan. Finally, it had attained a magic veto over diversion proposals in all the other Great Lakes states without the concern of retribution or the burden of regulating its own consumptive water use. That was a power that other states would come to regret, as later chapters in this book will show.

After WRDA, the idea of forging a consensus over Great Lakes water withdrawals was lost. From here on out, on the U.S. side of the border at least, water diversions would be decided by a straight up-and-down vote. Those who wanted a binding diversion law had finally gotten it. Governors who worried that the Charter's consensus format was too weak now had the comfort of a veto pen in their pocket. But was it constitutional? Many experts didn't think so. The main problem was that the document lacked any guidance on how diversion applications should be judged—forcing the governors to make up the rules as they went along—and not necessarily requiring them to treat all water applicants by the same standards. In addition, the law provided no opportunity for spurned water applicants to appeal. That left WRDA highly vulnerable to allegations that the law was arbitrary and capricious, if not unconstitutional.

Unlike the Charter, with its clear procedures for "prior notice and consultation," WRDA laid out no such procedure for how governors should go about exercising their newfound water veto powers. Did they have to meet in person? Did the veto have to be in writing? Was a consultation required first, or could a governor just veto the project by making a phone call after reading about it in the newspaper? "For many of us at the time, [WRDA] was viewed as an abomination. And as it's grown it's become a bigger abomination," says attorney R. Timothy Weston, a former Pennsylvania state official who helped draft the Charter. "It's really one of the worst pieces of legislation created . . . It provides no due process, it provides no standards, [and] it creates an entirely political and unaccountable arrangement for casting vetoes—which is one of the silliest ways for managing natural resources imaginable."

What a difference a few years of anti-diversion hysteria can make. The governors and premiers had gone from having no regimen for regulating Great Lakes diversions to having two very different and somewhat awkward water-management systems. One was voluntary, but international. The other was binding, but domestic—and of questionable constitutionality. Once WRDA passed, some states lost all enthusiasm for adopting the Charter's legislative standards as law. It certainly helped give Michigan the out it was looking for. "What [WRDA] did was provide us with a framework to approve and deny any diversions," says Jim Bredin from Michigan's Office of the Great Lakes. "And that's what we were mainly concerned about. We really didn't need to address it through state legislation." In the wake of the triple whammy, Great Lakes politicians had rallied to the cause of preventing diversions. But the result was a patchwork of policies that few were thrilled with. The Charter and WRDA were both imperfect in their own ways, but a lot of political capital had been spent pulling them together. By the late 1980s there was little energy to do anything more. Regional officials would have to live with what had been adopted and hope it provided the protections for the Great Lakes they were looking for.

PART II

Battle Lines and Skirmishes

~

Chapter 5

Reversing a River

IN THE LATE 1800s CHICAGO was a bustling urban center well on its way to becoming one of world's great cities. Having rebuilt itself after the Chicago Fire of 1871, it was a thriving metropolis of approximately a million people. But it also was a filthy place with wretched sanitation problems, and nothing exemplified that more than the squalid Chicago River. Virtually an open sewer, laced with visible filth, some of the river's worst pollution came from its urbanized tributaries. "Bubbly Creek" was an ecologically dead branch of the river that was filled annually with enough rotting stockyard offal to equal the pollution from a sizable city. "In the summer, when a hard brown scum settled on its surface, cats and chickens could be seen scurrying across it," writes Donald Miller in his book, City of the Century.[1] There were times, thanks to discharges from the slaughterhouses, when the river ran red with blood.[2] After heavy rains it was not unusual to see the rotting carcasses of dead cats—or even horses—floating in the river's sewage slick as it streamed far out into Lake Michigan. In some cases the polluted plume even neared the city's drinking water-intake structures two miles from shore.[3] The fear of water-borne illness was constant.[4] "Cholera, and later typhoid, were a problem," says Richard Lanyon, director of research and development at the Metropolitan Water Reclamation District of Greater Chicago, the metro region's wastewater treatment agency. "The other problem was just plain old nuisance conditions. The river smelled terrible and, depending on which way the wind was blowing, various parts of the city were 'treated' to this aroma."

By 1885 Chicago's leading citizens were fed up with the embarrassing, unhealthy condition of their river. The solution was bold and ambitious: to definitively reverse the stream's flow. The primary goal was to flush Chicago's sewage far away from the city's Lake Michigan water-intake pipes, though there was also a desire to use the reversed river for navigation.[5] Reversing the river had been tried before, in 1871, when a less ambitious effort led to limited and very temporary success.[6] This time, city leaders, with the eventual support of the state legislature, were determined to reverse the river's flow decisively and permanently. Their plan was to construct a twenty-eight-mile canal connecting the Chicago River to the Des Plaines River near the village of Lockport southwest of the city, where Chicago's pollution would then flow into the Illinois River and ultimately the Mississippi. Unlike the first attempt to reverse the river, this project was built to divert a large amount of water from the Lake Michigan waterfront: 10,000 cubic feet per second. The diversion channel eventually became known as the Chicago Sanitary and Ship Canal, and the diversion itself is called the Lake Michigan diversion at Chicago (also known as the "Illinois diversion," or colloquially as the "Chicago diversion").

Groundbreaking began in 1892. The canal took 8,500 workers eight years to construct; it was 25 feet deep, ranged from 160 to 300 feet in width, and cost $31 million (at the turn of the century) to build. Though much of the canal was dug through flat, soft terrain, roughly fifteen miles were blasted through solid bedrock. The Sanitary and Ship Canal was an unprecedented engineering feat that paved the way for the Panama Canal just a few years later.[7] Chicago would never have grown into the city it is today were it not for the clean, safe, dependable water supply that the Sanitary and Ship Canal ensured by diverting the city's sewage away from Lake Michigan. "Chicago was a city made possible by the largest engineering project undertaken in an American community up to that time, the river reversal and the installation of a new sewage and water system," writes Mr. Miller in City of the Century. "Now the fourth-largest city in North America, it was capable of doing big things and doing them well, and this became part of its permanent reputation."[8]

But there was a negative side to the Chicago River's reversal. It was the largest and most controversial project ever to divert water outside the Great Lakes Basin. Engineering feat or not, it stands as a polarizing example of precisely what water managers and politicians throughout the Great Lakes region would like to never see happen again. "The Chicago River [reversal] is one of the primary transformations of the Great Lakes ecosystem," says Henry Henderson, an attorney and former environment commissioner for the City of Chicago. "[It] is the poster child of bad behavior in the Great Lakes."

~

EVEN BEFORE the canal project was finished, it was marked by controversy. Despite Chicago's claims that pollution in the reversed river would be harmlessly diluted after a matter of miles, many downstream residents were doubtful. Chief of the skeptics was the

Photo 5.1. Construction of the Chicago Sanitary and Ship Canal circa the late 1890s. (Photo courtesy of the Metropolitan Water Reclamation District of Greater Chicago © MWRDGC2002-7)

City of St. Louis, which worried that the reversed river's sewage would taint the Mississippi—the city's drinking-water source. As the canal was nearing completion, word spread that Missouri planned to petition the Supreme Court to prevent Chicago from dumping sewage into the waterway. The news prompted Chicago's wily leaders to uncharacteristically take a pass on pomp and circumstance and surreptitiously open the canal during the early morning hours in the dead of winter. On the morning of January 2, 1900, ice-clogged water began to flow from the reversed river into the fresh-cut channel of the Sanitary and Ship Canal, and Missouri had lost its opportunity to prevent the canal from opening.

The following day the Chicago Tribune published a detailed and entertaining description of the Keystone Cop–like, weather-plagued effort to get the water flowing before Missouri could file suit.[9] Once word got out that the river had been reversed, it became national news. On January 14, 1900, the The New York Times trumpeted, "Water in the Chicago River now resembles liquid. The impossible has now happened! The Chicago River is becoming clear!"[10] Two weeks after the water began to flow in reverse, workers twenty-eight miles downstream put the finishing touches on the southern end of the canal, finally connecting it to the Des Plaines River (see figs. 5.1 and 5.2).[11] That same day word arrived that Missouri had finally gotten around to filing its injunction on behalf of St. Louis, but it was too late—at least to prevent the reversed river from opening, and the Supreme Court denied Missouri's request.[12]

In 1905 the situation heated up again when Missouri filed another Supreme Court challenge against the Sanitary and Ship Canal, blaming the new waterway for an increase in typhoid cases in St. Louis. Illinois's response to Missouri's court filing argued that Chicago's sewage was completely diluted by the time it reached St. Louis and thus there was nothing to worry about. In a comment that exemplified the bitterness of the time, Missouri's attorney general said, "The action of the Chicago authorities in turning their sewage into the Mississippi River for the people of St. Louis to drink is criminal, and Chicago knows it."[13]

The Great Lakes Water Wars

Development of the Chicago Sanitary and Ship Canal

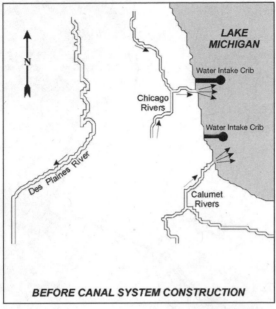

BEFORE CANAL SYSTEM CONSTRUCTION

CHICAGO SANITARY AND SHIP
CANAL SYSTEM COMPLETED

Fig. 5.1. The reversal of the Chicago River reworked much of the natural hydrology of the Chicago metropolitan area. (U.S. Army Corps of Engineers)

Lake Michigan Diversion at Chicago

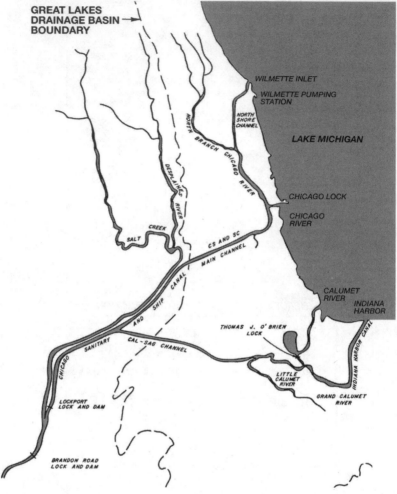

Fig. 5.2. *The Chicago Sanitary and Ship Canal in relation to the Great Lakes Basin boundary.*

Finally, in 1906, after reams of legal filings had been submitted in the case, the Supreme Court ruled against Missouri. The Court found that there was ambiguity in the factual record in the case, and that the contradicting experts failed to prove or disprove Missouri's allegations that Chicago's sewage was tainting St. Louis's drinking water. The Court determined that raw sewage from

Missouri was being discharged into the Mississippi upstream of St. Louis's water intakes. The justices ruled that this local source of contamination put the burden on St. Louis to install a modern water-treatment system that would take care of all the pollution—the local sewage, and the alleged contamination from Chicago.

Nonetheless, Missouri's tardy and unsuccessful legal challenge made history of sorts. It was the first salvo in what would become an acrimonious, century-long legal dispute involving the Illinois diversion—making the Chicago River one of the most heavily litigated bodies of water in the United States. The litany of lawsuits not only pitted Illinois against downstream states such as Missouri, but it also eventually prompted legal challenges from the federal government and just about every other Great Lakes state in the Basin. In fact, the Chicago River's burdensome legal legacy is not over. The terms of the diversion continue to be dictated by a highly complicated and much-fought-over Supreme Court decree that controls the water supply for some seven million people in the greater Chicago area. Any effort to change the Illinois diversion in the future would require the approval of a majority of the nation's nine most influential jurists.

~

FRESH FROM ITS VICTORY over Missouri, in the early 1900s Chicago was feeling cocky and began taking measures to expand the geographic breadth of its diversion. While other sewage-treatment technologies were available, the city took the regressive approach of embarking on a full-fledged regional effort to use dilution as the solution to its pollution. During the next several years city officials expanded the Illinois diversion, much to the dismay of the other Great Lake states and provinces. Between 1907 and 1910, on Chicago's North Side, the city dug a canal known as the North Shore Channel, and in 1911 it started another canal on the South Side called the Cal-Sag Channel.[14] In just ten years the city had rapidly expanded its diversion of Lake Michigan water at three different points, sending it all into the Sanitary and Ship Canal, and eventually down the Mississippi.

Meanwhile, Chicago kept ramping up the amount of its diversion.[15] In 1900, the flow started out at 4,167 cubic feet per second (cfs); by 1912 it had increased to 6,016 cfs; and by 1922 it had grown to 8,500 cfs. All of these increases came in the absence of a federal permit. As a result, during the early 1900s the U.S. government and Illinois spent a lot of time suing each other in federal court. Then in 1922—the same year the Cal-Sag Channel was completed—Wisconsin filed suit against Illinois, claiming the state was illegally expanding the diversion and blamed Chicago's actions for historically low Great Lakes water levels. Later, Wisconsin amended its complaint by asking the court to halt the diversion altogether. Wisconsin was eventually joined in the suit by Michigan and New York. The City of Big Shoulders was having its way with Lake Michigan water and there was little anyone could do about it. But Chicago's diversion was also driving a wedge through the heart of the Great Lakes Basin—a situation that would repeat itself time and again in years to come.

While the diversion's volume had nearly doubled in twenty years, Chicago still wanted more water. Illinois congressmen introduced legislation in 1924 to increase the diversion to the maximum the Sanitary and Ship Canal could handle—10,000 cfs, which prompted Canada to file a complaint. Meanwhile, lake levels continued to drop. Then in 1926, in a historically ironic turn of events, downriver states like Missouri, Tennessee, and Louisiana came out in support of Illinois' request to increase the diversion. As time passed, it seems, Missouri and other downstream states began to view Chicago's effluent in a more positive light.

Later that year, thanks to all the litigation, the Supreme Court appointed a judge to intensively study the issue and make recommendations (such appointees are called "special masters"). Finally, on April 21, 1930, the Court decided the case of State of Wisconsin v. State of Illinois—and Chicago suffered a rare loss. The Court gave the Sanitary District roughly a decade to wean itself from most of the water it had been diverting. The Court forced the district to impose a gradual though radical nine-year reduction from 8,500 cfs to 1,500 cfs by January 1, 1939. During that same period Chicago

The Great Lakes Water Wars

was to expand its sewage-treatment program to replace the need for this 7,000 cfs in dilution water that it would lose.

The Court had spoken, but the regional bitterness engendered by the Illinois diversion would linger for years. In the early 1900s, that bitterness was not just about pollution, but was laced with the angry belief that the Illinois diversion was having an enormous effect on water levels in the Great Lakes. Stanley Chagnon, emeritus chief of the Illinois State Water Survey, captures this anger in a comprehensive report he edited and partially wrote for the National Oceanic and Atmospheric Administration in 1994.

> Few would argue that through the late 1800s, Chicago residents faced serious health problems due to the quality of their drinking water. Few would argue that Chicago residents deserve, as much as any other people, clean water for household use. Many, however, have argued that Chicago (through the [Sanitary District] and often with the blessing of state and federal governments) did not have the right to divert water from Lake Michigan for its own use and then return that water in a contaminated state and to pollute other waters . . . Especially in the early 1920s, opponents of the diversion also argued that Chicago did not have the right to improve its own navigational interests at the expense of similar interest among the states and Canadian provinces that border the Great Lakes. Newspaper accounts from those years are full of accusations that the diversion was intended to do just that."[16]

Throughout the 1930s, Illinois moved several times to increase the amount of the diversion, even trying a few end arounds to avoid the Court ruling by seeking legislative action from Congress instead. All of these requests failed except for one in 1940, when another special master recommended that the diversion be increased to 10,000 cfs for just ten days during a period of drought to help remedy deteriorating water quality in the river. This was the first time that Chicago had been permitted to increase the flow of the diversion because of drought conditions. It was not the last time that happened, however. A decade and a half later, in 1956, dry weather prompted another new and unusual precedent. Four years of low rainfall had sapped water flows in the Mississippi and Illinois rivers, and the state of Illinois asked the Court for an emergency in-crease in the diversion. The Court approved an 8,500 cfs increase that lasted for seventy-six days starting in December 1956. This was a noteworthy decision with implications for the Great Lakes region in future years. It was the first time that the Illinois diversion had been increased solely to serve the needs of people from outside the Great Lakes Basin.

~

AFTER WORLD WAR II, Chicago's metropolitan region expanded rapidly, reaching five million people by 1950. Officials in northern Illinois and southern Wisconsin began noticing an alarming de-cline in regional wells—up to fifteen feet per year.[17] Chicago's sprawling suburbs were the main reason for this increased load on regional groundwater. Because the 1930 Court decision put no limit on the amount of water that Chicago could use for "domestic pumpage" (mainly drinking water), in 1958 the U.S. Army Corps of Engineers approved a plan to relieve pressure on the aquifer. The suburbs of Elmhurst, Villa Park, and Lombard obtained permission from Illinois, and a permit from the Corps, to tap into Chicago's Lake Michigan drinking water in an effort to slow the rapid ground-water decline. All three of these suburbs were outside the Great Lakes Basin line, a distinction that would have growing political importance in future years.

Wisconsin saw the political significance immediately and chal-lenged this geographic expansion of Chicago's metropolitan water network by filing another lawsuit. Among other things, Wisconsin argued that treated effluent from the Illinois diversion should be re-turned to Lake Michigan and not be sent down the Mississippi.[18] Illinois then countersued on behalf of the suburbs, specifically denying there was a need for returning treated water effluent to the lake.

For a third time the Court appointed a special master to study the situation—and the process dragged on for years. Finally, in 1967, the Court issued a decision on the Illinois diversion that was dramatically different, and significantly more complex, than the

Court's initial ruling in 1930. First, the Court sided with Chicago by boosting the total amount of the diversion from 1,500 cfs to 3,200 cfs. That meant that the diversion could total 2.1 billion gallons of water per day. But while the Court upped the amount of the diversion, it also tipped its hat toward Wisconsin by forcing Illinois to count water that it had never been required to keep track of before. For the first time Chicago drinking water and other "domestic pumpage" (which had been virtually ignored) had to be included in the 3,200 cfs number.

Interestingly, the decree also required Illinois to undertake a seemingly impossible task: calculate the annual amount of rainfall that fell in the 673-square-mile Chicago River watershed. This rain used to end up in Lake Michigan after running off into the once-natural flowing Chicago River. But with the diversion that rain ended up trickling into a backward-flowing Chicago River and was therefore a hydrologic loss to the Lake Michigan system. The Court (again nodding to Wisconsin) wanted Illinois to include that rainfall amount as part of the new 3,200 cfs number.

But the most important part of the Court's decision was a resounding victory for Illinois. In a key move, that had enormous implications for future growth in the greater Chicago area, the Court permitted Chicago's suburbs to tap into the city's Lake Michigan drinking-water system—even if the suburbs were far beyond the Great Lakes Basin boundary. In addition, the Court gave Illinois full authority to decide which communities could be added to the Lake Michigan drinking-water system—again, as long as the state stayed below the 3,200 cfs limit. The Chicago suburbs that were experiencing groundwater problems had suddenly found a new water source that would allow the metropolitan area to expand unhindered for the foreseeable future.

That some of Chicago's western suburbs—located far beyond the Great Lakes Basin line—are drinking Lake Michigan water seems patently unfair to contemporary opponents of Great Lakes diversions. And there are a number of water-troubled communities in other Great Lakes states that would love to access Great Lakes water, but because these areas lie outside the Basin line their water access has been limited. Residents of these communities look to Chicago's suburbs with an envy that borders on anger. One of them, Waukesha, Wisconsin, even approached Illinois to see if it could tap into the Chicago diversion as well, but was told that only Illinois communities qualify under the Supreme Court decree (chapter 13 discusses Waukesha more thoroughly). Chicago's polluted history sparked a series of historic events and judicial decisions that legally solidified the right in modern times for northeastern Illinois's suburbs to access Lake Michigan water. This is a unique and unprecedented right that most Chicago suburbanites don't fully appreciate.

A growing number of water-starved communities in the region are discovering just what a cherished privilege the Illinois diversion is turning out to be. "Everybody thinks Chicago gets special treatment," says Richard Lanyon at the Metropolitan Water Reclamation District of Greater Chicago. "Well, I guess so . . . But [other communities] never tried to get what we have. They fought us, and by fighting us have kind of eliminated the opportunity [for themselves]." But many environmentalists and legal scholars see the reversal of the Chicago River as an environmental abomination that should never be repeated. "The Chicago River diversion is an aberration," says Cameron Davis, executive director with the Alliance for the Great Lakes. "It is certainly an example of something that would never happen today."

With the terms of the 1967 Court decree, the purpose of the Illinois diversion changed significantly. In 1900 the bulk of the diversion was used for diluting and carrying sewage away from the city. "The original reason for the Chicago River diversion was to keep sewage from going into the drinking-water supply—Lake Michigan," Mr. Davis says. But by the late 1960s better sewage-treatment technology made it possible to allocate a growing percentage of the diverted water as drinking water for people who lived outside the city. Yes, part of the diversion was still being used to flush dirty water south, but over time that flush water was making up a smaller and smaller proportion of the total diversion allotment. Meanwhile, as Chicago needed less water to dilute its pollution, it needed more water for its collar communities to drink.

∽

CONTROVERSY OVER THE Illinois diversion flared again in the 1980s after an Army Corps of Engineers report looked at tripling the diversion's flow. The 1981 study concluded that tripling the diversion was technically possible, but that the increased flow would create a number of hydrologic headaches immediately downstream.[19] Then in 1988 a drought lowered water levels on the Mississippi River by several feet, hampering the river's billion-dollar commercial barge traffic. Barges, and other vessels, were forced to dodge numerous exposed—and unexposed—sandbars in the low water, if they could move at all. Democratic senator Jim Sasser from Tennessee, speaking for several Mississippi Valley politicians, encouraged President Ronald Reagan to use emergency powers to temporarily divert additional water from the Great Lakes via the Illinois diversion to help alleviate low flows on the Mississippi. Several bills were introduced in Congress to do just that.[20]

While those bills went nowhere, Illinois governor Jim Thompson shocked his Basin neighbors by supporting the call for an increase in the diversion all the way up to 10,000 cfs—the maximum that the Sanitary and Ship Canal could handle. That was an addition of more than 4 billion gallons per day—an enormous, though temporary, boost in the diversion. A 1985 study by the International Joint Commission had found that the Illinois diversion had already dropped water levels by 2.5 inches in Lakes Michigan and Huron.[21] What would this new increase do to the lakes? New York had tainted the spirit of the Charter in 1985 by contemplating Great Lakes water for the Big Apple. Now, just three years later it appeared that Illinois had its own diversion desires.

With this latest idea from Illinois, the situation looked like 1956 all over again: a proposal was on the table to divert water from the Great Lakes to aid people who lived hundreds of miles outside the Basin. This was precisely the kind of out-of-Basin diversion precedent that the Great Lakes Charter and the Water Resources

Development Act had tried to prevent. Governor Thompson's decision infuriated his colleagues in the Great Lakes Basin, who immediately labeled him a turncoat. The idea that a fellow Great Lakes governor would come out in favor of such a proposal sparked a political maelstrom—particularly because this governor already ruled over the largest and most controversial diversion ever to send water outside the Great Lakes Basin. Governor Tony Earl of Wisconsin still remembers how angry and incredulous the rest of Great Lakes governors were. "Very early after the Charter was signed . . . Jim Thompson came and said, 'Gee you guys, we've got to divert more water so we can float the barges [on the Mississippi]," Governor Earl recalls. "We all said 'Jim go powder your ass!'"

Governor Thompson's proposal even caught other Illinois officials off guard. "I was in St. Louis when that happened," says Neil Fulton, one of the governor's top water managers at the time. "I never got on a plane so fast in my life." Contacted nearly two decades later, Mr. Fulton was more than happy to distance himself from the governor's diversion idea, saying that he was not consulted before the announcement was made. "That proposal was never staffed," Mr. Fulton says. "We just spent a lot of time picking up the pieces."

More importantly, Governor Thompson's plan didn't make hydrologic sense. Water engineers pointed out that while expanding the diversion would affect water levels in the Illinois River, it would have a nominal impact on the flow regime of the mighty Mississippi—particularly by the time the additional water reached places like Tennessee and Louisiana. "The Mississippi's a huge waterway, and the amount of water you could get from Lake Michigan down there really isn't that significant," says Dan Injerd of the Illinois Department of Natural Resources (DNR). "There probably will never be another suggestion to try to use an increased diversion to alleviate drought conditions on the Illinois or the Mississippi." Maybe so, but while Governor Thompson's proposal went nowhere, it was the kind of scenario that anti-diversion advocates had worried about for years: that during a period of severe, long-term national drought, panicked politicians from outside the Great Lakes region would come groping for Great Lakes water—only to have one errant Basin governor break ranks and sell out.

~

IN THE 1990s the Illinois diversion made headlines yet again, this time for entirely different reasons. High water levels in the Great Lakes were making it difficult for Chicago to stay within the Supreme Court–mandated diversion limits, which further exacerbated regional water tensions. Officials discovered that more Lake Michigan water was entering the Chicago River than the Court allowed—a lot more. Because water levels can fluctuate, the Court's Chicago River decree permitted Illinois to occasionally exceed the mandated 3,200 cfs limit, as long as Illinois made up for that surplus water in later years. What mattered, the Court said, was that the amount of water diverted over a forty-year timeframe should not exceed an average of 3,200 cfs. At no point, however, was Illinois permitted to exceed the 3,200 cfs limit by an average of more than 2,000 cfs per year. But that's exactly what Illinois did for more than a decade. From 1988 through 2000, the diversion exceeded the 2,000 cfs arrearage limit every year. In fact, at the peak of excess diversion in 1993, Illinois was so far out of compliance that its annual water debt was running almost double the maximum ceiling allowed by the Court: 3,725 cfs.[22]

Once again the other Great Lakes states rallied to challenge Illinois's illegal water behavior, and this time Michigan was leading the charge. Officials in Lansing notified the U.S. Department of Justice that they were planning to file a petition with the Supreme Court asking the justices to reopen the Chicago diversion case because Illinois was so clearly in violation of the Court decree. Illinois said don't blame us, blame Mother Nature. During the late 1980s and early 1990s lake levels in the Great Lakes were at historic highs. Lake Michigan's water levels were so high that at times the lake was literally pouring over the top of a steel bulkhead that controlled how much Lake Michigan water flowed into the Chicago River. Illinois also admitted that there were a lot of leaks in the system, but said some of them were the responsibility of other entities (like the Army Corps of Engineers) and that the high water levels were pushing extra water through these holes in the "dike" as well.

Michigan was undeterred by the blame Mother Nature defense and forged ahead with its legal action. But lawyers with the Clinton administration's Department of Justice intervened and convinced Michigan to take an alternate approach. Rather than asking the Court to reopen the case—which history had shown would take many, many years and cost millions of dollars in legal bills—the Department of Justice talked Michigan and the other Great Lakes states into negotiating an out-of-court settlement with Illinois. The Canadian provinces of Ontario and Québec attended the negotiations as active observers.

The result of these negotiations was something that became known as the Memorandum of Understanding, or MOU, of 1996. Among other things, the MOU required Illinois and the Corps to fix the various leaks in the system. It also required Illinois officials to install a pump so that if notable amounts of water ever did leak

Photo 5.2. The mouth of the Chicago River (looking west), the flow of which was reversed in 1900. (Photo from Robert Cameron, Above Chicago [San Francisco: Cameron, 1992])

The Great Lakes Water Wars

into the river again—by flowing over the top of the bulkhead, for example—the water could be pumped back into the lake to make up the difference. Most notably, perhaps, the MOU also required Illinois to pay back its illegal water debt under a rigid, multiyear schedule that set specific targets to be met by certain dates. The MOU required Illinois to get back to a zero balance by 2019. Illinois responded with a number of engineering projects and changes that, in combination with extended drought years and much lower lake levels after 2000, helped the state achieve compliance much more quickly than most people (including Illinois officials) anticipated. By the end of 2005, preliminary figures suggested that Illinois had attained a zero balance on its water debt and was on its way to putting water back in the "bank" to draw on in future years.

~

BY THE EARLY PART of the twenty-first century roughly seven million people in more than 170 communities in northeastern Illinois—including Chicago—were getting their drinking water from Lake Michigan. Dan Injerd, the Illinois DNR's diversion supervisor, says that his department is adding an average of one new community every two years to the Lake Michigan drinking-water system. Any community that wants access to Lake Michigan water has to clear some state regulatory hurdles first. To start with, communities are required to show that Lake Michigan is the least expensive water source available—not the *only* one available, but the *least expensive* one available. Second, if a community is withdrawing water from the deep aquifer, it must agree to cease using groundwater within five years after drawing water from Lake Michigan. "The deep-water aquifer was vastly overutilized in this region, and we want to use Lake Michigan water as a tool to help balance resource use," Mr. Injerd says. "We want to get them off the deep-water aquifer and preserve that for those who are outside whatever will be the ultimate cost-effective Lake Michigan water supply service area."

Many of these suburban water permittees are well beyond the edge of the Great Lakes Basin boundary. "The most distant [Illinois] community that I'm aware of that is in the process of getting Lake Michigan water is the Village of Plainfield," Mr. Injerd says. "It's certainly a lot farther away from the lake than Waukesha [in Wisconsin]." But if Mr. Injerd is adding an average of one suburb every two years to the Lake Michigan water system, it begs the question, How far out from Lake Michigan will he go before telling a suburb or small town that it's just too far away to receive Great Lakes water? Rockford? Springfield? East St. Louis? Carbondale? What *is* the geographic limit of Illinois's Lake Michigan water supply service area?

"We don't know," Mr. Injerd says.

When pressed further, he unveils two hypotheses. The first one, which could be called the "rosy scenario," predicts that Illinois will continue to squeeze out enough water from the diversion's 3,200 cfs limit to meet the needs of all the suburbs that ask for it—until finally someone walks through the door from such a faraway place that it's just no longer cost-effective to consider connecting them to the end of the pipe. The other scenario, which is decidedly less rosy, goes like this: domestic water use in northeastern Illinois "becomes so significant that we run out of water—that we don't have enough Lake Michigan water [in the Illinois diversion] to meet the needs," Mr. Injerd says. "We would just have to say, 'No, sorry. We're out of water. We'd like to give you some, you meet the tests, it's cost effective, but you can't have any because we don't have it.'"

This raises an obvious question, of course. If Mr. Injerd is adding roughly one suburb every two years to the Lake Michigan drinking-water system, isn't he ultimately bringing about scenario number two, the less rosy scenario? After all, 3,200 cfs is a finite amount of water. How many growing communities can he squeeze into that limit before he runs out? Not to worry, he says. His department has done long-term water forecasting to 2020, and based on those calculations he's confident that there will be enough water to go around. But what about in 2120? "I don't know anybody who can say where we're going to be in 120 years. I've never heard of anybody doing a hundred-year forecast." That said, however, Mr. Injerd doesn't see a water crisis looming in the Chicago area's future. "I think Illinois will be able to live within its 3200 cfs limit for a long time to come—way past 2020."

Other water experts don't share Mr. Injerd's confidence. Robert Sasman worked as a hydrologist in northeastern Illinois for the State Water Survey for nearly forty years. He has been around so long that he actually testified before the Supreme Court's special master whose research eventually led to the Court's 1967 decree on the Illinois diversion. Retired and in his eighties, Mr. Sasman is troubled by what he sees as serious water problems in the Chicago area's future. "I think it's going to be a major crisis in the years to come," he predicts, "I don't think people realize it at all." The problem, he says, is that the metro area is sandwiched between the limitations of the Court decree on one side, and declining groundwater supplies on the other.

Sasman is so concerned that in March 2006 he gave a talk to the Illinois section of the American Waterworks Association about alternative water supplies for the Chicago metro area. In an interview for this book he suggested sinking new wells inside the Great Lakes Basin to try to tap into Lake Michigan groundwater. He also proposed that the metro area consider tapping the Kankakee, Illinois, and Rock rivers. But he didn't stop there. He said it's only about a hundred miles from his home in Chicago's western suburbs to the Mississippi River. "There is a tremendous amount of water in the Mississippi, and why not use some of it?" he asks. "The pipelines in the West and Southwest are much more extensive than this kind of proposal." There is something paradoxical, however, in a proposal that suggests that the largest metropolitan area in the water-rich Great Lakes region might some day depend on a pipeline from the Mississippi River to sustain its growth. That credible scientists are even contemplating such measures is telling.

Others argue that there's an easier way to deal with future water problems: ask the other Great Lakes states for permission to increase the Illinois diversion. "This is my personal opinion [and] I guess it reflects my working out West before I came back to Illinois," says Stephen Burch, a hydrogeologist at the Illinois State Water Survey. "We're going to have to make a deal with the other states to buy water from them . . . Like, say, Wisconsin, or Michigan, or Indiana, or whoever. Everybody has a certain claim to the Great Lakes, and if we are the big gorilla then maybe what we need to do is work out some arrangement institutionally over the next fifty years or hundred years or whatever. And maybe that's how we will go forward." Regardless, Illinois governor Rod Blagojevich is so worried about his state's water future that on January 9, 2006, he issued an executive order asking officials to develop a comprehensive statewide water-supply study in an attempt to help alleviate future shortages.[23]

Why is Dan Injerd so confident about water when some of his colleagues aren't? He's banking on water conservation. Once on the Lake Michigan water system, a suburb must adhere to specific water-conservation measures (water conservation is strongly encouraged in the Supreme Court decree). Water meters are required for all new construction, lawn-watering restrictions are mandated between May 15 and September 15, and communities must set water rates that "discourage excessive water use." Interestingly, for many years, these strict rules only applied to suburban users who were added to the Lake Michigan water network. Chicago, on the other hand, was permitted to waste all the water it wanted without penalty. Prior to 1982, water meters in the city of Chicago were virtually unheard of on private residences. After 1982, meters were required on new homes and rehabs. But existing homes paid a flat fee for unlimited use, which brought admonition from around the Great Lakes Basin—and from suburban Chicago. While lawns in the burbs were turning brown because of mandated lawn-watering restrictions, Chicago residents could lay down water with glee.

Then Mayor Richard Daley decided to bring Chicago's paternalistic water system into the twenty-first century. In April 2003 Mayor Daley announced—to the surprise of just about everyone— that Chicago's era of flat-rate water was coming to an end. Residents of roughly 320,000 houses and small apartment buildings were told that in coming years they would have to install water meters. For the first time all Chicagoans would be expected to pay for water on an as-used basis.[24]

Metering should reduce water use in Chicago as sticker-shocked residents scale back on their spigots. But water use throughout the city has already been on the decline. Trends in water use show why Mr. Injerd is so confident that conservation will give him the wiggle room to continue adding communities to the Lake Michigan water system. State-encouraged changes to Chicago's infrastructure have played an important role, like the replacement of approximately fifty miles of old, leaky water mains per year since 1994.[25] But economic changes have influenced water use in Chicago as well. Many of the heavily water-dependent industries—particularly steel—fell on hard times, and with their decline came a notable reduction in regional water use. The statistics speak for themselves. In 1988 Chicago's water use peaked at almost 850 million gallons per day (mgd), but during the following twelve years water use declined by nearly 25 percent to 650 mgd. "Since 1989 [water use] has been about flat, even though we've added well over a million people to Lake Michigan water," Dan Injerd says. "Well over half of the population of the entire state is dependent on Lake Michigan water."

Cameron Davis, at the Alliance for the Great Lakes, is surprised that other Great Lakes states—particularly those that border Lake Michigan—aren't paying closer attention to Illinois's expansionist practices. Mr. Davis can't help wondering if, given the way things are going, eventually Illinois will return to the Supreme Court and ask to increase its diversion. "If I were Wisconsin, Indiana, or Michigan, I'd be mad as hell because obviously Illinois is able to play by different rules and continue hooking up communities," he says. "Once these communities are hooked up, the ability to unhook them, politically, is pretty much zero."

During the early part of the twentieth century, Wisconsin served as the lead Illinois diversion watchdog, quickly challenging anything suspicious. But Michigan has since usurped Wisconsin's long-standing position as the diversion's nemesis. Mike Leffler, who runs the environment division in the Michigan attorney general's office, has been following and working on the Illinois diversion file since the early 1990s. Mr. Leffler says that because Illinois has spent years repeatedly adding suburbs to the Lake Michigan water system, the state could have a difficult time convincing the Supreme Court to increase the Illinois diversion in the future. "I would not expect uncontrolled development or bad land-use planning to be adequate justification for increasing the diversion," he says. "You don't build in areas where the resources will not support growth and then complain that you don't have the resources to support growth." When Stanley Chagnon, emeritus chief of the Illinois State Water Survey, was asked if Mr. Injerd's practice of adding one suburb every few years to the diversion's finite water supply was sustainable, his response was, "It obviously isn't."

What's more, legal scholars wonder if the Chicago River's reversal leaves the Great Lakes vulnerable to a lawsuit demanding that other out-of-Basin communities be granted access to Great Lakes water too. In an era when officials in the Great Lakes are becoming increasingly interested in preventing large-scale diversions, how can these same officials deny water to others outside the Basin when Chicago is sending 2.1 billion gallons of water down the Mississippi every day? Some legal experts have suggested that if a parched community outside the watershed were ever denied Great Lakes water (like Lowell, Indiana, was; see chapter 8), the spurned town could use the Chicago River precedent as a reason to file a water-discrimination lawsuit. "What about somebody outside the Basin saying, 'Well, this has been okayed before. [The Illinois diversion] sets a precedent for allowing a withdrawal of water," hypothesizes attorney Henry Henderson, who lectures on environmental law at the University of Chicago. "There's an inappropriate privileging of an in-Basin community that is discriminating against an out-of-Basin community."

~

IT HAS BEEN FASCINATING to watch how the exotic species issue has influenced the debate over the Illinois diversion as well. Exotic species are nonnative plants and animals that, once introduced to an ecosystem, can spread rapidly in the absence of natural controls. The diversion, of course, serves as an artificial, human-made link between two drainages that were never meant to be connected—the Great Lakes Basin and the Mississippi River watershed. That connection, via the Chicago Sanitary and Ship Canal, not only transmits water from one watershed to another, it also serves as a vector for exotic species. Nonnative species in the Great Lakes can work their way into the Mississippi and vice versa. One way to shut down this pathway, of course, would be to rereverse the Chicago River, permanently severing the unnatural connection between the Great Lakes and the Mississippi. A natural-flowing Chicago River—connected once again to only the Great Lakes—would no longer be a diversion nor would it be a vector for exotics. All the used water would be treated and sent back to Lake Michigan where it started, and species that are not native to one watershed would be unable to pass harmfully to the other.

As recently as the early 1990s if someone were to suggest rereversing the Chicago River they would have been considered uncredible. But unexpectedly, a growing number of people have suggested that it may be time to start discussing how to sever the artificial connection between the Great Lakes and Mississippi watersheds. And the reason has nothing to do with water levels, federal statutes, or Supreme Court decrees. It has everything to do with Asian carp. Asian carp are a voracious, fast-growing, ugly fish that was brought to the United States (with U.S. Department of Agriculture approval) to help Southern catfish farmers keep algae under control in their catfish ponds. Over a period of decades some of these carp escaped from these catfish ponds in states like Arkansas and Mississippi and made their way into the Mississippi River system.

The carp—three species of them are on the loose—aren't just slimy and ugly; they also rapidly grow to enormous sizes (more than one hundred pounds) and reproduce at a disturbing rate. They have expanded so rapidly and have devoured so much plankton that they are permanently altering the food web in parts of the Mississippi River, one of the most expansive watersheds in the United States. Some Asian carp species are startled by motors, and they jump into the air as boats pass by; these large airborne fish have sent boaters

and water-skiers to the hospital. Biologists consider the introduction of Asian carp to be an ecological disaster and they are
desperate to keep them out of the Great Lakes, which is why a $7
million electronic barrier has been installed in the Sanitary and
Ship Canal in an attempt to keep them out.

Could the lowly Asian carp prompt the Chicago River to flow
naturally again? Highly unlikely. Dan Injerd soberly cautions that
most people who suggest rereversing the river generally don't grasp
the magnitude of the task. It would require reworking the plumbing
throughout most of the Chicago metropolitan area. Right now that
plumbing, in essence, is tilted ever so slightly toward the Mississippi. Rereversing the Chicago River would require tilting all that
plumbing ever so slightly toward Lake Michigan—not an easy
thing to do. "You have to understand this whole region was developed with this plumbing over one hundred and some years. You
can't just say, 'Oh, let's just shut it off and turn it the other way.' It's
not that simple," Mr. Injerd warns. "It's not just a question of is the
quality of the water good enough to send back to the lake. You're
talking phenomenal flood-control issues, storm-water management,
navigation . . . all of these things will be impacted significantly one
way or another by any concept that would reestablish some physical
separation" between Lake Michigan and the Mississippi River watershed. But exotic species come with enormous costs too. The federal government estimates that nonnatives cost the U.S. economy
$137 billion per year.[26] They cost billions of dollars annually in the
Great Lakes as well.[27]

~

HISTORY HAS BEEN KIND to the Illinois diversion. A century of
legal challenges has altered the diversion, but not stopped it. And
for the most part, the city of Chicago and the suburbs around it
have received the water they wanted. But will the twenty-first century be as tolerant of the Illinois diversion as the last one? The era
of unchecked water use in the Great Lakes Basin is over. Communities throughout the region are sitting on dwindling or contaminated aquifers, and those communities that lie beyond the edge of

the Great Lakes Basin—at least outside Illinois—continue to be judged by a different standard. That means special exceptions like the Illinois diversion—and the unique suburban water privileges that come with it—will be scrutinized like never before. Illinois officials such as Dan Injerd will be called upon to justify their decisions more than they have in the past. And communities throughout metropolitan Chicago will find it more and more difficult to take Great Lakes water for granted.

It will not be a surprise if calls to rereverse the river only increase with time. Some officials privately suggest that rereversing the river would make an excellent federal project, bringing jobs to the region for a generation. Others argue that since most of the Chicago area's aging plumbing system needs to be overhauled anyway—with hundreds, perhaps thousands, of miles of leaky water mains in need of repair—why not spend the extra money to point the system in the right direction this time around?

The costs of retrofitting the plumbing system for seven million people are likely to be prohibitive. But environmentalists will continue to remind voters that there are also costs to doing nothing. "I think the Chicago River diversion has gotten to the point of absurdity," Cameron Davis says. "I've called the question: does the Chicago River diversion make sense any more? I don't think it makes sense—certainly when you compare it to its original purposes." Mr. Davis's question seems more rhetorical than literal. But throw a few water lawsuits into the mix and add a few million Asian carp, as well as a more environmentally conscious water culture in the Great Lakes region, and today's rhetoric could end up looking more like tomorrow's reality.

Chapter 6

Long Lac and Ogoki

I T'S A HOT JULY DAY in the lake country of northwestern Ontario when the DeHavilland Beaver floatplane lifts off from a lake 150 miles north of Thunder Bay. The small craft jostles and jags in a stiff wind as it rises above the rugged and remote country that blankets the watershed north of Lake Superior. As the plane climbs into the midafternoon sun, the full extent of the region's expansive boreal forest becomes clear. There are trees as far as the eye can see, and lakes dimple the landscape, sprinkled like so many watery sequins on the woodlands below. As the miles pass by, the serpentine logging roads, blotchy clear-cuts, and other signs of civilization slowly fade away until there's nothing left but pure, unadulterated Canadian wilderness.

Suddenly, after about thirty minutes of flight, an incongruent scene emerges from the forest below. In the middle of nowhere rests a dam. It's not a particularly large or noteworthy structure. Many dams are bigger. What is unusual is where it's located—in a roadless area. This is Ontario's Summit Dam, so named because it sits on the tip of the divide that separates the Lake Superior and Hudson Bay watersheds. And as strange as it looks out here in the wilderness, Summit Dam is not alone. Just a few minutes' flight to the north sits the Waboose Dam, and it *is* a noteworthy structure. Spanning 1,700 feet—or more than five football fields—it's much larger than the Summit Dam and is more than 450 feet longer than the Hoover Dam on the Colorado River.[1] The Waboose Dam is so large, yet so remote, that it strikes a surreal pose in the northwestern Ontario wilderness.

Photo 6.1: *The Waboose Dam across the Ogoki River in northwestern Ontario backs up the river's flow over the edge of the Great Lakes Basin divide, and the water then flows south toward Lake Superior. (Photo by Peter Annin)*

Why are these dams here? They are the primary hydrologic structures behind the giant Ogoki diversion, by far the largest inter-Basin water transfer project ever built in the Great Lakes region (fig. 6.1).[2] The Waboose Dam serves as the diversion's backstop, cutting through the upper reaches of the Ogoki River and blocking off water that would otherwise wind its way to Hudson Bay. Stretching from one bank of the Ogoki to the other, the Waboose Dam steals water from the upper reaches of the river, backing it up into a sprawling man-made reservoir that feeds toward Summit Dam. If Waboose is the plug that creates this giant diversion, Summit is the outlet—and the tap is almost always open—pouring billions of gallons of reversed Ogoki River water daily toward Lake Nipigon and ultimately into Lake Superior.

With an average estimated flow of about 4,000 cubic feet per second (cfs), the Ogoki diversion is 25 percent larger than the highly contentious Illinois diversion (at 3,200 cfs). But unlike the Illinois diversion, Ogoki is practically devoid of controversy—

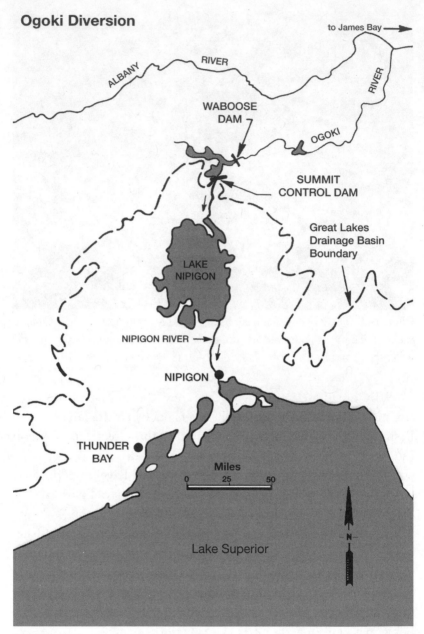

Fig. 6.1. *The Ogoki diversion transfers water from the Albany River basin to Lake Superior.*

Illinois diversion, Ogoki is practically devoid of controversy—
boring by comparison. Most people don't even know it exists. Its remoteness lends to its obscurity, and so does its age—it was completed in 1943. But the Illinois diversion is four decades older, and
it still makes headlines. What is it then that makes the Ogoki diversion so noncontroversial? Perhaps because it diverts water into
the Great Lakes instead of out of them. "It's a giver, not a taker,"
says Ralph Pentland, a Canadian water expert. That, more than
anything else, sets it apart from the more controversial diversions
in the Great Lakes Basin.

When people do hear about the Ogoki diversion, it's usually
lumped together with a neighboring diversion at Long Lac (fig.
6.2). That diversion, also known by its English name Long Lake, is
approximately eighty miles east of Ogoki and operates on much the
same principle—by diverting water from the Hudson Bay watershed into Lake Superior.[3] Long Lake's diversion starts with a dam
that blocks off the upper portions of the Kenogami River and
pushes that water back over the edge of the Great Lakes Basin
divide—or what Canadians often refer to as the "height of land."
By damming the Kenogami River on the north side of Long Lake,
and blasting and cutting a channel on the south side, engineers
managed to funnel the diverted water into the Aguasabon River,
which flows into Lake Superior near the town of Terrace Bay.

At roughly 1,500 cfs, Long Lac is no small diversion either. But
when Ogoki and Long Lac are lumped together, they become
huge—the equivalent of adding a large new river to the Lake Superior ecosystem. They not only raised water levels on Superior—the
largest surface area of freshwater in the world—they also raised lake
levels on every other Great Lake in the system. According to the
International Joint Commission, Long Lac and Ogoki have boosted
Lake Superior water levels by 2.4 inches, Lake Michigan and Lake
Huron by 4.3 inches, Lake Erie by 3.1 inches, and Lake Ontario by
2.8 inches.[4] Long Lac and Ogoki are so large that they more than
offset other divisions that have sent Great Lakes water out of the
Basin, including Chicago's. "There's an accidental balancing," Mr
Pentland says. "It's not good planning. It just happened."

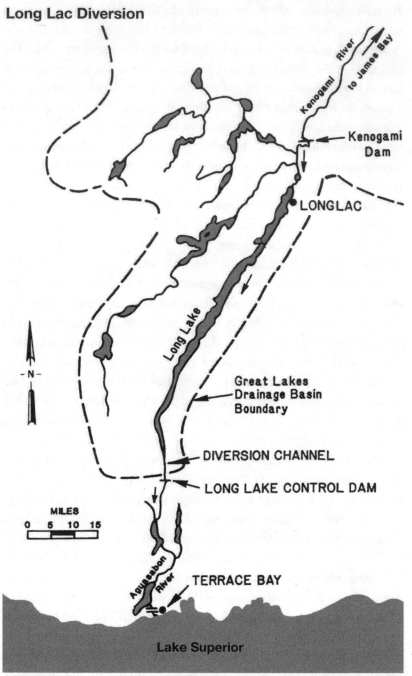

Long Lac Diversion

Kenogami River
to James Bay

Kenogami Dam

LONG LAC

Long Lake

Great Lakes
Drainage Basin
Boundary

DIVERSION CHANNEL

LONG LAKE CONTROL DAM

- N -

MILES
0   5   10   15

Aguasabon River

TERRACE BAY

Lake Superior

Fig. 6.2. *The Long Lac diversion imports water from the Albany River basin.*

Inadvertently atoning for the sins of others has made Long Lac and Ogoki more historically palatable. Rightly or wrongly, diversions into the Great Lakes Basin are considered to be less newsworthy than diversions out of it. Despite the benign reputation of these two water projects, they have had their own social and ecological costs—which helps reinforce the notion that water belongs in its natural watershed and not someplace else. "I don't think there will ever be any more diversions of this magnitude—not without significant political or social change," says Karl Piirik, a water engineer with Ontario Power Generation, which owns and operates the two diversions. Long Lac and Ogoki are anachronisms, symbols of bygone times when the whims of the drafting table ruled the day, while ecosystems—and people—were expected to adjust accordingly. As Mr. Pentland puts it, "They are dinosaurs from another era."

~

THE TALE OF THESE TWO diversions is rich and historically significant. Long Lac came first after Ontario made a Depression-era deal with four American paper companies to harvest trees in the surrounding watershed.[5] The companies needed a dependable pulp supply; Ontario needed jobs for its citizens and revenue from natural resources. The timber contract covered a vast and inaccessible area—2,600 square miles—larger than some national forests on the U.S. side of Lake Superior. In return, the companies agreed to pay $300,000 toward diversion construction, build a pulp mill, and employ at least four hundred men for the subsequent two decades.

With no way to economically get the timber to market without a diversion, construction began during the summer of 1937. By that time Canada had begun negotiations with the United States to secure hydro rights to water from the Long Lac diversion as the water passed through Great Lakes generating stations. Canada wasn't interested in sending bonus electricity to the United States and wanted to lay claim to this additional water before the diversion came on line. But the Long Lac hydro negotiations bogged down in horse trading that was already underway regarding development of the St. Lawrence Seaway. The Americans wanted the seaway, but many Canadians were opposed, fearing the transportation alternative would compete with Canadian railways, which were already running deficits. Because the United States wouldn't sign over Long Lac's hydro rights until the St. Lawrence Seaway issue was resolved, the Long Lac negotiations stalled.

While the talks bogged down in Ottawa and Washington, the roughnecks continued their arduous chores in the field constructing the diversion works. Northwestern Ontario's bitter winters and mosquito-choked summers were a challenge to the work crews. The remoteness of the Long Lac diversion site made for some extraordinary logistical obstacles as well. During the warmer months, a hundred men and their material were moved by boat from the remote village of Longlac to a work camp at the Kenogami Dam site ten miles outside of town. Everything they took with them—food, tools, heavy equipment, building supplies—had to be portaged around a sixteen-foot waterfall via a quarter-mile rail track that had been built for the project. After freeze-up, workers used a temporary winter road to access the dam site. They cut lumber with a portable sawmill and hauled gravel from a pit they dug nearby. Most cement-pouring was done in subzero temperatures during the winter of 1938. "The quality of the facilities that they made in these remote locations is quite extraordinary," says Karl Piirik. "From an engineering point of view, it's fantastic." Although construction wrapped up by the summer of 1939, the full diversion did not begin until the hydro rights issue was resolved with American negotiators. Finally, in 1940, diplomatic notes (sort of a temporary, quickie version of a treaty) were exchanged between the two countries, and the gates to the Long Lac diversion were thrown open early the following year.

While construction on Long Lac was wrapping up, Canadian officials started talking about adding the larger diversion at Ogoki. The motivation behind Ogoki was very different however, and much more urgent. In 1939 Britain and Canada entered World War II, and Canada was desperate to boost its hydro capacity in order to power the war effort. "I remember as a boy, later in the 1940s when lights would go off in the city of Toronto," remembers Frank Quinn, a retired water-policy advisor at Environment Canada.[6] "And this was *after* the war," he says. "With Canada entering the war in 1939, there must have been a lot of pressure," he adds, to find additional energy sources. To resolve the energy crisis, engineers proposed a large diversion eighty miles west of Long Lake to send Ogoki River water south to Lake Superior. There was a brilliant simplicity in the Canadian plan. Much of Ontario's hydro capacity was at Niagara Falls, between Lake Ontario and Lake Erie, but the Ogoki's "surplus" water was hundreds of miles away on the north side of Lake Superior. How to get that water to Niagara? By dumping it into Lake Superior and letting it flow downstream, winding its way through the upper Great Lakes until it reached Ontario's generating facilities at the falls. The plan would allow Canada to boost electrical output without building new hydro facilities in remote stretches of northern Ontario or erecting extensive new transmission lines to ship power south. Rather than bring the infrastructure to the water, they brought the water to the infrastructure. Though the diverted water would also generate power at hydro facilities in Sault Ste. Marie (and on the Nipigon River), delivering water to Niagara was what the Canadians were really after (fig. 6.3).[7]

Building Ogoki's diversion works in the remote Ontario bush was even more challenging than constructing the diversion at Long Lac. Construction began in the middle of winter, December 1940, and used winter roads and bush planes to transport men and equipment over the edge of the Lake Superior basin divide. A massive 820-man crew built the 50-foot high, 1,700-foot-long dam at a boiling stretch of the Ogoki River known as Waboose Rapids.[8] Several other smaller earthen dams had to be constructed to round out the edges of the eighty-nine-square-mile reservoir that would hold the backed-up river water. "Ogoki was different," explains Simon Peet, an area supervisor with the Ontario Ministry of Natural Resources, who wrote his thesis on the Long Lac diversion. "It required the construction of a reservoir, whereas Long Lake didn't—there was a lake system already there." At the southern end of the Ogoki

Ogoki/Long Lac/Niagara

Fig. 6.3. The Long Lac and Ogoki diversions generate power throughout the Great Lakes, but Canada was most interested in capturing the power hundreds of miles away at Niagara Falls. (Based on the original from the Department of Geography, University of Waterloo)

Reservoir, the 405-foot-long, 23-foot-high Summit Dam was erected across a channel that had been cut through the "height of land" that divided the Lake Superior and Hudson Bay watersheds. From there, the diverted water would spill through a series of lakes and a river, entering Lake Nipigon and ultimately rushing down the Nipigon River into Lake Superior east of Thunder Bay.

World War II was well underway when the Ogoki diversion finally came on line in July 1943. Because Canadian negotiators had lumped the hydro rights for the Ogoki diversion into the diplomatic note discussions for Long Lac, Ogoki didn't suffer any political delays before the spigot was turned on. Signed in October 1940, the diplomatic notes regarding the hydro rights for Long Lac and Ogoki were haughty and unnecessarily obfuscating, but they served their purpose. "There is apprehension in both countries over the possibility of a power shortage," the U.S. note read, stating that America would "interpose no objection" to Canada claiming the hydro rights to both diversions.[9] The correspondence emphasized that the notes were meant to be a temporary agreement until more formal treaties could be signed. That occurred a decade later when the notes were recognized in the Niagara Treaty of 1950, which updated the international hydro rights at Niagara Falls.[10]

The diplomatic notes estimated that the combined size of the two diversions was 5,000 cfs—4,000 for Ogoki and 1,000 for Long Lac—but in reality the diversions have varied widely over time. In a 1985 report, the International Joint Commission found that the combined total of the two diversions had been as low as 2,530 cfs and as high as 8,020 cfs. These extensive fluctuations have continued. Between March and August 2004 the two diversions racked up an enormous six-month average of 8,410 cfs.[11] Though the diversion didn't remain at that level for long, this flow was nearly 70 percent higher than officials expected the diversions would be when they signed the diplomatic notes in 1940—and a variance of that magnitude obviously can affect Great Lakes water levels.

Because lake levels fluctuate extensively without the help of Long Lac and Ogoki, at times people have suggested using the two diversions to counterbalance the lakes' natural variability. While coastal freshwater ecosystems thrive on fluctuating water levels, humans prefer lake-level stability (see chapter 3). More than once, Canadian officials have been asked to turn off the Long Lac and Ogoki diversions during periods of high water, and in the 1950s and 1970s they even agreed to do so.[12] "We did [shut them down] for some years," says Frank Quinn, the former water-policy advisor at Environment Canada. "But in the more recent period of high water, Ontario Hydro said, 'Well, too bad. We're making so much money from this import, we're just going to keep doing it.'"

Over time Great Lakes environmentalists, biologists, and water managers have become united in their opposition to using artificial diversions as a means of regulating Great Lakes water levels. "From time to time you get this idea from various people that you can manipulate Great Lakes levels by manipulating diversions—in other words, turning these taps on and off," says Ralph Pentland. "But that was studied by the [International Joint Commission] and was determined to be infeasible."[13] Because diversions like Long Lac and Ogoki are profitable to hydroelectric entities, at times some have also suggested that they be expanded. "[There was] a brief period when Ontario and Canada considered increasing diversions— either at Ogoki and Long Lake or [adding] new diversions," Mr. Quinn says. "It became a little controversial there in the early '70s, and we dropped it."

While it's easy to find Great Lakes environmentalists to criticize the Illinois diversion, the same spokespeople are usually perplexed when asked to comment on Long Lac and Ogoki. When contacted for this book, for example, Susan Howatt, the national water campaigner with the Council of Canadians—one of the most vocal groups on water issues north of the border—was stumped when asked about Long Lac and Ogoki. "I don't really have a position on that, to be honest," she said. "I know almost nothing about it." And when Paul Muldoon, executive director of the Canadian Environmental Law Association (CELA) was reached for comment, he passed the question to his colleague Sarah Miller, CELA's project coordinator. Ms. Miller said that while her organization didn't have an official position on the Long Lac and Ogoki diversions, that didn't mean that CELA supports diversions into the Great Lakes Basin. But she admitted that it was inconsistent for environmentalists to be so adamantly opposed to diversions out of the Great Lakes, like the one at Chicago, but comparatively ignorant about major diversions into the lakes, such as those at Long Lac and Ogoki. Did she see any lessons to be learned from the Long Lac and Ogoki diversions? "[That Canadians] have manipulated more waterways than just about any other nation," she said. "I think people in power now truly believe that that's harmful—in large-scale degrees—but at the same time, I think that's a reversible position depending on the conditions in the world."

~

THE REMOTENESS of the Long Lac and Ogoki diversions has led to a lack of awareness and has muffled opposition—but not among the indigenous First Nations people who live in the Long Lake and Ogoki watersheds. They have been negatively affected more than anyone, and to them these diversions remain a contentious issue. Their voices just aren't being heard. Perhaps no community has shouldered the burden more than the Long Lake No. 58 First Nation reserve on the north side of Long Lake. Chief Veronica Waboose says that the Long Lac and Ogoki diversions may not be controversial in Toronto, or Ottawa, or Chicago, but they are to her.

There are 1,200 members in her Ojibwa community, but there's only room for 400 on the square-mile postage stamp of a reserve that the government has given her people. The other eight hundred live elsewhere and are waiting for Chief Waboose to come up with more land. That has been difficult, she says, thanks to unsympathetic government officials and the fact that the Long Lac diversion washed away or inundated 142 acres on her tiny reserve—including a large portion of the tribal cemetery. "[Much of] our graveyard has been washed away," she says. "The people who had buried their loved ones there don't have anywhere to go [to pay their respects]." Prior to the diversion, the cemetery was on a hill, but now that hill is an island. The power company surrounded the island with rip-rap to prevent more graves from washing away, Chief Waboose says, and the company built a one-lane cemetery access road, but she remains concerned about the threat of higher water levels.

Chief Waboose says that tribal lawyers continue to negotiate with Ontario Power Generation to lower lake levels and thus resolve the myriad problems the higher water has caused for her people. But an agreement has yet to be reached. The main thing her community needs is more territory—to make up for land lost to the

Long Lac diversion and to make up for historical injustices, like the size of her band's small reserve. "We want more land, that's what we're fighting for," she says. "I'm not saying give us money for free, I'm talking about resources for our people so that they could live like other Canadians."

~

EROSION WAS A SERIOUS PROBLEM at the Ogoki diversion as well, in part because soil that was not accustomed to being exposed to waves washed away or sloughed off into the rising diversion waters.[14] This increased turbidity and degraded water quality and fish habitat, particularly in the biologically productive areas near the water's edge. The roaring rapids below the Waboose Dam were tamed too—nothing but a damp boulder garden remains. Similar changes were seen for several miles below the Kenogami Dam as well. What kind of effect have these diversions had on the Hudson Bay watershed? The limited research that has been done has focused on the effects immediately downstream from these dams and has showed that the loss of diverted water created a decline in fish forage, disrupted spawning and fish migrations, and created declines in species diversity.[15] This research also found that during periods of high water and spring snowmelt infrequent water releases from these dams mimicked spring flooding, but once the dam's sluices were shut down, fish and other aquatic animals could become stranded in the receding waters.[16]

Canadian officials argue, however, that farther downstream, where the Ogoki and Kenogami rivers meet up with the Albany, there's so much water roaring through the watershed that the loss of water from the Ogoki and Long Lac diversions becomes imperceptible. That's particularly the case, they say, when you get to the enormous water-rich ecosystems at James Bay or Hudson Bay. While that may be true, there's no evidence that Canadian officials have ever actually studied the ecological ramifications that these two diversions have had downstream in the Albany River drainage basin. "Almost nothing is known of the impacts on the Albany watershed below the points of diversion," Frank Quinn says. "This is, of course, a very sparsely settled region, and aboriginal communities well downstream nearer to James Bay would not have noticed much difference in flow." But it seems hard to imagine that a diversion that could have such a wide-ranging effect on one of the world's largest collections of freshwater lakes has not left the ecosystem wanting on the other side of the watershed divide. In 2005 the Long Lac and Ogoki diversions completed an extensive long-term review process during which officials from the Ontario Ministry of Natural Resources asked Ontario Power Generation to slightly increase the nominal average daily flows from both diversions into the Albany River watershed (these "flows" are essentially the leakage of a few cubic feet per second that happens to squeeze through the Waboose and Kenogami diversion dams). Ontario Power Generation, however, has been reluctant to do so.

What scientists do know is that the diversions caused unexpected water-quality problems in the Long Lake and Ogoki watersheds—particularly with mercury. Chad Day, an emeritus professor at Simon Fraser University in British Columbia who supervised research projects about Long Lac and Ogoki, says that when the diverted waters inundated new land, they washed over ambient mercury in the ground. The mercury eventually made its way into regional fish populations, creating a spike in contamination levels that decreased over time. "The mercury goes into solution and it goes right through the ecosystem," Mr. Day says. "It's in those fish that the Indians have to eat, and they end up with excessive amounts of mercury in their bodies."

The diversions had effects on regional outfitters as well. Fly-in fishing camps are found throughout the area, especially in the Ogoki watershed. During the early years of the diversion these outfitters were rarely if ever warned about impending water-level changes. So during periods of high water, when hydro officials would release pressure on the ballooning Ogoki Reservoir by opening the floodgates at Waboose Dam, downstream outfitters were often caught off guard. "I don't know if it's any different today, but [these releases] were very insensitively handled because they wouldn't even tell anybody that the water was coming—especially on the Ogoki," Mr. Day says. "Some of the outfitters downstream [would have] their cabins flooded and their materials being swept down the river because the water came up and they didn't know it was coming."

~

FROM A PURELY ECONOMIC PERSPECTIVE, the Long Lac and Ogoki diversions brought solid and tangible benefits to the Canadian economy. People need to remember, Professor Day says, that Britain needed Canada's help in defeating Hitler, and Canada needed help from Long Lac and Ogoki to provide electricity for the war effort. It was an era when governments didn't give much thought to social or environmental impacts of hydro projects—particularly when national security was at stake. "It was a wartime decision. I was alive at the time and I'll tell you people were just terrified about the thought of the Germans and the Japanese coming here and taking North America," Mr. Day says. "People forget about how serious that was." While there were ecological and social impacts in northern Ontario, Mr. Day says the diversions at Ogoki and Long Lac provided a relatively quick fix to a severe wartime energy crisis by delivering hydro capacity right where Canada needed it most—Niagara Falls. Depression-era jobs were created through construction of the diversion works and in harvesting trees in the Long Lake watershed.

Simon Peet, who grew up in northern Ontario, wrote a thesis on the Long Lac diversion and he still works in the region. He is troubled by the negative social and environmental effects that the diversions have created, particularly on native communities, but from a broad perspective, he says it's hard to be critical. "My assessment of it overall was that it was positive," Mr. Peet says. "There were some people who were displaced and negatively impacted from erosion and that sort of thing . . . [But] you have this major project and people don't even know it exists—that must tell you that it has a fairly benign impact." On that point, Mr. Peet and Chief Waboose might have to agree to disagree. But perhaps they can both take comfort knowing that no one envisions diversions like Long Lac and Ogoki ever happening again.

Chapter 7

Pleasing Pleasant Prairie

PLEASANT PRAIRIE, WISCONSIN, is a modest community spliced into the faceless suburbia that sprawls north along Interstate 94 from Chicago to Milwaukee. Located in the extreme southeast corner of Wisconsin, the town of eighteen thousand people is bordered by Illinois to the south, the city of Kenosha to the north, and the rich blue waters of Lake Michigan to the east. Pleasant Prairie also happens to straddle the edge of the Great Lakes Basin. In some parts of the Great Lakes region, the watershed boundary lies more than 150 miles inland from the lakeshore. But in Pleasant Prairie, the watershed is a remarkably narrow strip just a few miles wide, which means the Basin divide cuts right through the middle of the village. Rain that falls on western Pleasant Prairie doesn't find its way to Lake Michigan; it eventually ends up in the Mississippi River instead.

No one in Pleasant Prairie paid much attention to all this watershed business until the early 1980s. That's when officials discovered that some of their groundwater wells were contaminated with radium, a naturally occurring radioactive element that was present in the village's groundwater at four times the level allowed by the federal government. Discovering that you have a cancer-causing agent in your groundwater is bad news. But fortunately most people in Pleasant Prairie didn't drink the town's notorious well water anyway. The taste was terrible, and the water was so stained that it ruined clothes in the washing machine. Sheets hanging out to dry in the backyard on a summer day would be marred if water from an errant lawn sprinkler made contact. Some people found that it was possible to shower in the water after running it through a water softener, but everyone else found it useful for just one thing. "Flushing the toilet," says Michael Pollocoff, administrator for the Village of Pleasant Prairie. "Most people got their [drinking] water from someplace else."

Whether people drank the water or not, the federal government still considered it a health hazard. The village investigated a wide array of alternative water options, including treatment to remove the radium from the water supply. But that was expensive, and radium concentrations in the sludge would create all sorts of disposal headaches. Given that the community rests on the shores of Lake Michigan, turning to the Great Lakes seemed like an obvious alternative. The City of Kenosha, just to the north, already pulled its drinking water from Lake Michigan. And as luck would have it, Kenosha's water lines were so close to Pleasant Prairie's that one section of eight-foot pipe was all it would take to connect the two water systems. Kenosha had the capacity and inclination to bring Pleasant Prairie on line; all the two communities needed was clearance from state water officials.

That clearance would have been easy to obtain just a few years before, but by the late 1980s diverting water from the Great Lakes had entered a new and more complicated era. In 1985, the Great Lakes governors and premiers signed the Great Lakes Charter, which called for a regional "consultation" before diversions of more than 5 million gallons per day (mgd) could be approved. And in 1986, Congress passed Section 1109 of the Water Resources Development Act, which required unanimous approval from all eight Great Lakes governors before a single drop of water could be diverted outside the Great Lakes Basin—at least on the American side of the border (see chapter 4). What did all this mean to the people of Pleasant Prairie? Because their proposed diversion was only 3.2 mgd, they fell well below the 5 mgd trigger of the Great Lakes Charter. That meant the Canadians wouldn't have to get involved. WRDA did apply, however, and local officials weren't quite sure what that meant because the federal anti-diversion statute had never been used before. Pleasant Prairie was about to become a guinea pig for the first federal Great Lakes anti-diversion law ever passed in the United States. And while the village's water application was minuscule compared to the giant diversions at Chicago, Long Lac, and Ogoki, times had changed in the Great Lakes region. Pleasant Prairie's water application was about to undergo a vetting that most underestimated at the time. Like any trial run, the road was going to be bumpy. But few, including the Great Lakes governors who would ultimately decide the village's fate, realized what a bizarre test case Pleasant Prairie's diversion application would turn out to be.

~

ON MARCH 29, 1989, Wisconsin governor Tommy Thompson sent a letter to the Council of Great Lakes Governors requesting permission to divert 3.2 million gallons per day from Lake Michigan to Pleasant Prairie.[1] On May 15, 1989, Governor Richard Celeste of Ohio, who happened to hold the rotating seat as chairman of the council, sent a letter to all eight governors alerting them to Wisconsin's diversion request. Even though it wasn't required, as a courtesy in the spirit of cooperation exemplified by the Great Lakes Charter, the provinces of Ontario and Québec were notified about Pleasant Prairie's proposal as well. Based on the informal feedback that Wisconsin was getting, there was a lot of confidence in the state capitol that Pleasant Prairie's diversion proposal would be approved. "They were saying 'This should be a no-brainer,'" remembers Bruce Baker, deputy administrator of the Water Division at the Wisconsin Department of Natural Resources. "[Pleasant Prairie] doesn't have a water supply, it's a public health issue, it's a very small amount. It's totally insignificant in the realm of Great Lakes water quantity . . . The consensus of the group was, 'This is a good one to say yes to.'"

Almost immediately responses started to arrive from around the Great Lakes Basin. In a letter dated May 30, 1989, Governor Rudy Perpich of Minnesota consented to the diversion. Good news. That was followed by letters from the Illinois, Ohio, and Indiana governors who said they had "no objection" to the proposed

Pleasant Prairie diversion. The government of Québec also sent a memo saying that because the diversion didn't meet the 5 mgd threshold of the Great Lakes Charter, Québec too was in favor of the diversion. But not all the correspondence was affirmative. In a letter dated June 1, 1989, word came from the Ministry of Natural Resources in Ontario saying that officials there would prefer a solution that didn't require a diversion. If a letter like that had come from a governor, under WRDA, Pleasant Prairie's diversion proposal would have been history. But because that letter came from an official working for a Canadian premier, who had been notified as a courtesy, the lack of an endorsement was a disappointment, but not a deal breaker.

The bigger concern was that Wisconsin still had not received letters from Pennsylvania, Michigan, or New York. A little rooting around determined that Pennsylvania was remarkably disengaged in the process. "It was hard to get any consistency out of Pennsylvania," remembers Chuck Ledin, director of the Great Lakes office at the Wisconsin DNR. "This was like a nothing issue for [them]." The situation could not have been more different with the state of Michigan. The governor there didn't send a letter, but one of his staffers requested a meeting to discuss the Pleasant Prairie proposal. That ended up being the first of numerous meetings, phone conversations, and letter exchanges between Wisconsin and Michigan about the proposed diversion. "We were meeting at the Milwaukee airport, we were meeting at the Detroit airport," Bruce Baker says. "They asked for all kinds of information like the land-use plan in the area, [sewer] background, 'What's your water-conservation program in Wisconsin?' Just tons of information." The consultations with Michigan dragged on for months. Meanwhile, Wisconsin officials spent a lot of time on the phone with New York. Governor Mario Cuomo's staffers didn't participate in any of the meetings with Michigan, but they wanted to be kept abreast of what happened at the meetings, and they asked for copies of some of the information that Michigan received. If Michigan was the lead scrutinizer of the proposal, New York wasn't far behind. But no one else on the U.S. side of the border seemed all that interested. In the end, Mr. Baker says, officials in New York told him, "We're fine with it, but we won't approve it unless Michigan does."

Suddenly a diversion proposal that had seemed like a sure thing, was hanging in the balance. Mr. Baker heard through back channels that staffers had sent a memo to Governor James Blanchard in Michigan recommending that he sign off on the Pleasant Prairie diversion, but the recommendation was kicked back. Then, at the insistence of Michigan, Wisconsin offered up what's known in the Great Lakes Basin as a "return-flow" requirement. State officials would require Pleasant Prairie to eventually retrofit its sewage system to return the diverted water back to Lake Michigan after it was used and treated. This would not be required immediately because Pleasant Prairie had two new wastewater treatment plants that discharged into the Mississippi River watershed, and the debt load for those plants would be on the books for decades. So Wisconsin floated an offer to have Pleasant Prairie complete the return-flow requirement by 2010, the year Pleasant Prairie was due to retire its treatment-plant debt. This meant, of course, that the water loss from the diversion would be temporary—a key factor that seemed to break the logjam for Michigan. After a face-to-face meeting with Michigan officials in July 1989, Wisconsin's negotiators finally thought that they had answered all Michigan's questions and that an approval letter would soon be on its way.

But to Wisconsin's consternation, the back and forth continued. Michigan officials said that while many of their questions had indeed been answered, they still needed those answers in writing. The key issue for Michigan's negotiators became how the water was going to be used. They had no problem, it seemed, with helping the people of Pleasant Prairie out of their drinking-water bind. But Michigan was very suspicious that Pleasant Prairie officials were asking for more water than they really needed. Michigan worried that village leaders would use the diversion to spur future economic growth in their sleepy town. One of Michigan's chief negotiators was J. D. Snyder, then director of the state's Office of the Great Lakes. In a letter dated August 10, 1989, Snyder complained that he continued to have "deep concern regarding the full extent of the proposed diversion, which includes allowances for population and economic growth in addition to addressing current public health needs."[2]

Wisconsin officials provided numbers, letters, tables, facts, and charts to show that the diversion would be primarily used by humans, not corporations. But two people can sometimes read the same information differently, and five months after Governor Thompson sent his diversion request, Michigan still needed convincing. "You have indicated that the justification for the proposed 3.2 [million gallons per day] temporary diversion is based solely on the need to provide a potable water supply to address public health concerns. Nevertheless, the proposed diversion may provide substantial water for commercial and industrial development," Mr. Snyder said in a September 7, 1989, letter. "Michigan strongly maintains that any warranted diversion of Great Lakes water must be used to address public health concerns and should not be used for commercial and industrial development."[3]

~

NINETEEN DAYS after J. D. Snyder wrote his letter, Governor Thompson broke ground on a new LakeView Corporate Park on Pleasant Prairie's far-west side—the end of town that sits outside the Great Lakes Basin. Though this might at first suggest that Wisconsin was negotiating in bad faith, state officials argue that the situation was more complicated. The plan for LakeView was to take water from Kenosha, funnel it through Pleasant Prairie's west side, and then return the water to Lake Michigan. As a new corporate development, this return-flow plumbing could be installed from the start. So, the thinking in Wisconsin was that LakeView would use Lake Michigan water, but because it was *not* discharging its wastewater into the Mississippi watershed, it would not be a diversion. Or at least that was Wisconsin's interpretation of WRDA. But since WRDA never defined what a diversion was, it was hard to say if Wisconsin was right. As the statute's first test case, these kinds of issues had not been worked out by officials in the Basin. In fact, Wisconsin didn't even submit the LakeView water plan for regional review. Years later, sending water across the Basin line and then returning it would be seen as a diversion that required a unanimous vote by all eight Great Lakes governors (see chapter 10.) But for the time being, the LakeView project managed to squeak through without further consideration.

Even before the LakeView development was built, the Kenosha Water Utility had been diverting water outside the Great Lakes Basin since 1964. With roughly 20 percent of the city lying outside the Basin line, the utility continued to add customers to the Lake Michigan water system long after WRDA was passed. Each time Kenosha's water service was expanded outside the Basin, the Wisconsin DNR approved the extensions without requiring the city to submit its water application for review by the other governors. "Did we continue to add customers? Absolutely," says Edward St. Peter, general manager of the Kenosha Water Utility, adding that as far as he could tell, Wisconsin officials didn't consider what he was doing to be a diversion—as long as the sewage came back. But he acknowledged that not everyone in the Great Lakes region shared Wisconsin's interpretation. "Other states, especially Michigan, felt that any water that went out [of the Basin] was a diversion," he says, which led to a debate about "what's a diversion? . . . I'd like to see something in writing that says what a diversion is." The legal language in WRDA didn't answer that question, and if a water withdrawal with return-flow constituted a diversion, "then what we were doing was illegal," says St. Peter.

While Kenosha continued to operate under the radar, Pleasant Prairie was not so lucky. Michigan continued to have serious reservations abut Pleasant Prairie's proposal, and the village's own consultant worried the LakeView water deal could derail the diversion's approval. George Loomis was a Lansing lobbyist whom Pleasant Prairie had paid $30,000 to help get its water application approved in Michigan. In a confidential memo to the village on September 29, 1989, he warned of "significant problems down the road should the future water use of the LakeView Corporate Park ever be claimed to constitute a diversion of water from the Great Lakes

Basin and, therefore, to require the approval of the Governors of the Great Lakes."[4]

While Wisconsin was having difficulty getting approval from Michigan, state officials were having a hard time determining exactly what the problem was—all they knew was that Michigan kept requesting more and more paperwork. On October 9, 1989, Wisconsin tried to calm Michigan's fears by sending a three-page single-spaced letter from Bruce Baker that included numerous attachments. The letter gave J. D. Snyder at Michigan's Office of the Great Lakes the costs of the other water options that Pleasant Prairie had explored and had determined to be "infeasible." Mr. Baker also tried to reassure Michigan that Wisconsin had adequate water-conservation statutes regarding diverted Great Lakes water. But the bulk of Mr. Baker's letter dwelled on the commercial and industrial water-use issue. It included an estimate that 88.5 percent of Pleasant Prairie's diverted water would go to residential use, and none of the diverted water, he said, would go to LakeView. "Future industrial growth in this portion of the Village of Pleasant Prairie will occur within the LakeView Corporate Park; a development which has an existing water supply connection to the City of Kenosha and thus, will not be served by the proposed diversion." In his closing paragraph Mr. Baker made it clear that Wisconsin was getting very tired of being strung along. "I again state my earnest hope that all of Michigan's concerns regarding the proposed diversion have been answered by this letter and the preceding correspondence of May 9, June 8, July 20, and August 16, as well as the July 20, 1989 consultation meeting in Milwaukee," Mr. Baker wrote. "Your reticence in approving this proposal has placed the citizens of the Village of Pleasant Prairie and this Department in an untenable position."[5]

Michael Pollocoff was feeling irked as well. As Pleasant Prairie's administrator, he had been dispatched to resolve the water issue, and the locals were getting restless. Mr. Pollocoff's neighbors had difficulty understanding why he was having such a hard time accessing water that many of them could see from their front doorstep. Their water was contaminated with *radiation*, what else did anyone need to know? "We had water that you couldn't stand to smell . . . you didn't like looking at it, and we couldn't clean it up," Mr. Pollocoff says. "To our utility customers we looked like a bunch of knuckleheads." And when you go to bed at night knowing that there's radioactive contamination sitting in your toilet, it's kind of hard for the average citizen to understand why some bureaucrats on the other side of Lake Michigan would play hardball.

The situation even spawned a lot of small-town conspiracy theories that Michigan was trying to stifle economic development in Wisconsin to gain a regional competitive advantage. Then Mr. Pollocoff got a phone call from George Loomis, his Michigan lobbyist, who told him, "I think your case needs to be made to the public over here." A few weeks later a Michigan paper sent a reporter and photographer over to do a story about Pleasant Prairie's proposed diversion. In the article Mr. Pollocoff reiterated all the details of why his community had submitted its request for Great Lakes water. "There was a picture of me on the front page of the paper holding up a mayonnaise jar of what looks like Kool-Aid but it was water," Mr. Pollocoff says. And the lobbyist was right, the publicity seemed to help. "Not long after that we got this kind of begrudging okay [from Michigan]," Mr. Pollocoff says. "The governor didn't even sign the letter."

Michigan did finally send a letter, and it was like no other Wisconsin had received. The December 12, 1989, dispatch insinuated approval of the Pleasant Prairie diversion, but it never actually came right out and said it. Instead the letter said supplying Pleasant Prairie with Michigan water "is not unreasonable . . . The state of Michigan, however, remains opposed to any diversion of Great Lakes water for purposes of supporting growth and expansion in any area unable to provide its own public water supply."[6] To Wisconsin, the letter was an eerie echo of Michigan's correspondence of the last several months. It suggested that Michigan would support the diversion if Pleasant Prairie's current population remained stagnant. But if the water ended up spurring population growth or economic development, Michigan would be opposed. There was another problem. The letter was not from the governor, which WRDA seemed to require. Instead, it was from David Hales, the director of Michigan's DNR. Critics continue to argue that Michigan's unusual letter doesn't meet the legal requirements of gubernatorial approval required under WRDA. For the first time ever, in an interview for this book, an official from the Wisconsin government agreed with that assessment. "Clearly it's not an approval letter under WRDA," Bruce Baker admits. "They just played games with the letter."

Contacted more than fifteen years later, David Hales's memory of the letter was a bit fuzzy. "My guess is we didn't want to come across as saying, 'Gee we are incredibly callous about this whole thing.' But at the same time, we wanted to take a clear stand on principle," he said. "We could be reasonable about meeting existing [water] needs, but we didn't think that any capacity to create the ability for growth should be included in any of those plans." Jack Bails, who works as a consultant in Michigan, was Mr. Hales's deputy at the time. He describes the Pleasant Prairie letter as a "punt" on Michigan's part. While his memory has faded as well, his guess is that Mr. Hales was dispatched to draft the Pleasant Prairie letter in such a way as to give Michigan full deniability that it ever approved a diversion, while allowing Wisconsin just enough wiggle room to move forward. "I suspect what happened," he says, "is that rather than have the governor respond, this would be responded to by an agency head to provide some political cover."

That was an unusual way of handling things, but at least Michigan sent a letter. The situation with New York remained so noncommittal that officials from Governor Cuomo's administration never ended up putting anything on the record in writing. "After [Governor Blanchard] did what he did they couldn't figure out what to do," Mr. Baker says. "We never did get a letter from New York." Pennsylvania didn't send a letter either.

This put Wisconsin officials in an awkward position. WRDA seemed to require a strong affirmative vote from all eight Great Lakes governors before a diversion proposal could go forward. But after months of waiting, phone calls, and wrangling, Wisconsin's file on Pleasant Prairie was missing letters from two states and contained a confusing letter from a third—and that letter wasn't even from a governor. In addition, the courtesy notification sent to Ontario had resulted in an objection from that government, even though technically, Ontario had no standing under the Great Lakes Charter or WRDA to object. It was a tough call, and Bruce Baker and Chuck Ledin sent the final decision upstairs to Governor Tommy Thompson's office. After much deliberation and consternation, the decision was made to go ahead. The feeling was that Michigan's letter gave Governor Thompson enough political leeway to sign off on the Pleasant Prairie proposal, while giving Michigan's governor the ability to deny to his constituents that he had ever approved a diversion. New York and Pennsylvania had been given more than enough time to cast a veto, if that had been their intent. "We went through the process, we did what we had to do," says Mr. Ledin. "We can't make somebody else respond. So in the absence of getting a yes or a no, we went ahead with the project."

While Pleasant Prairie heard the news immediately, the official written go-ahead from the state didn't arrive until early January of 1990. Since all it took was one section of eight-foot pipe to make the connection, Mr. Pollocoff decided to forgo hiring a professional construction crew. "We did it ourselves," he says. "We went out there with a crew and said, 'Let's get this pig hooked up.'" After months and months of delays, making the actual connection to Kenosha's water system took less than a day. "We did make some subsequent other connections so we had a redundant system. [But] the bulk of the problem was solved within a few hours," Mr. Pollocoff says. At first the water consumption rate in town didn't change much—the original diversion was only 250,000 gallons per day—but once people became convinced that their water was potable, water consumption started ramping up at a steady clip. Today Pleasant Prairie's diversion averages about 2.3 mgd, still well below the ceiling of 3.2 mgd. Mr. Pollocoff says the village will have no problems meeting the 2010 date for ending the diversion. One treatment plant that dumps water into the Mississippi River watershed will be retired in 2006 or 2007, he says, and the other will be retired by 2009. When that happens, the people of Pleasant Prairie will still be drinking Great Lakes water, but their treated effluent will flow back into Lake Michigan, rather than into the Mississippi River watershed.

~

WHAT ABOUT THE GROWTH that Michigan was so concerned about? There's no doubt that gaining access to Lake Michigan changed Pleasant Prairie into a sprawling exurb. From 1980 to 1990, when the town's water was undrinkable, the population remained stagnant at twelve thousand. When Michael Pollocoff arrived at the village in 1985, he says only one home was added that year, and it came on a truck. But after the new water came to town, the village's size increased 50 percent during subsequent years. In 2005 the population was 18,000, and 250 homes have gone up annually since the year 2000. In the early 1990s, Pleasant Prairie was a place to drive through, but it has since become a destination in itself. The village's daytime population swells to 35,000 people, most of them frequenting the LakeView Corporate Park and the shops out by I-94, all outside the Great Lakes Basin. Regarding the corporate park, and economic development, LakeView is now valued at $560 million. Mr. Pollocoff boasts that Pleasant Prairie—the village of 18,000 people—has the fourth-largest industrial tax base in the state, behind Green Bay, Madison, and Milwaukee, which have populations of 100,000, 220,000, and 600,000 respectively. "We're not a bedroom community anymore," Mr. Pollocoff says.

Pleasant Prairie's diversion may have been the first test case of WRDA, but it wasn't a pretty one. Legal doubts have dogged the diversion from the beginning. Environmental groups and officials in other Great Lakes states have questioned whether the diversion would survive a court challenge. At a minimum, most officials believe Pleasant Prairie falls into a gray area legally. Not having letters from New York and Pennsylvania leaves Wisconsin vulnerable to obvious criticism for having gone ahead with the proposal. And the confusing letter from Michigan makes both states look bad. Some officials from neighboring states have gone so far as to suggest that the correspondence from Ohio, Illinois, and Indiana was not even properly worded. Those letters, these critics argue, said the governors did "not object" to the diversion, which is different from actually casting a vote in favor of something.

"There are some people who still feel that Pleasant Prairie might be illegal. But no one has ever challenged it," says one former Great Lakes official who asked not to be identified. "It's one of the unspoken issues in the Basin. People accept Pleasant Prairie as being approved and I can make an argument that it was approved. But there are only four letters on file from governors saying that they approved it." More than once over the years, the Michigan attorney general has criticized the Pleasant Prairie diversion, threatening to take legal action to challenge it in court. At one point, those grumblings caused enough of a stir in Wisconsin that a legislative hearing regarding the diversion was held. But as many times as the legality of Pleasant Prairie has been raised, the situation has always calmed back down again without incident.

The Pleasant Prairie case also attracted a lot of negative attention to WRDA. Many Great Lakes officials believed that the federal law's first test run uncovered many problems with the statute. The two-page law left a lot of key questions unanswered and a lot of details yet to be filled in. Yes, the law said every diversion of Great Lakes water—no matter how small—needed the approval of all Great Lakes governors. But what was a diversion? Was taking water out and returning it after use a diversion? Many didn't think so. Others did. The statute, unfortunately, was no help in resolving such disagreements. And how exactly was a state supposed to go about obtaining approval from the other governors? Were letters on file enough? If so, how should they be worded? Is "not objecting" the same as an approval? Or do the governors have to use the word "approve" in their correspondence? Or was a formal vote in person or by conference call what the law had in mind? These were just some of the many unanswered questions swirling around the Basin in the wake of the Pleasant Prairie case. Wisconsin, in particular, was interested in filling these gaps in WRDA, because it had water-quality problems in many other communities that were straddling the edge of the Great Lakes Basin divide. "[Pleasant Prairie] clearly demonstrated to us that the system was a mess," Bruce Baker says.

"We asked the Council [of Great Lakes Governors] to get the other states together to try and develop an agreement on how these [proposed diversion cases] would be handled in the future . . . but we could not get all the states to agree."

The Pleasant Prairie experience left a lot of scar tissue in Wisconsin. Yes, the state's small diversion application went forward, and that was a local victory. But the difficulties in the process had a chilling effect on future diversion applications from the state. Chuck Ledin says that in the years after Pleasant Prairie went through, he regularly counseled water-troubled communities in his state not to submit new diversion requests. The expense, frustration, and uncertainty were just not worth it—especially since he could not guarantee the results. "If somebody wants to get Great Lakes water, they had best be prepared to spend some money and do a good technical justification for the need, and be prepared to defend their request," he says. "Rather than thinking of Great Lakes water as an option, they best be thinking of it as a last resort." That was a lesson that Lowell, Indiana, was about to learn the hard way.

Chapter 8

Sacrificing Lowell

L OWELL, INDIANA, is a quiet Midwestern town of 7,900 people nestled in the flat pastoral countryside that lies about an hour's drive south of Chicago. This is corn and soybean country, marked by tree-lined fencerows and creek beds. Lowell's quaint downtown stretches for just a few blocks, with old brick buildings that contain storefront shops with names like "Midtown Hardware" and "Hawkeye's Restaurant." Despite its proximity to Chicago, Lowell is more country than city. It's a place where strangers politely say hello as they pass on the sidewalk, where store clerks seem genuine when they say "Have a nice day." Some locals commute to jobs in Chicago; others work in the steel mills just up the road in Gary, but the backbone of the town's culture remains agriculture. "Lowell is a farming community," says David Gard, the gregarious president of the town council. "It's kind of the best of both worlds. We're rural, but we're on the fringe of the big city."

Throughout its recent history, however, Lowell has been haunted by one thing: water woes. For years its main problem was that its water stunk, literally. A high hydrogen sulfide content gave the water an essence of rotten eggs. Some people didn't notice the taste; others got used to it. But there were those who have never been unable to tolerate Lowell's water, even though things have improved. "I've never had any trouble with it, my kids have never had any trouble with it," Mr. Gard says. "But my wife can't drink the stuff."

Lowell's tolerant residents put up more of a fuss, however, when fly larvae started coming out of the tap. Midge flies are tiny mosquito-like insects that some fish love to eat, but that people are not fond of drinking. In the juvenile or larval stage, midge flies live underwater—usually in ponds, lakes, and streams—before emerging to sprout wings and take flight. But in Lowell the midge fly's thin quarter-inch larvae seemed to prefer hanging out in toilet tanks on the east side of town.[1] Officials assured local residents that the larvae were harmless, but they couldn't blame people for being disgusted. The problem seemed to be centered in just one of Lowell's water towers, so workers drained, scrubbed, and blasted the inside of the tower with high-pressure hoses. But the larvae returned. "We did everything," remembers Jeffery Hoshaw, former superintendent of the Lowell water utility. But the flies kept coming back. Finally, the town considered using modest chemical treatments, including hydrogen peroxide and other disinfectants, "but by the time we were ready to put something into practice," Mr. Hoshaw says, "they were gone." Neither he nor anyone else was really sure why.

Then the U.S. Environmental Protection Agency (EPA) came to town, and the stoic people of Lowell met their match. In December 1987 the federal government sent an administrative order to local officials declaring their water a health hazard and demanding that Lowell resolve the issue on a strict timeline. This time the problem had nothing to do with the smell or the larvae. Instead, tests showed that Lowell's problematic groundwater had yet another fault: exceedingly high levels of fluoride. Fluoride in low doses is good for people, especially their teeth. But high fluoride levels can leave teeth stained, and over time it can cause increased bone density, with crippling results.[2] The EPA order required local officials to notify all residents of the health hazard, and the agency gave Lowell six months to find a solution to the problem and two years to implement it. If Lowell failed to meet this deadline, the EPA would either fine the town or take it to federal court, where the penalties could be as high as $25,000 per day.[3] Though Lowell didn't realize it at the time, the EPA's order would end up snatching the town from obscurity and thrusting it to the forefront of the of the Great Lakes water-diversion debate. The experience would leave the community battered and bruised, and Great Lakes officials would walk away questioning the functionality of the anti-diversion policies they had worked so hard to create.

~

AT FIRST LOWELL'S residents took the news from the EPA in stride. After many meetings and public hearings the town narrowed its choices to two water options. One was to drill new shallow wells on farmland on the outskirts of the town. The other option was to look less than thirty miles north to Gary, Indiana, which lies at the southern tip of Lake Michigan—the largest body of water wholly within U.S. borders. Officials in Gary were willing to ship Lake Michigan water to Lowell, for a fee. The Lake Michigan water was more expensive, but to many residents the money seemed worth it.[4] Lake Michigan water was higher in quality, and seemingly as endless as the lake itself, and there was a concern that the shallow-well option could become unreliable during droughts. The town's residents were surveyed and three-fourths of the responding citizens voted for the Lake Michigan option.[5] But that survey was nonbinding and the final decision was up to the town council. So in early April 1990, Lowell residents packed the council chambers with a capacity crowd that had come to witness the final decision. The tally wasn't even close; the council vote was unanimous—the crowd applauded as council members decided that Lowell would buy Lake Michigan water from the Gary-Hobart Water Corporation, a privately owned utility a half hour up the road.[6]

But in the months that followed, it became clear that Lowell wasn't going to get by that easily. Town residents started reading stories about the Great Lakes Charter of 1985, and the Boundary Waters Treaty of 1909, and the Water Resources Development Act of 1986. These stories, and the public meetings that followed, were confusing to the residents of Lowell. But it was becoming clear that the Lowell Town Council didn't have the authority to import water from Lake Michigan. The problem? Lowell lies less than five miles south of the Great Lakes Basin boundary. Water shipped to Lowell, and then discharged by its water treatment plant, wouldn't flow back to Lake Michigan, but would head south toward the

Mississippi and ultimately the Gulf of Mexico, resulting in a net water loss to the Lake Michigan ecosystem. Under federal law (WRDA), and an international agreement (the Great Lakes Charter), this was a very important distinction.

The good news was that because Lowell was asking for less than 5 million gallons of water per day (mgd), the Great Lakes Charter did not apply. (Lowell wanted to divert 1 mgd from Lake Michigan with the option to increase the flow to 3.8 mgd over time.) The bad news was that WRDA applied to diversions of any size from the Great Lakes Basin, which meant Lowell's diversion proposal would need the approval of all eight Great Lakes governors. This came as a surprise to the leaders of Lowell and their citizens, who viewed WRDA as a form of water regulation without representation. Snaking through such a convoluted bureaucratic gauntlet appeared daunting, but there was reason for hope. The governor of Indiana would surely vote for it, and the Village of Pleasant Prairie, Wisconsin, had managed to squeak out a similar diversion the year before (see chapter 7). So how could Wisconsin deny Lowell's water request? Despite the bureaucratic challenge, Lowell was quietly confident that ultimately its diversion request would be approved. "We didn't see this as such a big deal," says John Hughes, who was Lowell's town attorney at the time. "We felt it was just a matter of explaining our problem, and intellectually, people would just agree with us." After all, what was the big deal about sending water just five miles beyond the edge of the watershed? Who would oppose such a proposal when a classic heartland town like Lowell needed help?

The governor of Michigan for one. A year after Lowell's residents applauded their town council's vote to acquire water from the Great Lakes, Governor John Engler of Michigan issued a press release dashing the town's hopes. "We want to give Indiana a fair hearing," Governor Engler's press secretary was quoted as saying in April 1991. "But a veto is probable."[7] Governor Engler asked for a meeting with Indiana governor Evan Bayh to discuss the issue. The press release put Lowell—and the rest of the Great Lakes Basin— on notice that Governor Engler was leaning against approval of Lowell's request for Lake Michigan water. Pleasant Prairie,

Wisconsin, may have slipped through, the governor seemed to be saying, but that was under a prior Michigan administration. There was a new team of officials in Lansing now, and they were watching Lowell's situation closely.

A meeting to address the Lowell proposal was scheduled in Indianapolis for early June 1991. Michigan and Indiana would be there, of course, and the other Great Lakes states and provinces would be invited to send representatives as well. In essence, the meeting became a "consultation" like that envisioned under the Great Lakes Charter. WRDA didn't dictate how water-diversion proposals should be reviewed, so the charter's consultation guidelines were followed instead. And even though the withdrawal request was below the trigger level of the charter, Ontario and Québec were invited to participate. Officials from the Town of Lowell would be making the main presentation, but others would be allowed to speak. Behind the scenes, Indiana was trying to get a sense of where the various states stood on the issue. Who, besides Michigan, needed convincing? After quietly surveying the Basin, Indiana concluded that the only other potential weak link seemed to be New York. Every Great Lakes state and province except Minnesota and Pennsylvania sent representatives to the meeting.[8]

John Hughes, Lowell's attorney, was one of the key presenters. He argued that alternative sources of water had been explored, as had other options, such as treating the contaminated groundwater. Consultants could not assure the town that new wells would produce the quality and quantity of water needed. Based on the town's research, the Lake Michigan option was the most dependable long-term solution. Regarding water conservation, Hughes mentioned that the town had implemented a sprinkler ban and that a weekly news column included tips on how to save water. But he admitted that Lowell didn't have any specific institutional controls. He also said that while the town had originally requested 1 to 3.8 mgd, officials were reducing the maximum request to 1.7 mgd. Hughes expected that 1.1 million gallons would meet the town's daily needs for the next two decades.

Jim Hebenstreit from the Indiana Department of Natural

Resources also spoke at the meeting. As the assistant director of the state water division, he had been shepherding Lowell's diversion request from the start. He told the gathering that he didn't think an outright denial of Lowell's request would withstand a court challenge. He pointed out that Indiana—because it diverted water *into* Lake Michigan at other areas—would still be providing a net surplus of water to the lake, even after the Lowell diversion went into effect. And he warned the Great Lakes governors and premiers that they would be facing an "enforcement nightmare" if they attempted to regulate small diversions and consumptive uses in the region.

Some who attended the meeting remember how shocked Lowell officials were at the widespread interest in their proposal. Both Canadian provinces sent representatives, and Ontario made statements questioning Lowell's proposed diversion. John Hughes remembers wondering why the Canadians were even there, given that they had no vote under WRDA and the Charter didn't apply. "'Why are they so vocal about this when they don't really have a say in it?'" he remembers thinking. Tim McNulty, who was executive director of the Council of Great Lakes Governors at the time, had a different perspective. "I'll never forget the beginning of the formal process, sitting in Indianapolis," he says. "With the Town of Lowell officials—very solid Hoosier people—kind of reflecting the state of Indiana. And then you've got the cultures of all of the other states, including two Canadian provinces present—someone speaking French. I found it heartening because I thought this is really what this is all about—finding a sense of community in this resource that you share."

Dennis Schornack, who went on to become the U.S. cochair of the International Joint Commission, remembers how unconvinced he was by Lowell's evidence. At the time, he was Governor Engler's point man on the Lowell case and he spoke at the Indiana meeting. "They had some huge ten-inch diameter irrigation wells outside of town that were privately held by farmers, so there was a lot of irrigation going on from the same aquifer," he said. "We went through this whole series of questions. They didn't have any kind of best practices in place with the irrigators who were drawing from the same aquifer . . . It was just sort of pump it at will."

Despite these issues, a number of states tipped their hand at the meeting, making it clear to Lowell, and to the rest of the Indiana delegation, that they wouldn't object to the diversion. Dick Bartz, from the Ohio DNR, suggested his state would not object. Minnesota and Pennsylvania weren't there but were leaning toward approval, and Illinois had already sent a letter signing off on the diversion. The other three states—Michigan, New York, and Wisconsin—said they needed more information. Nevertheless, having five out of eight votes in hand was movement in the right direction. But because of the way WRDA was written, it only took one state to pull the plug. Mr. Hughes says he wasn't worried about Wisconsin, "but we weren't getting very good signals from Michigan, and we were also concerned about New York."

While Lowell officials were making their case in Indianapolis, the EPA was busy suing them in federal court. On the same day as the Indianapolis meeting, June 7, 1991, the EPA filed a suit arguing that the fluoride-remediation deadline of 1989 had long since passed, and Lowell's residents were continuing to drink tainted water. The suit asked the judge to force Lowell to clean up its water and requested that the town be slapped with a penalty of up to $25,000 for each day of the violation. One would think that the suit would make Lowell feel even more besieged, but town officials actually had the opposite spin. They thought the suit might help their case with the governors, making the situation seem even more urgent and possibly creating sympathy for their cause.

Sympathy was hard to come by, but the Indianapolis meeting set off an intense round of behind-the-scenes jockeying and negotiations coordinated by the Council of Great Lakes Governors. Indiana put significant pressure on the council to broker some sort of a deal that would get Lowell its water. Michigan and New York were the key skeptics, but Ontario was also aligning itself—albeit symbolically—in opposition. Mr. McNulty spent endless hours on the phone trying to forge a deal. He remembers the eight states breaking down into three distinct camps: Wisconsin, Illinois, and Indiana were generally willing to support limited diversions. Ohio, Minnesota, and Pennsylvania tended to be swing states. And New

York and Michigan were the most vigilant opponents, particularly Michigan.

There was the sense, in Michigan and New York, that Lowell hadn't exhausted all its options. More importantly, there was the issue of precedent. The case in Pleasant Prairie, Wisconsin, was arguably different. Pleasant Prairie was on the shore of Lake Michigan, and half the community was inside the Basin. But the entire town of Lowell was clearly and cleanly outside the Basin. Michigan's (and New York's) fear was not that Lowell's puny request would drain Lake Michigan. Hydrologists said that Lowell's proposal was so small that it would be hard to measure in Lake Michigan's massive 1.2 quadrillion gallon ecosystem (Indiana estimated that Lowell's peak diversion would lower Lake Michigan's water level by 0.000000365 feet).[9]

The issue was that if the Great Lakes governors made an exception for Lowell, how could they prevent dozens, scores, or even hundreds of communities from reaching for Great Lakes water during the next century? In a mere generation, they feared, the million gallons a day in Lowell could become precedent for cumulative diversions that added up to billions of gallons a day from who knows where. In addition, there was the question of where to draw the line once you breach the Basin? If the Great Lakes Basin was not the line, what was? Halfway down the state of Indiana? The borders of each Great Lakes state? Atlanta? Dallas? Phoenix? Los Angeles? There were a lot of unknowns. "We saw it as kind of the tip of the iceberg," Dennis Schornack says. "If one put the straw in at Lowell because it was a health concern for the drinking water, there were a lot of communities that ultimately would be coming to that door with the same kinds of requests. And it would have set, I think, a very bad precedent."

For many of the states, the problem wasn't Lowell's water application, but the lack of direction in the WRDA statute itself. Once again, like Pleasant Prairie, a test case had uncovered problems in the statute. What bothered many governors about the entire Lowell review process—including those who supported Lowell's diversion proposal—was that they had no standards or guidelines on what

The Great Lakes Water Wars

was a justifiable diversion. The statute gave the governors a veto, but didn't give them much guidance in how to use it. Tim McNulty couldn't fix WRDA, so he worked the phones for a compromise that everyone could live with, even begrudgingly. What he cobbled together was a compromiser's compromise. The boldest part of the plan was the imposition of a one-year moratorium on future diversions of water from the Great Lakes. The idea was to give the governors and premiers time to come up with a system to gauge and ultimately judge different diversion requests. "So the moratorium was to create the high ground for Michigan and New York," Mr. McNulty says. "They could clearly argue they had taken steps to prevent future actions that might be seriously damaging [until] we have a completely new framework in place."

In return, of course, Michigan and New York would have to approve the diversion, but not without more sacrifices from Lowell. Some officials wanted to require Lowell to return its treated wastewater to Lake Michigan so there was no net loss to the system, like had been required of Pleasant Prairie. Under initial drafts of Mr. McNulty's agreement, the return-flow plan was deemed to be impractical and prohibitively expensive for a town thirty miles from the lake. Lowell resisted the return-flow idea at first, but when it appeared to be a deal-breaker, it gave in. The town agreed to replace the water it was diverting from the lake. While Lowell's return-flow offer was genuine, the details were sketchy and patched together. "As we got closer to the vote we agreed to replace the diversion with a like amount of water," John Hughes says. "We weren't sure exactly how we were going to do it, but if we had to, we were prepared to sink some wells and pump water into a creek that flows to Lake Michigan."

~

BY LATE SPRING of 1992, New York had privately agreed to go along with the backroom compromise, and Tim McNulty says he was under the impression that Michigan had too. "I really felt that we had it," he says. "Dennis [Schornack] was working hard to represent his governor, but also reflect the team spirit of working as a region, and looking back I wonder if I didn't misread how far he could go." With the deal seemingly brokered, a date was set for the governors to take a final vote on Lowell's request, Friday, May 8, 1992. At the time, Lowell officials shared Mr. McNulty's cautious optimism. "We thought we had made a proposal that met all the issues they had raised," John Hughes remembers. "We really thought we had a chance."

The day before the vote, however, Michigan governor John Engler dropped a bombshell by releasing an advance copy of a letter he had written to Indiana governor Evan Bayh. The letter said that Governor Engler planned to veto the Lowell diversion proposal, and the news hit Lowell broadside. "I was shocked," Mr. Hughes says. Now that Michigan had shown its hand, Mr. Hughes had the distinct feeling that Governor Engler had made up his mind from the start, but that his team had kept Lowell—and much of the regional political establishment—needlessly scurrying around for months. Mr. Hughes was particularly offended that Governor Engler announced his veto before the parties even gathered for the vote. "For them to go and upstage the meeting that way—I just thought that was reprehensible," Mr. Hughes says. "I still do, and I'll tell Engler that to his face!" Mr. McNulty was caught off guard too. So was New York governor Mario Cuomo's aide, Frank Murray, who had spent so much time working with Mr. McNulty on the compromise. "I had long conversations with Frank that day. He was furious," Mr. McNulty says. "He had worked hard."

The next day, the vote went ahead as planned. The tally would be taken by conference call, with the call originating out of the Council of Great Lakes Governors office located on Wacker Drive in downtown Chicago (next to the reversed Chicago River). None of the governors was expected to take part in the call, deciding instead to pass the vote-casting authority on to senior staffers. Representatives from Ontario and Québec would be allowed to listen in, but not vote. In one of the more perfunctory moments in Great Lakes history, the representatives gathered for the conference call as scheduled, knowing full well that Michigan was going to cast a veto. The Town of Lowell sent a delegation to sit in on the call in Chicago and Mr. Hughes remembers walking into the office fuming with anger. Once the call got underway, the states were asked to cast their votes in alphabetical order. Illinois and Indiana both voted yes. Then Dennis Schornack cast Michigan's no vote and the polling stopped. Mr. Hughes remembers bitterly castigating Mr. Schornack during the call. "I told him off. I thought it was very, very inappropriate for Governor Engler to do that," he says. "If they were never going to approve it they never should have made us go through the hoops for eighteen months."

In his three-page letter to Governor Bayh, Governor Engler tried to explain the reasoning behind his veto. The letter said that Michigan's attorney general, as well as its natural resources and public health departments, unanimously opposed Lowell's diversion proposal, and that both houses of Michigan's legislature had passed resolutions against it as well. "The issue of diverting Great Lakes water out-of-Basin is an extremely important and sensitive issue to the citizens of Michigan who clearly have nothing to gain from diversions," the letter read. "While we are sensitive to the needs of the citizens of Lowell to reduce high fluoride levels in their public water supply, we believe that the first priority and obligation of the Great Lakes states and provinces must be to ensure continued protection of this invaluable resource." Governor Engler also highlighted the potential landmark status of Lowell's request. "Perhaps the most important reason that we oppose the Lowell diversion is the precedent-setting nature of the proposal." The letter went on to say that the governor envisioned cases in which a diversion request could be approved, but only when there was a true emergency like "an imminent danger to public health, safety, and welfare." He added that a diversion should only be considered when there were no other feasible water supplies to draw from and that any diversion proposal should be accompanied by return-flow and strict conservation measures. "The assertion by the Town of Lowell that there are no feasible and prudent alternative water supplies other than Lake Michigan is not persuasive." Governor Engler believed that

Lowell, while obviously in a bind, was not facing a water emergency—the town had other options that it was choosing not to pursue.[10]

More than a decade later, Governor Engler's perspective hadn't changed much. In an interview for this book he said he always thought that Lowell looked at the Great Lakes as the first option rather than an alternative of last resort. "That would absolutely qualify as the old way of doing things," he said. "I had to marvel at how the proponents of keeping Great Lakes waters in the Great Lakes Basin were strong and righteous, but then could look the other way when suddenly it was time to do something in their own backyard." He also confessed to being "dubious from the beginning" about Lowell's diversion application, saying that he "wanted to defend a point of view" about the Great Lakes being protected from potential precedent-setting diversions. "Since Michigan sits entirely in the Basin, if we don't care, it's hard to imagine that others will."

~

MANY YEARS HAVE PASSED since the 1992 Lowell veto, and the case has been nearly forgotten by much of the general public, but not by regional water experts. Lowell marked a turning point in the Great Lakes diversion debate. For the first time since federal water-diversion legislation had been passed, a community that wanted to ship water outside the Great Lakes Basin had been turned down. "Lowell was a key moment in Great Lakes water-management history because somebody finally said no," notes Jeff Edstrom, a former official with the Council of Great Lakes Governors. On the surface, it appeared that WRDA had worked in the Lowell case. A proposal was made, it was evaluated fully for months, and then there was a vote. Some liked the outcome, some didn't, but the system appeared functional—at least to the public. Behind the scenes, however, there was a lot of grumbling. Some were starting to suggest that the water-management system in the Great Lakes Basin was inadequate and needed to be changed.

Governor Engler said as much in his veto letter to Governor Bayh. "Reaching a timely decision has been made difficult by the lack of clearly defined procedures and criteria for evaluating diversion requests," he complained. "Neither the [Great Lakes] Charter nor the federal law provide adequate procedures or criteria to evaluate diversion proposals." Governor Engler said he would prefer that the Great Lakes governors establish diversion-review criteria "before any new diversions are allowed, not after."[11]

Many governors began to wonder about the effectiveness of WRDA as a piece of water-management law and, in particular, about the infringement it imposed on state sovereignty. What kind of monster had they created? Michigan, the only state completely within the Great Lakes Basin, could simply veto every diversion request that came down the pipe, never having to worry about the political repercussions. The tensions surrounding the Lowell decision had shown what an emotional issue this was, and many wondered if the next diversion application might get uglier. "I thought if we can't . . . work through this on Lowell, the stakes are going to be much higher in other cases and you won't be able to jury-rig something," Tim McNulty says. "To me it wasn't just [about] the merits of the Lowell petition . . . I could see [similar cases] on the horizon."

WHATEVER HAPPENED TO LOWELL? Did it end up suffering a slow, dehydrated death? After some tense times in town, a lot of soul searching, and more than a few contentious public meetings, the community went on to sink new shallow wells south of town—an option that the citizens had rejected a few long years before. They also settled their legal case with the EPA, paying a fine of $65,000 in 1993. But not long after those shallow wells went on line, Lowell started experiencing problems. The wells were so shallow that they proved inadequate and unreliable, particularly in times of drought. Water rates increased markedly. By 2001—ten years after the town council voted to divert water from Lake Michigan—there was growing concern that Lowell would start to suffer severe economic hardship if a more reliable water source could not be found. A nearby quarry was considered as a source of water, so was a reverse osmosis treatment system. The town even toyed with the idea of asking for Lake Michigan water again.[12] Finally, in late 2002, a decision was made to sink some new wells in a field about three miles outside of town. "So we punched a well down," says David Gard, town council president, "and we hit water. Lots, and lots, and lots, and lots, and lots, and lots, and lots, of water." It's not clear why all the water consultants Lowell hired ten years before were unable to locate this mother lode. Lowell has been able to mix the new well water with old well water in an attempt to stretch out both resources. "So that's where we are today," Mr. Gard says. "We're pretty confident about our water quantity. We're very confident about our water quality."

Does that mean Governor Engler was right? Many spurned residents in Lowell would have a hard time admitting it, but Dennis Schornack and Governor Engler think so. Even Mr. Gard admits that he can understand the logic behind Governor Engler's denial of Lowell's diversion request. Mr. Gard says he has been to Las Vegas and seen the conspicuous consumption of water that occurs there, with opulent golf courses in the desert and celebrated water fountains on the strip. To a guy from Lowell, Las Vegas's green desert lawns and unbridled growth don't seem like they can last—unless water is shipped in from someplace else. "This is probably an unpopular opinion [in Lowell], but I almost understand them not giving us the water. You know, obviously, selfishly, at the time I wish they would have. But where do you stop? If the Basin's the barrier, is it one *foot* outside the barrier, or is it one *mile* outside the barrier? Or is it *ten miles* outside the barrier? So now you tell a community three miles out, 'Yeah, you can have it.' Then the guy four miles out says, 'Well what about me? I'm only four miles out.' Then, 'I'm only four hundred miles out.' Then, 'Well, I'm only two states away.' Then, before you know it, we're looking at wrecks at the bottom of Lake Michigan . . . because there's no water there either. People look at Lake Michigan and think it's an unending supply—it's not," Mr. Gard says. "The Great Lakes are very fragile. People think, 'Oh, they're going to be there forever because I can stand on the shore in Indiana and not see [the state of] Michigan. It's an unending supply of water.' That's a fallacy."

Governor Engler couldn't have said it better himself.

Chapter 9

Tapping Mud Creek

GAZING AT A MICHIGAN MAP, it doesn't take long to recognize that the outline of the state's lower peninsula resembles a mitten. Michiganders are very familiar with this unique attribute of course. One of the most geographically recognizable parts of the state is an area that locals refer to as the "Thumb"—a broad peninsula due north of Detroit, bordered by Lake Huron to the east and the shallows of Saginaw Bay to the west. Long ago, Huron County laid claim to the tip of this peninsula—the thumbnail, if you will—and today the area is sparsely populated and highly agrarian, with a town named Bad Axe as its county seat.

Prior to European settlement, this area likely held some of the most impressive old-growth forests in all of the Great Lakes. David Cleland, a landscape ecologist with the U. S. Forest Service, says that the soil conditions and hydrology of the area made it particularly well-suited for growing large, stout white pine and hemlock, many of which could have reached five hundred years of age. During the last ice age, the northern Thumb region was scraped pool-table-flat, and the land drained very poorly, leaving the forest floor dented with wetlands and water-filled potholes. The result was classic old-growth Great Lakes forest that only exists in small remnants today. "In that area, white pine would have been as large, old, and as high quality as anywhere," Mr. Cleland says. "This was the perfect white pine/hemlock system."

Nineteenth-century lumber barons dreamed about these kinds of forests. The prized white pines were likely the first trees to be cut. The hemlocks would have been the next to go—their bark being an integral ingredient in tanning leather at the time. Once the hemlocks were gone, lumberjacks would have clear-cut whatever hardwoods were left. The shaded, damp old-growth forests of the Great Lakes were some of the most fire-resistant timber stands in the world. But by removing the old-growth canopy, and leaving behind slash and kindling to dry in the hot sun, the lumber barons of the 1800s created an unnatural tinderbox that would bake and bake, until a lightning strike, or some other source, set off a conflagration. Two such ground-clearing wildfires swept through the Thumb in the late nineteenth century, the first in the early 1870s and the second a decade later.

With the landscape cleared and torched, a new wave of settlers moved in—the farmers. But before any serious agriculture could get underway, the hydrology of the region had to be altered. The flat, poorly draining land needed to be ditched and/or tiled to dry out the soil for spring planting. Long ago, most farmers in Michigan's Thumb laid drainage tiles three feet underneath the surface of their fields to help gently send water to ditches at the field's edge. "This area was swampland and woods and if it's not tiled, it can't produce. That's the bottom line," proclaims Jim LeCureux, who worked as an agricultural extension agent in Huron County for more than twenty years. Slowly, as farmers laid more and more subsurface tile, the Thumb's wetlands—like the forests before them—disappeared as the hydrology of the entire area was reworked to maximize the land for agriculture.

While farmers did everything they could to dewater their fields in the spring, the land was often left wanting during the peak growing season, when the Thumb becomes one of the most arid spots in the region. "Historically, there's a four- to six-week window in the summer that if we could have some rain, it would make a tremendous difference to the crops," Mr. LeCureux says. The right rain at the right time could help the yields of crops like corn and soybeans, and the well-timed water was precious to high-value cash crops like sugar beets and navy beans. Many farmers made do with what the clouds provided; others irrigated with water from the ground or nearby streams. But in the Thumb many streams were small and intermittent, making them an unreliable water source. And groundwater was spotty—new wells often came up dry or produced water that was too salty for crops or drinking. With the Thumb jutting out into the seemingly endless waters of Lake Huron, it was only a matter of time before local farmers started looking to the Great Lakes for irrigation.

In 1983, that's exactly what happened when three Huron County farmers walked into Jim LeCureux's office, armed with a grand plan. As the local agriculture extension agent, Mr. LeCureux's job was to serve as a conduit of information and expertise between the agricultural researchers at the state's universities and the farmers in the field. He also acted as a sounding board for farmers' ideas. In this case, the farmers who had come to call had developed an elaborate irrigation scheme that grabbed Mr. LeCureux's attention. The farmers had done their research, starting with an obscure irrigation law passed in the 1960s by the Michigan legislature following a period of low water levels. Under that law, farmers were allowed to form irrigation districts for the sole purpose of withdrawing water from the Great Lakes. But by the time that law had passed, the drought that had prompted it was over, so the statute fell dormant on the books.

Sixteen years later, these farmers were proposing to dust off the law and put it to use in an ambitious way. Their plan was to pump millions of gallons of water from Saginaw Bay and pipe it due south along an abandoned railroad right-of-way, watering communities and farms along the way. It was one of the most enterprising water projects ever proposed in the area. Most brilliantly of all, the plan called for subirrigation to deliver water to crops. Subirrigation is an efficient means of water delivery that pumps water into drainage tiles underneath farmers' fields to irrigate from below, substantially reducing water waste and evaporation that can often accompany overhead irrigation networks. Mr. LeCureux remembers being impressed by the breadth and scope of the farmers' vision. "I was like 'Wow, this is unique!'" he says. Little did he know, however, that the farmers' plan would morph into an important and controversial case study in the history of the Great Lakes Charter.

LIKE ANY GOOD extension agent would, Jim LeCureux passed the irrigation idea along to his superiors. Meanwhile, the farmers approached their local congressman to ask for financial help. Fortunately for them, their congressman was Bob Traxler, a seasoned Democrat in the House of Representatives who held seats on the appropriations and agriculture committees. Congressman Traxler had a reputation for bringing home the bacon, and in this case he let his constituents know that things were looking good. People in Huron County were getting excited. Then came the stumbling blocks. The first problem was that the 1967 law only permitted creating irrigation districts for agricultural purposes, meaning the local communities were on their own. The next problem was bureaucratic. Agriculture officials in Michigan, while impressed with the farmers' grand plan, wanted the state's first irrigation district to start off small—a limited pilot project that would draw less negative publicity if it didn't work out. Congressman Traxler managed to shake loose some research funds, and during the next several years a wide array of feasibility studies were conducted in Huron County to determine how and where to set up the irrigation pilot project.

"We analyzed the hell out of that [land]," remembers Mike Gregg, with the Michigan Department of Agriculture. "We went through that whole area with ground-penetrating radar to understand the subsoils, to know where they could subirrigate. There was a lot of money invested." As part of the research, Mr. LeCureux planted a series of irrigation test plots and found that timely application of water during the dry season could increase yields more than 25 percent for cash crops like dry beans and sugar beets. So much research was produced that two hardcover volumes— containing more than six hundred pages of detailed information— were published on the project.[1] "There were a whole lot of studies," Mr. LeCureux says. "All this work was funded by money from Traxler." No cost, it seemed, would be spared to make sure that the pilot project was a success.

Finally, officials decided to locate the irrigation district in the northwest corner of the Thumb, on 2,500 acres of land just a few miles south of Caseville, near a straight, mile-long ditch with the unassuming name of Mud Creek. On February 26, 1990, more than a dozen farmers submitted a petition to form the Mud Creek Irrigation District. Under the irrigation plan, the Mud Creek ditch, which traditionally flowed into Saginaw Bay, would be deepened so that water would end up flowing in reverse, allowing Great Lakes water to be used to irrigate farmers fields. At the inland terminus of Mud Creek, a series of irrigation pumps would be installed to send the water throughout the 2,500-acre district. In the formal language of the irrigation petition, the farmers pledged that their project would "not materially injure other users of the waters of the Great Lakes" and that it would not "prejudice the state in its relations with other states bordering on the Great Lakes." The Mud Creek pilot project was much smaller than the grand plan that had been hatched seven years before, disappointing many farmers who were turned away. But those who didn't make the cut were buoyed by assurances that if the Mud Creek plan succeeded, irrigation likely would be expanded throughout the area, if not beyond.

～

BEFORE FARMERS could contemplate expansion, however, they had to get the original Mud Creek plan approved. The irrigation petition landed on the desk of David Hamilton, who was then the chief of the Michigan Department of Natural Resources Water Management Section. He recognized its significance immediately. "I pulled together a team within the department," he says. "Because it was pretty clear that there were a lot of potential implications of this." The team came up with roughly a dozen significant environmental questions that the farmers would have to answer in order to get an irrigation permit from the DNR. Mr. Hamilton remembers the farmers had a hard time understanding what all the fuss was about. "Their attitude was, 'We just want to grow our corn. This is just water, what's the big deal?'" he says. Finding the answers to many of the DNR's permitting questions was not going to be cheap, and the farmers were unwilling to put up their own money for the research needed to provide the answers. So they went back to

The Great Lakes Water Wars

Congressman Traxler. "If the federal government hadn't been willing to put money into this," Mr. Hamilton says, "It never would have gotten anywhere."

The farmers used federal funds to hire a team of consultants who put together a polished, thirty-page report outlining the details of the irrigation district, complete with charts, maps, and a thorough hydrologic analysis—all designed to alleviate the DNR's concerns. In the report, the consultants referred to Mud Creek's potential precedent-setting nature by saying that a number of agricultural agencies and farming groups had expressed "widespread interest" in this "first of its kind" project. The report went to great lengths to emphasize that the irrigation district suffered from a dearth of surface and groundwater options, and it reiterated that the irrigation would be seasonal, only taking place for fifty to eighty days per year, starting around early June and continuing through early August. In addition, the report said that the farmers only planned to irrigate 1,800 of the 2,500 acres and that when the pumps were running the farmers would use an average of 8.6 million gallons of water per day (mgd). During a severe drought year, the consultants said, that could potentially increase to 14.4 mgd. The report juxtaposed the Mud Creek withdrawal with the much, much larger Illinois diversion of 2.1 billion gallons per day, stating that Mud Creek was puny by comparison.[2]

While this comparison was certainly valid, a more telling comparison might be with Lowell, Indiana (see chapter 8). That village of 7,900 people was denied a 1 mgd diversion request in 1992 thanks to a veto by Michigan governor John Engler. On an annual basis, Lowell's diversion request would have totaled 365 million gallons per year. By comparison, the consultants were estimating that the Mud Creek Irrigation District was planning to use 430 million gallons of water annually. That's 20 percent more water than Lowell planned to use. It's worth noting that Mud Creek's water would be used by a handful of farmers during just a few weeks, all for the purpose of increasing the farmers' profit margin on crops—and some of those crops were already produced in surplus. Lowell's diversion, by contrast, would have provided water to a village of several thousand people that was under a federal order to improve the safety of its drinking water. The Mud Creek/Lowell comparison is a case study in how much water agricultural irrigation uses compared to "domestic" use in an urban setting. This helps explain why irrigation remains the single-largest consumer of Great Lakes water in the Basin.[3]

But there was a key difference between Mud Creek and Lowell. Lowell was a diversion outside the Great Lakes Basin, while Mud Creek was a "consumptive use" inside the Basin, meaning that the water withdrawn would not breach the Basin boundary even though some would be lost to the system. Irrigation water that did not evaporate, or end up in the crops, would eventually trickle down to the local aquifer, or even drain back into Lake Huron. Like Lowell, the Mud Creek project alone would have had an imperceptible effect on levels and flows in the Great Lakes. Mud Creek's consultants anticipated the project would drop the level of Lake Huron by an infinitesimal 0.0000455 feet.[4] More importantly, however, the project would not set a diversion precedent.

Dave Hamilton gladly accepted the consultants' report. But his team was growing increasingly concerned about a new and emerging environmental issue that the report did little to address—zebra mussels. During the early 1990s zebra mussels were a major concern in the Great Lakes, clogging water-intake pipes and costing regional power companies and municipal water utilities millions of dollars in repairs and maintenance. The fingernail-sized invasive species had likely been transported to the Great Lakes in the ballast water of oceangoing ships. With no natural predators in the Great Lakes, they spread pervasively. By early 1993 Mr. Hamilton's team was so worried about the spread of invasive species that they determined the zebra mussel issue to be a deal breaker. The problem was that the zebra mussels' larvae were practically microscopic and seemed all but impossible to filter out. Pumping them through a large twenty-seven-inch pipe was bound to contaminate the entire irrigation district and adjoining inland waters with this unwanted species. Mr. Hamilton told the irrigation district which way his experts were leaning, and the farmers asked for more time. Eventually the farmers found special filters fine enough to strain the mussel larvae out, and the irrigation district was back on track for approval.

While Mr. Hamilton was worrying about zebra mussels he was also getting political pressure from above. During 1992, Governor Engler's office was struggling with Lowell's diversion request, and his political operatives didn't want news of the Mud Creek application to create a political sideshow to the whole Lowell affair. Aides told Mr. Hamilton to stall Mud Creek to prevent both Great Lakes water requests from showing up in newspapers at the same time. "The governor's office wanted us to slow down," Mr. Hamilton says. "They didn't want [Mud Creek] to come up right then. So as soon as Lowell was past, Mud Creek was ready, and so we went forward."

By obtaining the zebra mussel filters, the farmers had gotten closer to their permit. But there was one more hurdle yet to jump, and it was not an insignificant one. With an average usage of 8.6 mgd, the Mud Creek irrigation plan was large enough to trigger the Great Lakes Charter, which covers diversions or consumptive-use applications greater than 5 mgd (see chapter 4). That meant Michigan needed to seek the "consent and concurrence" of all the other Great Lakes states and provinces before moving ahead with Mud Creek. (Because Mud Creek was a consumptive use, and not a diversion, the federal Water Resources Development Act did not apply.) Though the Charter was nonbinding, the signatories had pledged to uphold a lofty "spirit of cooperation" regarding water-management issues. Governor Engler would have to send a letter to all the other Great Lakes governors and premiers notifying them of the proposed withdrawal. If just one of those officials requested a "consultation," a public hearing would have to be organized so water experts from throughout the Great Lakes could vet the project.

~

ON NOVEMBER 4, 1992, six months after Governor Engler vetoed the Lowell diversion request, he sent a letter to all the Great Lakes governors and premiers notifying them of the Mud Creek consumptive-use proposal. That letter was followed by a packet that included the consultants' thirty-page report. Those materials set off a flurry of activity throughout the Great Lakes Basin, as six governors and premiers sent back a stack of letters all requesting or supporting a consultation on Mud Creek.[5] Michigan responded by scheduling a consultative hearing about Mud Creek for April 28, 1993, at a hotel near the Detroit Airport.[6]

Interestingly, a representative from every Great Lakes state and province attended the consultation. But there were very few members of the public. Only twenty-nine people were in attendance; of those, just three were nonbureaucrats—two environmentalists and one Saginaw Bay marina operator. Everyone else was an official of one sort or another. The meeting lasted all day. Every state and province took advantage of its opportunity to ask questions and level concerns about Mud Creek, and some of the discussions were quite stern. Illinois, Indiana, and Québec all accused Michigan of inconsistent water-management policy, arguing that it was hypocritical for Governor Engler to oppose the Lowell diversion while supporting the Mud Creek consumptive-use proposal. Illinois's representative, Dan Injerd from the state's DNR, went so far as to suggest that Michigan either needed to deny the Mud Creek proposal or revisit its veto of the Lowell diversion.

In one of the meeting's more memorable moments, Jim Hebenstreit from the Indiana DNR asked the Michigan delegation to explain exactly how the Lowell case differed from Mud Creek. Dennis Schornack, who represented Governor Engler at the meeting, said that Michigan residents considered consumptive uses—where the water use remains within the Great Lakes Basin—to be different from diversions of Great Lakes water outside of the Basin. Michiganders believed that as long as water was applied on the ground within the Basin it would eventually make its way back to the Great Lakes. Diversions, meanwhile, would be lost forever.[7]

Terry Yonkers, the representative from Great Lakes United, a binational environmental group, hammered the project and argued that using a subsidized irrigation system to raise crops that were already in surplus smacked of the "disastrous" federally subsidized water projects of the American Southwest. Like many in the room, he questioned whether such a project was a "reasonable" use of Great Lakes water, arguing that the Mud Creek project would be using Basin water on the "wrong crops, in the wrong place at the wrong time." By the end of the consultation, both Canadian provinces and the state of Indiana made it clear that they had serious reservations about the Mud Creek plan, and many other states were far from supportive. When the consultation was over, only one thing was clear: the group had not come close to meeting the consensus that the Great Lakes Charter demanded.

Governor Engler was undeterred. On May 7, 1993—exactly a year to the day after he announced his veto of Lowell's water request—he sent a letter to the governors and premiers alerting them that, despite the concerns raised at the consultation meeting, his staff would recommend that the Mud Creek proposal be approved. His letter made no reference to the fact that regional consensus had not been met. "We feel confident," Governor Engler wrote, "that the rigorous requirements of the Mud Creek proposal will set new standards of excellence for consumptive water use in the region."[8] He gave the other governors and premiers just thirty days to send any final written remarks, as he expected the project would be voted on in coming weeks. Under Michigan law at the time, the governor didn't have final say over the approval of irrigation districts. That approval had to come from the seven gubernatorially appointed members of the state Natural Resources Commission, which often follows the recommendations of the state DNR. (In this case, because the zebra mussel issue had been resolved, the DNR recommended approval of the Mud Creek project.)

Governor Engler's May 7 letter set off an unprecedented volley of angry, critical, and sarcastic correspondence from his peers around the Great Lakes Basin. Democrats as well as the governor's fellow Republicans were equally critical of the project. The first response was written on June 1, 1993, from Governor Jim Edgar, a Republican from Illinois.[9] While Governor Edgar said that Illinois "will not object" to Mud Creek. Illinois remained "concerned with the appearance of inconsistency" on Governor Engler's part.

Governor Edgar concluded his letter by saying that Illinois remained unsatisfied with the current system of judging Great Lakes water withdrawals, and he hoped that the Council of Great Lakes Governors might find a way to "restore regional unity" in the Great Lakes Basin.

Ontario premier Bob Rae and Minnesota governor Arne Carlson (a fellow Republican) openly chided Governor Engler for providing subsidized water for the production of surplus commodity crops. Meanwhile, some of the stiffest criticism came from Governor Evan Bayh. If anyone was going to oppose the Mud Creek water proposal, it would be the governor of Indiana. "The utilization of Great Lakes water for the economic benefit of such a small number of individuals does not represent a prudent water management philosophy for the Great Lakes," Governor Bayh wrote. Then, in a section of the letter dripping with sarcasm, he said that if Governor Engler's support of Mud Creek was a sign that he had changed his position on the use of Great Lakes water, then by all means "we would welcome the opportunity to re-open discussion of the Lowell diversion proposal. Certainly that proposal would reap far more public benefit with less negative impact on the Great Lakes than the Mud Creek proposal." For these reasons, Governor Bayh concluded, he was objecting to the Mud Creek plan under the Great Lakes Charter.

DESPITE ALL THE CRITICISM, there's no sign that any of these letters had any effect on Governor Engler whatsoever. So on June 10, 1993, after a decade of studies, debate, hearings, heated correspondence, and hand-wringing, the Michigan Natural Resources Commission convened to consider the Mud Creek proposal. In a 5-to-1 decision, the commissioners followed the recommendation of the Michigan DNR and adopted the Mud Creek irrigation plan.

The vote of 5 to 1 may suggest agreement, but anyone who had followed the discussion realized there was nothing approaching agreement in executive offices around the Basin. As it turned out, the commissioners were completely unaware of the flurry of heated

The Great Lakes Water Wars

letters from the governors and premiers that had been landing in Governor Engler's office the week before their vote. For reasons that remain a mystery, the letters somehow didn't make it to the DNR nor even to the Michigan Office of the Great Lakes—the two departments charged with briefing the commissioners on any last-minute developments before the vote. Cynics smelled a conspiracy. They accused Governor Engler's staff of burying the letters in his office until after the commissioners voted. But the governor's staff would later blame the snafu on simple incompetence in managing the paper flow in his office. Whatever the case, G. Tracy Mehan, head of the Office of the Great Lakes at the time, was in the dark when he sent a memo to the commissioners on June 9—the day before the Mud Creek vote—stating that no complaints had been received from governors and premiers. "As of this date, we have received no notice or information from the Great Lakes States and Provinces that the Mud Creek project would materially injure other users of the Great Lakes or significantly affect the levels of the Great Lakes," his memo read. He added that the project "does not appear to jeopardize Michigan's relations with other states bordering on the Great Lakes."[10]

That was a surprising claim. Even in the absence of the most recent heated gubernatorial correspondence, it seems bizarre for Mr. Mehan to have assured commissioners that the Mud Creek proposal would not jeopardize relations with other states. Indiana had definitely expressed its disappointment about Mud Creek at the April 28 consultation meeting. It should have been obvious to Mr. Mehan—and everyone else on the commission—that if nothing else, the Mud Creek proposal would have damaged relations with at least one other Great Lakes state. Why is that important? Above and beyond the consensus approach that the Great Lakes Charter requires, one could argue that Michigan's own laws prohibited an irrigation plan that created friction with its neighbors. Remember the old dusty irrigation law that the farmers were waving about in Jim LeCureux's office back in 1983? That law specifically states that water shall not be withdrawn from the Great Lakes if such a withdrawal will "prejudice the state in its relations with other states bordering on the Great Lakes."[11] A number of officials and environmental advocates appear to have failed to do their homework on that point.

When word of the letter mix-up became public, Governor Engler suffered a severe beating in the newspapers. One commissioner who voted for Mud Creek told the *Grand Rapids Press* that he now felt as if he hadn't properly considered the issue. The same article quoted Kent Lokkesmoe, director of the Minnesota DNR's water division, as saying that there was a "feeling that Michigan is hypocritical" when it comes to Great Lakes water use. An editorial in Michigan's *Bay City Times* said the commissioners had acted "hastily" in approving the Mud Creek project. The *Kalamazoo Gazette* said that Governor Engler had "decreed that Michigan will operate under one standard while applying different standards for others."[12] But the most fervent criticism came from an editorial in the *Grand Rapids Press* published on July 25, 1993. Under the headline "Diversion by Omission," the editorial said, "Gov. John Engler threw cold water in the face of anyone who thought he was a strong advocate for the Great Lakes. He has shown contempt for the lakes and international agreements in his handling of [Mud Creek] . . . The governor looks like a hypocrite." The editorial added that obviously the Mud Creek withdrawal would have no physical impact on Lake Huron's water level, but that wasn't the point. "The issue is principle, not quantity. Any removal of water—whether it's to a Great Lakes drainage basin or not—should be allowed only when there's a serious public need and obvious benefit. Neither is the case with the Lake Huron proposal." The controversy prompted environmental groups to ask the Natural Resources Commission to reconsider its vote, but the commissioners refused.

Back in the Thumb, the Mud Creek Irrigation Board was euphoric—most notably because the affirmative decision came just before a $700,000 federal construction grant for the project was due to expire. Once approved, it took three more years for the irrigation district to be completed (the main holdup was convincing the state officials that the zebra mussel filters worked as promised). On August 8, 1996—thirteen years after three farmers walked through Jim

LeCureux's door—Michigan released a boosterish press statement marking Mud Creek's completion. "This project is a tribute to those who work the land," Governor Engler cheered in the statement. In a reference to the $2 million in federal subsidies, he added that the Mud Creek project "shows public and private partnerships at their finest." The statement boasted that Mud Creek was the first irrigation project of its kind in the Great Lakes region and that Governor Engler had "led the effort and consulted other regional governors about the consumptive use of Great Lakes waters." Buried toward the end of the press release, officials mentioned the $2 million price tag and added that during the "start-up phase" only five farmers would participate in the district, irrigating just seven hundred acres. That works out to a federal subsidy of $400,000 per farmer.

HOW MANY FARMERS stayed in the Mud Creek Irrigation District? A total of four, according to Phil Leipprandt, who happens to be one of them. Mr. Leipprandt is a solid, broad-shouldered man with a friendly, unassuming demeanor and the strong, callused hands of someone who has spent his life working the land. His ancestors were some of the first people to settle the area during the late 1800s, and he's more than happy to show a stranger around the Mud Creek pumping station. He uses Mud Creek water to raise corn, sugar beets, and alfalfa on 260 acres, which is just a fraction of the land that he owns in the area. The irrigated lands regularly outperform his other acreage, particularly during droughts. "We've had three dry summers in a row and it's sure been helpful to have a few good fields," he said during an interview on his farm during the fall of 2004. But in 2003, he said, it was so dry that the water levels in Saginaw Bay dropped to a point where water no longer flowed into Mud Creek; he and his fellow irrigators were out of luck. What's the historical significance of that? The 1967 irrigation law was specifically passed by the Michigan legislature to give farmers a new weapon in combating drought. But ironically, when the first irrigation district created under that law was confronted by drought, lake levels fell to a point where irrigators were unable to deliver Great Lakes water to their fields. The Mud Creek irrigation plan didn't work when farmers needed it most.

As he walked around the Mud Creek pump station, Mr. Leipprandt explained that there were actually two pumps, but only one was in use thanks to a lack of interest by irrigation district farmers. "If a lot more people signed up, we'd use them both, but we're just using the big one now." The zebra mussel filters that caused so much delay—and so much extra expense—are no longer in use because the mussels have become so pervasive that officials have given up trying to prevent their spread to Great Lakes tributaries. Mr. Leipprandt explains that when the irrigation district was originally set up, the farmers hoped to have a little extra money left over to cover some of the electrical expenses (that way the farmers wouldn't have to carry that burden). But when the zebra mussel filters were added, "that took care of that," and all the extra cash was gone. As a result, he said, some of the farmers who signed up for the irrigation district bowed out; the razor-thin margins of modern agriculture prompted them to balk at paying the electrical bills that come with using irrigation water. "That sort of separated the serious ones from the not-so-serious ones," Mr. Leipprandt says. "Now it's down to four of us, and just two of us are actually using it."

When a visitor points out that the irrigation pilot project doesn't sound like a success, Mr. Leipprandt says, "It's been a success for me, but you can't force people to use it." But he admits that he doesn't see any other irrigation districts popping up around the Thumb soon. If you can't make it work with extensive federal assistance, he says, "How can you make it work when you have to pay the building expenses out of your own pocket?" According to statistics supplied by the state, annual water usage by the irrigation district peaked at 73 million gallons in 1998 and then dropped to 21 million gallons the following year. Since then the district hasn't used more than 10 million gallons in any one year, and in 2000, 2001, and 2005 farmers didn't use any—either because they received enough rain, lake levels were too low, or a combination of the two.[13] Looking back, Mr. Leipprandt says, the multiple layers of bureaucracy and all the various setbacks with the Mud Creek project proved to be a bitter turn-off for many of the farmers in the irrigation district. Even as one of the few farmers who has stuck with the project, he's not exactly thrilled with how things have ended up. "If I had to do it over again," he says, "I don't think I'd go through it."

~

WITH AN ENDORSEMENT like that, the experiment at Mud Creek can be considered a $2 million flop. But the Great Lakes Charter proved to be a failure as well. The ineffectual Mud Creek consultation was a damning revocation of the spirit of the Charter and an indictment of the document's nonbinding status. The cooperative *esprit de corps* that marked the signing of the Charter in 1985 was shattered by Governor Engler's decision to promote the interests of a tiny political constituency at the expense of Basin-wide consensus. Many of his peers were offended that Michigan would approve a project that seemed so lacking in merit, despite their objections. Others were disappointed that the first consumptive-use test case under the Charter had such a divisive outcome. Sure, there was a good airing of views, but what good is that if there's no attempt to forge a consensus? Dick Bartz, who had helped draft the charter, attended the Mud Creek and Lowell consultations for the Ohio DNR. He says some states and provinces were "incredulous" that Michigan approved the Mud Creek project. "There's this geopolitical tension," Mr. Bartz says, "[and] some distrust of Michigan that continues today."

There aren't many people who think that the Charter worked as planned at Mud Creek, but the few who do are from Michigan. G. Tracy Mehan says the Mud Creek case brought out some fundamental differences among states and provinces in the Basin about consumptive uses. "People sort of used [Mud Creek] as a forum to vent about consumptive uses, saying, 'Hey, why was Michigan doing this when they opposed Pleasant Prairie or Lowell, Indiana,'" he says. "Of course, the difference was we're residents of the Basin. This is a consumptive use within the Basin, so it's not the same case at all . . . Maybe there was some failure to dot the i's and cross the t's under the Charter, but this thing was heavily reviewed by technical staff," he says. "At the end of the day the key issue was whether it was within or without the Basin. It was within the Basin. That's Michigan's good fortune, which a lot of people begrudge. But when you have almost your entire state within the watershed, it's a big difference. Watersheds mean something."

Governor Engler is unapologetic about how the Mud Creek case ended up. "We looked at Mud Creek as completely in the Basin. That was simply the distinction," he says. "That [water] wasn't going anywhere." What's more, he says that from the beginning he saw the complaints about Mud Creek as an attempt to seek revenge for his veto of Lowell's water application, especially with regard to Indiana. "I just assumed that it was a little bit of payback time, more than a principled criticism of what water policy ought to be." But he adds that the Mud Creek episode was also a sign that the Charter had already started to deteriorate. Talk had begun about the need to implement a more comprehensive regional water-management paradigm in the Great Lakes region. "I think part of what we did at Mud Creek probably showed that the Charter itself needed to be fixed," he says. "[The charter] represents a statement of intent, but . . . they just never took the next step to turn it into a binding agreement." When he was told about what a multimillion dollar flop the Mud Creek project had become, Governor Engler declined to call the experiment a mistake. But he didn't defend it either. Instead he suggested that perhaps the best lesson to be learned from the experience is that both the farmers and the environmentalists appear to have exaggerated their claims about the project. "From both sides it probably was an overreaction," he says. "For the proponents [of Mud Creek] there weren't nearly the benefits, and for the opponents there wasn't nearly the impact [on the ecosystem]. It became almost a nonevent."

By the mid-1990s, with the Mud Creek case fading in the Basin's collective memory, many Great Lakes officials were hopeful that the distrust and negative feelings from the project could somehow be channeled into improving the regional water-management system. But it would take a few more years, and a few more controversial test cases, before the collective opinion in the Great Lakes region would reach a point where officials were finally prompted to act.

Chapter 10

Akron Gets the Nod

B ACK IN THE EARLY 1900s Akron, Ohio, had a serious problem on its hands. Its population had boomed by 60 percent during the previous decade, making the city of seventy thousand people so overcrowded that boarding houses were renting beds in shifts. The condensed living conditions were bad enough, but Akron's biggest problem was water. The local water supply had not kept pace with the booming growth rate—and what water there was, was so tainted that it often made people sick. Summit Lake, the shallow water hole that had long been one of Akron's main sources of supply, was growing increasingly fetid. In desperation, local water officials sank more than seventy wells in and around Akron during the early 1900s, but the overtapped gravel aquifer wasn't productive enough to meet the rising demand. When fire swept through town in 1909, there wasn't enough water in the city's system to pressurize hydrants, leaving firefighters helpless, and much of the city burned. Later that same year state officials in Columbus condemned Akron's water supply as a health hazard.[1]

Part of Akron's problem was that the city's water came from a derelict private utility called the Akron Water Works Company. Back in the late 1800s the company had no problem meeting local demand with a thirty-five-foot well. But as the town rapidly expanded, Akron Water Works was forced to tap Summit Lake, and that's when the water quality began to deteriorate. As demand for the city's water skyrocketed and the shores of Summit Lake became increasingly developed, water quality plummeted. Akron Water Works was either unwilling or unable to resolve the situation,

172

forcing city leaders to step in. "It may be said that the quality of water supplied by the Akron Water Works Company has never been satisfactory for any length of time," proclaimed a city report. "Conditions surrounding Summit Lake [are] seriously contaminated and vegetable organisms have been present in such quantity as to affect the physical character of the water [and] render it offensive to sight and smell."[2]

In January 1911 city leaders hired an engineering team to thoroughly examine Akron's water situation and propose a series of options. After months of study, the engineers recommended that Akron consider a completely new water source: the Cuyahoga River. They proposed placing a dam across the Cuyahoga upstream from Akron near the Village of Kent, thereby creating a reservoir from which Akron could pipe water roughly ten miles to its residents. The engineers estimated that the reservoir could store enough water to meet the needs of 350,000 people, and they suggested either acquiring the private water utility's infrastructure or replacing it with a new, modern urban plumbing system. In submitting the report to Akron's city council, the mayor strongly urged his colleagues to adopt the engineers' recommendations. "Akron is facing one of the most critical situations in the history of the city . . . we must act, and act at once."[3] And act the council did. On September 6, 1911, the council adopted the engineers' recommendations and then negotiated an option to purchase the Akron Water Works Company for $815,000.

While the engineers were drafting their plan for the Cuyahoga, Akron's politicians were busy working the halls of the statehouse in Columbus. What they wanted was unprecedented legislation granting Akron special water rights. The recent water crisis had given the city a scare, and officials wanted water that the city could own, not just use. Water rights are pervasive in the western United States, where the prior appropriation doctrine permits people to own water rights without the burden of having to share them with others. But in the eastern United States, water law is based on what's known as the riparian reasonable use doctrine, which is very different from western water law. Riparian reasonable use holds that those who own property along a lake or stream may withdraw all the water they need as long as their water use is "reasonable" and doesn't infringe on other property owners who also have access to the same water body. In other words, in the East people don't own water rights, but they have guaranteed rights to access water, within certain limits. That wasn't good enough for Akron. Instead, the city was asking the state legislature to take the unusual step of nudging aside the riparian reasonable use standard and granting the city special western-like rights to water from the Cuyahoga River watershed. That strategic decision would lay the groundwork for nearly one hundred years of water conflict in the greater Akron area. And by the end of the twentieth century, Akron would become one of the most heated water battlegrounds in the entire Great Lakes region.

~

AFTER AN EXTENDED PERIOD of political arm-twisting, the city finally got the water rights it was looking for. State legislation passed on May 17, 1911, declaring that Akron "and the inhabitants thereof" had the right to "divert and use forever" the waters of the "Tuscarawas River, the Big Cuyahoga and Little Cuyahoga rivers, and the tributaries thereto, now wholly or partly owned or controlled by the state and used for the purpose of supplying water to the northern division of the Ohio Canal, provided, however, and this grant is upon the condition that at no time shall said city use the waters of any such stream, to such extent or in such manner as to diminish or lessen the supply now necessary, to maintain the flow in and through the canal." The bill went on to grant Akron permission to build reservoirs on any of the rivers before stating that "the governor, upon behalf of the state, shall execute and deliver to the city of Akron . . . a grant of the right to use forever the waters of such streams, as herein provided."[4]

But it turns out that Governor Judson Harmon had reservations about the legislation. The debate over the Akron water bill was extremely contentious and, like all politicians facing these kinds of moments, he appears to have been worried about the political repercussions of granting Akron these special privileges. The governor failed to sign the bill—but he didn't veto it either. In Ohio, when that occurs—after a certain number of days—a bill becomes law anyway, and that's what happened with Akron's water legislation. Now that a law was on the books, the governor was required to draft a water-rights agreement for the city. But he hemmed and hawed for five months before releasing what is often referred to in Akron as the "governor's deed"—a document that mimicked the language in the 1911 legislation and essentially served as the legal title to Akron's water rights. The deed was followed by a city bond initiative to construct a dam upstream, and the initiative passed by a 10-to-1 margin. Not long thereafter Akron's leaders broke ground on a reservoir that would later become known as Lake Rockwell.

But critics were not going to let Lake Rockwell go through without a fight. In 1913 the community of Cuyahoga Falls, located just upstream from Akron, filed suit, challenging the legality of the governor's deed. Cuyahoga Falls, like a few other villages, sat along the ten-mile section of the river between the planned Lake Rockwell reservoir and Akron's city limits. Cuyahoga Falls didn't draw drinking water directly from the river, but rather used the river to replenish the aquifers that residents counted on for drinking water. The town also needed flow in the river to dilute its wastewater discharge. Like other communities sandwiched between Akron and its proposed dam, Cuyahoga Falls worried that the exclusivity of the governor's deed might prompt Akron to someday take all the water in the river. The exact legal grounds upon which Cuyahoga Falls based its argument are unknown because some years later the court record was lost or destroyed. What is clear is that Akron won the case, and during subsequent years the city repeatedly won several other court challenges to its unique water right. The Lake Rockwell reservoir was completed in 1915 with a capacity of 2.3 billion gallons. In later years it was followed by two other reservoirs constructed farther upstream: the East Branch Reservoir in 1939, with a storage capacity of 1.5 billion gallons, and the Wendell R. LaDue Reservoir in 1962, with a storage capacity of 5.9 billion gallons (fig. 10.1).

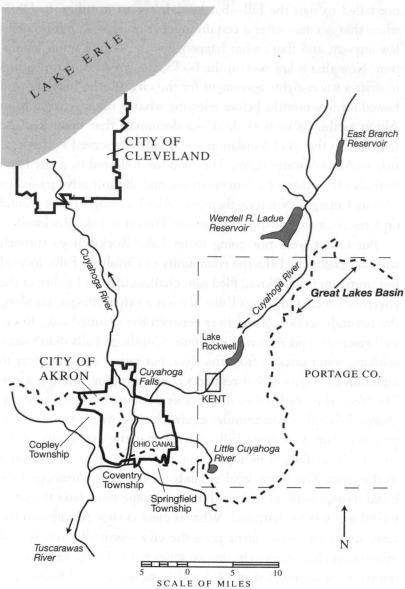

Fig. 10.1. The water of the Cuyahoga River, once so polluted it caught fire in Cleveland, has become a source of contention in the Akron metropolitan area. (Based on the original from the City of Akron)

~

WITH ITS WATER PROBLEMS SOLVED, Akron boomed. Located in the heart of steel country, and just a few hours drive from the auto factories of Detroit, Akron used its abundant water supply and central location to build itself into the leading supplier of tires for the American auto industry. Akron began billing itself as the "Rubber Capital of the World," and with good reason. Tire companies like Goodyear, General, and Firestone all eventually built offices and/or factories there. Akron had become the rubber buckle on the steel belt, and in 1969 the city's water use peaked at 61 million gallons per day. But as the steel belt began to rust, Akron's rubber economy went flat. Manufacturing plants aged and became less efficient; many tire-producing jobs moved out of state or overseas. Akron's unemployment rate climbed, and the once-thriving city center began to deteriorate as people fled for outlying communities. The city's water use also declined, and Akron found itself with a healthy water surplus.

Many surrounding communities discovered it was cheaper to tap into Akron's water system than create or expand their own. In some cases Akron annexed neighboring communities, but annexation proved bitterly controversial because towns despised losing their identities to the bigger city. In the face of this annexation opposition, Akron created something known as JEDDs—Joint Economic Development Districts. The JEDDs were a political compromise between Akron and its neighbors: the JEDDs allowed surrounding towns and suburbs to tap into the city's water system without the pain of annexation. In exchange, the employees and businesses in those communities had to pay Akron's 2 percent income tax. Akron had fallen on hard economic times, but it had found a way to turn its surplus water into cash. "The driving force [behind the JEDDs] was economic development," explains Michael McGlinchy, manager of Akron's Public Utilities Bureau, which includes the water department. "What we had as an asset to share was our water and sewer service."

But selling water to your suburbs can get a little complicated when you straddle the edge of the Great Lakes Basin. And Akron literally straddles the Great Lakes Basin divide (which is why it was an ideal place to build the Ohio and Erie Canal). Part of the town drains into the Lake Erie watershed, the other part drains into the Ohio River watershed. Smitten with its new idea to sell water to surrounding communities, in March 1992 the City of Akron sent a letter to the Ohio Department of Natural Resources outlining its plan to extend water service of 4 million gallons per day to areas outside the Great Lakes watershed.[5] Akron would pull water from the Cuyahoga River in the Great Lakes Basin and divert it to homes and businesses outside the Basin, where the water would be used, treated, and discharged into the Ohio River watershed.

Knowing that a diversion of this sort was a sensitive issue under Ohio law and with the Great Lakes governors, Akron came up with a plan to make up for that lost water. It would send replacement water back to the Cuyahoga River (and thus the Great Lakes watershed) just a few miles downstream via the Ohio and Erie Canal. Hence, the city argued in its letter, because the diverted water was replaced with water farther downstream it wasn't really a diversion at all, under Ohio law or under the federal Water Resources Development Act. What Akron didn't say, however, was that because of its circuitous return-flow plan, water would be withdrawn above Akron and returned below Akron, meaning that more than ten miles of river between Lake Rockwell and the city would never see the diverted water.

The letter went on to say that because the diversion wasn't really a diversion, Ohio didn't need to bother notifying the rest of the Great Lakes governors about the plan. (Keep in mind that at this time Lowell, Indiana's, diversion request remained active and hadn't yet been vetoed by Michigan.) Near the end, the letter said that if the Ohio DNR decided that it did need to notify the other governors about this nondiversion, Akron requested that "an informal interpretation" of WRDA be solicited "before any formal steps are taken to initiate the notice and consultation process under the Great Lakes Charter." For some reason, it seemed, Akron wanted to keep its water request quiet—at least for the time being.

Two months later, attorneys at the Ohio DNR determined that

Akron was right, at least in part. Because the water was replaced, the lawyer's determined that under Ohio law Akron's diversion was not really a diversion. But the federal law was less clear, and the attorneys said Akron's diversion request would indeed have to be reviewed by the other Great Lakes governors, just like the proposals from Lowell and Pleasant Prairie before it. The next month, Ohio DNR officials met with representatives from Akron to break the news, and Akron's delegation didn't like what they heard. The news sent the city into a cooling-off period for two years. In the meantime, Lowell's water request was vetoed, and the Mud Creek consumptive-use proposal was approved over the objections of other states and provinces (see chapters 8 and 9).

In April 1994 Akron officials approached the Ohio DNR again, ready to reignite their proposal. Although two years had passed, it was as if nothing had changed in many respects. Akron stubbornly maintained that its diversion was not a diversion. DNR officials were not so sure whether WRDA applied so they decided to "request an informal interpretation" from the Council of Great Lakes Governors. At the time, the state of Pennsylvania held the rotating chairman's seat on the governors council, and Joseph Hoffman, assistant director of the Pennsylvania Department of Environmental Resources, was chairing the council's Water Resources Management Committee. Mr. Hoffman agreed to informally review Akron's request.

Nine months later Akron again ended up with news that it didn't want to hear. Officials in Pennsylvania had studied the city's complicated water proposal— with all its circuitous make-up-water specifications—and had determined that despite the return-flow a diversion from the Great Lakes Basin was still a diversion and it needed to be approved by all eight Great Lakes governors. Mr. Hoffman had also closely examined Akron's water deed from the governor. He pointed out that the deed specifically stated that the Cuyahoga's waters could be used only for Akron and the "inhabitants thereof." He said that the proposed diversion, as he understood it, would "serve areas outside the city." Though interpreting the meaning of the governor's deed was an internal matter in Ohio,

Mr. Hoffman suggested that the city could not use the governor's deed to send water outside the city's limits.

~

UNDETERRED, AKRON went to work putting together a proposal designed to win over the Great Lakes governors. The city hired consultants (at a cost of $250,000) to prepare a comprehensive report on the proposed diversion, complete with charts, graphs, maps, and a narrative.[6] A video and color brochure were produced for distribution to the governors as well. Interestingly, neither the title nor the body of the brochure mentioned the word "diversion." Instead, it was called, *Preserving the Great Lakes through Regional Cooperation: A Proposal by the City of Akron, Ohio.* The brochure was short and to the point, explaining that Akron was located on the edge of the Great Lakes watershed and that the neighboring townships—with their contaminated wells and failing septic systems— were located "at least in part" in the Ohio-Mississippi River watershed. It emphasized Akron's greatest selling point: that thanks to its return-flow idea involving the Ohio and Erie Canal, there would be "no net loss" to the Great Lakes under this diversion proposal. "This ensures that water used by these townships will either be returned or replaced," the brochure read.[7]

The accompanying video hit that point even harder. In nine minutes of tape, the video mentioned the words "no net loss" a total of seven times. The city admitted it had fallen on hard economic times and that it was hoping to use surplus water as a way to create badly needed revenue. Just like the brochure, the video managed to describe the Akron water project without once using the word "diversion." The consultants' report contained less gloss and fluff and dove much deeper into detail about the project, estimating the maximum annual amount for the diversion at 4.8 million gallons per day (mgd). At the time the report was written, Akron had a population of 221,000 people and was using 47 mgd, well below the city's record water usage of 61 mgd. The townships had issues with contamination and water availability. The report said the most promising underground water source near these suburbs had a former "waste disposal site" directly above it that contained known carcinogens, and a nearby reservoir had water-quality problems.

On September 30, 1996, the report, video and brochure were forwarded to all the governors and their water managers in the Great Lakes Basin. At Akron's insistence, Governor George Voinovich requested that the proposal be reviewed informally and that all comments and criticisms be returned to representatives at the Ohio DNR. Any feedback from around the Basin would then be integrated into a final report that would be formally recirculated among the governors and premiers later for their ultimate approval. "Once the technical review is complete," Governor Voinovich wrote, "I will follow up with you again."[8]

It's important to note that by this stage there had yet to be a public hearing about Akron's proposed diversion. There had not even been a public announcement about the diversion plan. At Akron's request, officials had kept its proposal quiet. But once a draft diversion document starts circulating around the Great Lakes Basin, it's almost impossible to keep it under wraps for long. Sooner or later an environmentalist—or a journalist—is going to get wind of it. And that's precisely what happened on February 13, 1997. Reporter Bob Downing of the Akron Beacon Journal published a story about the diversion, quoting a number of environmental advocates criticizing the proposal as a "precedent-setting end run that numerous other municipalities just beyond the edge of the Great Lakes Basin would use to try to justify diversions." The main critics were two of the leading environmental groups in the Basin: the Canadian Environmental Law Association, in Toronto, and Great Lakes United, based in Buffalo and Montréal. The two environmental organizations had just published a comprehensive report on the history of Great Lakes diversions, and they saw the Akron proposal as the latest sign that water management in the Great Lakes was heading down a slippery slope toward more diversions.

An unexpected story on the front page of the local paper isn't exactly the coming out party that Akron had planned for its nondiversion diversion. A number of local communities along the Cuyahoga River—especially in the ten-mile stretch between Akron and Lake

Rockwell—were shocked to read that Akron was working quietly to cut a special water deal with the state. They were particularly insulted that Akron's deal had been quietly floated to governors in *other states*—without holding a local public hearing first. Many of these upstream communities had grown resentful over the years as they watched Akron hoard the river water during times of drought. "Akron more or less indicated that they owned the river," says Larry Valentine, former head of the Cuyahoga Falls water utility. And thanks to the 1911 governor's deed, these streamside communities felt powerless to do anything about it.

These towns already felt quite strongly that there wasn't enough Cuyahoga water to go around. And now Akron wanted to pump river water outside the Great Lakes Basin? The news put these towns into a state of panic. "The more we saw them pumping over the divide," Mr. Valentine says, "the less we saw coming down the river." Officials in Cuyahoga Falls had been unhappy with Akron's special water privileges ever since they filed suit against the governor's deed back in 1913. But by the 1990s Cuyahoga Falls had been joined by several other unhappy neighbors who were fed up with living on or near a river that Akron claimed to own. The list included the City of Kent, the City of Munroe Falls, the Village of Silver Lake, and even the Portage County Board of Commissioners. "How we found out about it is the thing that made everybody upset," says Mr. Valentine in reference to Akron's proposed diversion. "They knew we were going to get upset. They were trying to get all their ducks in a row before they even approached us."

~

DICK BARTZ SAYS he never saw the controversy coming. Mr. Bartz has been working at the Ohio DNR Division of Water long enough to have been involved in drafting the Great Lakes Charter. He was also one of the DNR's point people on the Akron diversion, and as a student of the Charter his main concern was making sure that Akron's plan satisfied his peers in the Great Lakes Basin. After watching the Pleasant Prairie, Lowell, and Mud Creek cases, his eye was on regional governors' offices, not on a handful of communities in the Cuyahoga Valley. "We walked into a Hatfield and McCoy pissing match," Mr. Bartz admits. "We got blindsided by that." He says that he and his DNR colleagues made a mistake in not informing the communities between Akron and Lake Rockwell about the proposed diversion, but he also says he had no idea that there had been such a longstanding level of antipathy and distrust. "Akron has kind of been the bully, in trying to bully these communities around using water, using sewer, using everything they can," Mr. Bartz says. "[Akron] completely excluded [Lake Rockwell] from recreation. The people in [Portage] County are very upset that they can't get to that reservoir."

While the controversy between Akron and the upstream communities simmered, on March 31, 1997, Governor Voinovich finally circulated the official, public version of Akron's plan to the other Great Lakes governors and premiers. One by one the various states sent in their approval letters signing off on the Akron diversion. Michigan, as usual, was the last state to give the nod. But in an odd way, for political reasons, Michigan needed the Akron diversion to go through almost as much as Ohio did. Michigan had lost so much credibility in the Basin after the Mud Creek debacle that if it vetoed Akron too, that could have sent interstate relations in the Great Lakes Basin into a tailspin. In addition, Michigan had recently confronted Illinois over the Chicago River diversion, prompting new, out-of-court negotiations in that case— negotiations that eventually led to the Chicago River Memorandum of Understanding of 1996. So Michigan was picking fights with many of its neighbors. "I think some hard questions were being put to [Michigan]," says Jack Bails, one of Akron's consultants. "Were they being unreasonable? . . . Were there *any* circumstances where they would approve use of Great Lakes water outside the Basin? Looking back, I think Michigan wanted to get back into the fold, if you will." Michigan officials realized, he says, that if they pushed things too far the other Great Lakes states might ask for WRDA to be altered or revoked. If support for WRDA were to erode among the Great Lakes states—because of Michigan's intransigence or for some other reason—many observers think Congress would willingly rescind WRDA or at least weaken it.

Akron's no-net-loss return-flow was designed to be politically palatable for the Michigan electorate, as well as the voters in Ohio, so that the governor of Michigan could approve the Akron diversion without suffering political damage at home. "We saw what happened with Lowell, we saw how Pleasant Prairie went," Mr. Bartz says. "And it takes a lot of objections off the table if there's return-flow . . . It was critical." In April 1998—exactly six years after Akron had first approached the Ohio DNR about their nondiversion diversion—state officials sent word to Mayor Donald Plusquellic that the Akron diversion had been approved by all eight Great Lakes governors. "Akron's proposal to extend drinking water service into Springfield, Coventry and Copley townships has obtained the approval of all the Great Lakes States' Governors as required," the letter read. "The City may now initiate provision of drinking water service as proposed."[9]

~

BUT AKRON'S WATER FIGHT was far from over. On April 17, 1998, just two weeks after Michigan gave notice that it had approved Akron's diversion, attorneys representing the disgruntled Cuyahoga River communities sued Akron in state court challenging a wide array of the city's water practices. The plaintiffs in the suit included some familiar faces: Cuyahoga Falls, Kent, Munroe Falls, and Silver Lake, as well as the Portage County Board of Commissioners—local upstream governments that had long been unhappy with the way Akron was using the Cuyahoga River. "Shipping water across the Basin line to those townships was the straw that broke the camel's back," says Jack Van Kley, the attorney for the disgruntled communities. "That really was what set off the war." The result was that the Cuyahoga—once known the world over as the chronically polluted river that caught fire in downtown Cleveland—has become one of the most conflict-ridden water sources in the Great Lakes region.

The heart of the communities' lawsuit was directed squarely at the 1911 governor's deed. They argued that Akron had taken its original water right and broadened it far beyond the deed's intended scope. The suit also attacked Akron's practice of fencing off Lake Rockwell from public recreation. But the lawsuit had a broader, more nationally significant theme. It argued that Akron's behavior was an affront to the riparian reasonable use doctrine upon which water law in the eastern United States is based. In their lawsuit these communities were arguing that Akron's actions were an "unreasonable use of water" that infringed on the rights of other riparian communities and landholders along the Cuyahoga. "Out West the person who grabs the water first has a right to it forever," Mr. Van Kley says. "In the East you don't appropriate water by possessing it. In the East you have the right to take water out of a river to which you own riparian rights" as long as the water use is "reasonable" and doesn't harm other riparian landowners. The communities argued that the 1911 governor's deed clashed directly with riparian reasonable use, and they were asking a judge to finally set the record straight. They wanted him to rule that the 1911 deed did not grant Akron ownership to all the water in the Cuyahoga, and later they would ask the judge to force Akron to provide a minimum flow in the river of 10.9 mgd.

Akron was unfazed. The day after the suit was filed, Mayor Plusquellic was quoted in the Cleveland *Plain Dealer* as saying, "They act like we don't have any rights to this water. We have purchased those rights . . . You're going into issues that were resolved decades ago."[10] In the years following the 1911 deed, Akron went up and down the river buying land and/or water rights from property owners. Others landowners took Akron to court. But according to Akron, under Ohio law citizens have twenty-one years to make a claim in such cases, and that statute of limitations had run out long ago. "In a nutshell," says the city's trial attorney Leslie Jacobs, "Akron's position is, 'You've got to be kidding! Where were you for the last hundred years?'" In its court filing Akron argued it "has the right, among other things, to possess the water of the Cuyahoga River" and that the governor's deed gave the city the right to use the Cuyahoga "forever, without limitation as to amount . . . and there is no restriction upon Akron's sale of water outside the city limits."

The Ohio media had a field day with the litigation. One mayor from a disgruntled community was quoted by the *Plain Dealer* as saying, "I just can't believe that the state of Ohio can sell a city a river . . . This to me is ludicrous. I don't care if it's 1911 or 1850. I don't think that can be done."[11] The *Akron Beacon Journal* later predicted that the trial would be moved to another part of the state because the controversy had reached the level of a "regional war for water."[12] Continuing the war analogy, on the eve of trial in January 2001, the *Beacon Journal* quoted Mayor Plusquellic, sounding particularly exercised: "If they say we're enemies, then fine. Let's do battle . . . I didn't start this fight . . . If I have to shut off water to little old ladies, and churches, and hospitals, I'm sorry. They're on their own." The same article quoted Bob Brown, manager of the Kent, Ohio, wastewater treatment facility, who said, "It's ironic we're sitting next to the largest freshwater supply in the world [the Great Lakes], and we're still fighting about water."[13] As the *Plain Dealer* put it, "This fight sounds like it should be taking place in the water-starved Southwest between Colorado and Arizona."[14]

Before the case even went to trial, Jack Van Kley filed a pretrial motion challenging Akron's claim that it owned the river based on the governor's deed. "We went for the jugular early on by filing that motion," he says. The motion resulted in Akron's first big setback in the case. In a key ruling on April 20, 2000, the judge found that the governor's deed did not grant Akron unlimited use of the Cuyahoga's water.[15] "We respectfully disagree with the judge's ruling," Leslie Jacobs was quoted as saying, adding that Akron would certainly appeal. "But to put it in context, if he had decided this in our favor—as we think the Ohio Supreme Court will do—the case would effectively be over."[16]

The trial lasted sixteen days and testimony included, among other things, Mayor Plusquellic denying that he was a "bully." A total of twenty-seven witnesses testified, and the stack of legal documents for the case stood eight feet high. The two sides spent a combined $4.3 million preparing for trial.[17] The state judge took eight months to render a verdict, and during the interim both sides made it clear that no matter what the judge decided, the case would be appealed to the Ohio Supreme Court. Finally, in October 2001 Judge John Enlow released his twenty-eight-page opinion, and while it was a split decision, Akron came out on top.

The judge ruled that while the governor's deed did not give Akron the right to sell water to other communities, because Akron had purchased land along the river upstream, the city was in fact a "riparian" landowner that could sell water to others. "Akron has a right as a riparian owner along the Cuyahoga River to take water for its own use, including the sale of water to others, as long as the amount of that taking is reasonable," he wrote. "This Court concludes that Akron's current taking of water from the Cuyahoga River at Lake Rockwell is not unreasonable."[18] But the judge also ruled that the city had to open Lake Rockwell to public recreation and suggested—though didn't require—that the city should continue to release 5 mgd into the river—about half what the communities had asked for. "We're quite pleased," Leslie Jacobs said after the verdict. "The judge's order sustains our position on all but two points."[19]

It turned out that Akron's victory celebration was short-lived, as both sides filed appeals the following month. The longer the case dragged on, the more abrasive and acerbic the court filings became. The briefs were punctuated with insulting words like "myopic," "concocted," "fairytale," "fable," "illogical," and "revisionist." It took two more years for the appeal to make it to court, where at times the jurists seemed unsympathetic to both sides. One judge asked Akron's lawyers if they felt they had the right to "box up" Cuyahoga River water and "sell it to the people of Biloxi, Mississippi?"[20] On March 31, 2004, Ohio's Eleventh District Court of Appeals handed down its decision, which reversed the lower court's rulings on many counts. The appeals judges said that Akron could restrict public access to Lake Rockwell, but ruled that the city must release a minimum amount of water from the reservoir every day. They declined to say exactly how much water, kicking that decision back to the lower court judge. The opinion, which ran for more than sixty pages, made plain that Akron didn't rule the river quite as solidly as it had alleged, agreeing with the lower court that Akron's claim to all the water in the river was without merit.[21]

The appeals court verdict was a clear victory for the upstream communities, and it was time for the plaintiffs to crow. "Akron held that it had an absolute right to the water in the river. We've already won the case because we've disproved that opinion," boasted Chuck Keiper, a Portage County Commissioner. "Portage County has for the first time in a century regained its right to that river, which is important to our growth and our future. From that point alone it's worth every penny."[22]

As promised, however, both sides appealed the case to the Ohio Supreme Court. On March 6, 2006, the state's most influential judges handed down their forty-page opinion, and while the Ohio media declared it a split decision, key segments of the opinion went against Akron. First, the justices agreed with the appeals court (and the lower court) in ruling that Akron didn't come close to owning the whole river, or its tributary water, as the city had claimed under the 1911 governor's deed. That, obviously, was a major victory for the plaintiffs. The only thing the governor's deed gave Akron, the justices said, was the water that flowed through the Ohio and Erie Canal. What's more, the supreme court decision forced Akron to ensure that a minimum amount of water flowed downstream from Lake Rockwell on a daily basis. This too was a coup for the plaintiffs, who worried that Akron might hoard water during droughts. Although the communities didn't get the 10.9 mgd minimum flow that they asked for, they came close, with the court requiring a minimum flow of 8.1 mgd to 9.5 mgd.[23]

The decision meant that Akron's disgruntled neighbors had finally attained the water security that they yearned for. It had been a long and bitter struggle. But of all the things that went their way in the courtroom, the communities were happiest to see that Akron's rigid claims under the 1911 governor's deed were thrown out. "The sweetest part," says their attorney Jack Van Kley, "was striking down their interpretation of the 1911 statute."

But Akron did not leave the courtroom empty handed. The justices pointed out that the city *did* have rights to the river—the rights that Akron obtained when it purchased the land upstream to create the Lake Rockwell reservoir. And while it was true that the governor's deed did not give Akron the right to sell Cuyahoga River water, the justices said that Akron's purchase of riparian rights did give the city the power to legally ship water to other communities. That meant Akron's contested diversion (the one that the Great Lakes governors had approved a few years before) could stand. And in another victory for Akron, the justices ruled that in order to protect the public water supply, Akron was within its rights when it banned public access to Lake Rockwell.

Given that the supreme court had finally ruled in the case, there was hope that Akron and its neighbors might finally begin the peace process in their water war. The court suggested as much in its opinion when it said, "We leave the task of resolving future water-allocation issues in this region to appropriate planning authorities."[24] That theme was echoed in an *Akron Beacon Journal* editorial a few days later: "The water war between Akron and its upstream neighbors on the Cuyahoga River is over, hopefully for good."[25]

∿

WHAT ARE THE LESSONS to be learned from the Akron case? The city's diversion proposal was approved a decade after the Great Lakes Charter and WRDA had been signed. During that time three communities and one irrigation district had come forward to ask for water. Pleasant Prairie, Wisconsin, got its water, but questions remained about whether the diversion had been legally approved. Lowell, Indiana, was turned down. Mud Creek, in Michigan, emerged victorious, but hapless. And now Akron, Ohio, was the first community to definitively receive unanimous support from all eight Great Lakes governors for its diversion.

Return-flow was the crucial ingredient in getting that approval—a factor that wouldn't be lost on future water applicants. While Akron had requested and received permission to divert

4.8 mgd, as of this writing the diversion continues to be much, much smaller than that. At its peak, the Akron diversion has only reached 700,000 gallons per day. Of that, 580,000 gallons was returned to the Great Lakes Basin via Akron's wastewater system. The remainder was returned via the Ohio and Erie Canal.[26]

The Akron case also showed that a Michigan governor could indeed approve a diversion outside the Great Lakes Basin under certain circumstances. It also showed that, after several awkward moments, the governors and premiers were finally formulating a system by which Great Lakes water-diversion requests should be judged. Precedent was being set, which would make it easier for future water applicants to gauge their chances of success. But the Akron case also served as a reminder that the governors and premiers are just one piece in the complex water puzzle in the Great Lakes region. Akron got its water, but then was hamstrung by a bitter legal case that cost millions and further soured relations with its neighbors. "Nobody likes the idea of someone else constraining his options," says Leslie Jacobs, Akron's attorney. "But deep down beneath it all, there is a recognition that even sitting on the edge of the Great Lakes, water is the principal constraining factor for economic development." In a region that has always taken water for granted, that may be the most important lesson of all.

PART III

New Rules of Engagement

~

Chapter 11

The Nova Group and Annex 2001

ONE EVENING BACK IN 1997, John Febbraro was lounging at home in Sault Ste. Marie, Ontario, when a narrator popped up on the television and began pleading for donations on behalf of the world's poor. As dolorous photos of impoverished faces flashed across the screen, the narrator talked about how—with just one dollar a day—viewers could change a person's life in the developing world. As Mr. Febbraro, a Canadian entrepreneur, listened to the sales pitch he realized that these people didn't just need food— drinking water was a problem for them as well. That's when he came up with a bold and daring idea of his own: to ship Great Lakes water to thirsty people halfway around the world. "They need water," he remembers thinking, "and literally we look in our back-yard and we have tons of it!" In the days that followed, Mr. Febbraro huddled with a partner at his diminutive consulting firm, the Nova Group, and they began fleshing out a plan to use bulk ocean-going freighters to ship cool, clean Lake Superior drinking water to Asia.

Mr. Febbraro, a former consultant to the Canadian space agency, spent the next several weeks contacting shipping companies, crunching numbers, and developing a business model. The more modeling he did, the more he became convinced of the project's viability. From a business school perspective, however, the model was somewhat unusual—a humanitarian effort on behalf of the world's poor that was also designed to make money. "It was a for-profit," he says unapologetically. "I mean, I'm an entrepreneur, right?"

The plan called for sending an empty bulk freighter out into Lake Superior a few miles northwest of Sault Ste. Marie, where the vessel would pump water into a large disposable liner inside the ship's hold. The water would be purified at a Great Lakes port before the ship continued on to the Far East. The plan was to start with a few shipping runs per year to see how it went and expand the operation from there. With his strategy mapped out, in early 1998, Mr. Febbraro went down to a government office and was surprised at how easy it was to find a permit application. "There was an application that says 'for the withdrawal of bulk water,'" he remembers. "So that is what we filled out, and what we sent in." He attached a brief business plan, and on March 31, 1998 (after a quiet thirty-day comment period that elicited no response from the public), he obtained the permit. The document gave the Nova Group permission to export 158 million gallons of water to Asia per year—one tanker at a time.

When news of Mr. Febbraro's water export scheme hit the papers, it spread rapidly through the Great Lakes Basin, prompting an extraordinary and heated anti-diversion debate. Ever since the Chicago River was reversed nearly a hundred years before, people had worried about additional diversions of Great Lakes water. But never before had someone stepped forward with a plan quite like this one. Although most people on both sides of the border agreed the Nova proposal was a bad idea, it created a time of heightened international water tension in the Great Lakes region. People were particularly alarmed that the proposal had managed to gain government approval without the public, the press, or politicians even knowing about it. "Nova identified a series of gaps," says Jeff Edstrom, who worked at the Council of Great Lakes Governors at the time. "It was something that wasn't really planned for. Today we think about water exports all the time, but before Nova, people's primary concerns were about pipes."

Mr. Febbraro found himself caught up in controversy and besieged by the media, politicians, and average citizens on both sides of the border. "I was on the news almost every day," Mr. Febbraro exclaims. "*Time* magazine, CNN, CTV, ABC, it didn't matter." The controversial nature of his proposal caught him completely off guard. "I was absolutely surprised by the media attention," he says. The most ferocious criticism came from environmentalists. "A lot of environmental groups really got on our case," Mr. Febbraro remembers. "[They were] saying, 'What the hell are you trying to do here? You're going to set a precedent.'" As usual, precedent was indeed the chief concern. Once Great Lakes water was turned into a bulk international commodity, how could Great Lakes officials turn off the tap? If the tiny Nova Group was allowed to export Lake Superior water, who could stop some of the largest international shipping conglomerates from lining up to do the same? And if it was okay to ship water to Asia, how could the region say no to the Ogallala or Nevada? While Mr. Febbraro was pummeled in the press, quiet alarm swept through government offices around the Great Lakes region. "It wasn't panic, and it wasn't really dread. At first it was confusion," Mr. Edstrom says. "No one really knew what the proposal was about. Nova had always talked about this water going to an Asian country, but no one could tell if they actually had a buyer. And there were a number of people who were concerned that Nova was a potential front for a big multinational corporation."

After more than a decade of trying to create a system to keep Great Lakes water in the Great Lakes Basin, John Febbraro had stumbled upon an embarrassing exception that left red-faced bureaucrats scrambling. In reality, there were enormous questions about the economic viability of Mr. Febbraro's scheme, but it raised new concerns about whether the Great Lakes were vulnerable to extraction under international trade accords like the North American Free Trade Agreement (NAFTA) or the General Agreement on Tariffs and Trade (GATT). For years, water use in the Great Lakes had been controlled by an awkward series of agreements and water regulations. The Great Lakes Charter was well-meaning, but nonbinding. The Water Resources Development Act was binding, but only in the United States—and only for diversions, not consumptive uses—and there was worry that WRDA would not withstand a legal challenge. Mr. Febbraro's business plan slipped right through these piecemeal anti-diversion mechanisms. Because the proposal came from Canada, the WRDA legislation didn't apply. And because the diversion was less than 5 million gallons of water per day, Nova's proposal didn't trigger the prior notice and consultation stipulations of the Great Lakes Charter. More important, at the time no laws in Ontario prevented the export of Great Lakes water. After messy squabbles concerning Pleasant Prairie, Lowell, Mud Creek, and Akron, water officials throughout the region had grown tired of dealing with a system that didn't really work. Nova prompted a rallying cry to do what officials should have done long before: go back to the negotiating table and create a modern, binding, international water-management system to regulate Great Lakes withdrawals for the next century and beyond.

~

AFTER LENGTHY NEGOTIATIONS, in late 1998 Canadian officials successfully pressured John Febbraro to withdraw his permit, under one condition: that if things ever changed in the future, the Nova Group would be first in line to export Great Lakes water. In truth, the controversy had an effect on Mr. Febbraro; he had no interest in becoming an anti-diversion pariah. Over time, he came to appreciate where the critics were coming from. "We understood that concern," he says. "So we said 'protect and maintain,' that's fine, and we won't be part of a precedent-setting application."

The following year, Ontario passed a sweeping anti-diversion law that prohibited the bulk removal of water from the Great Lakes, as well as from other major provincial drainage basins. That was followed by the passage of a federal law in Canada that banned diversions from the Great Lakes Basin—at least on the Canadian side of the border. While Canada was strengthening its anti-diversion statutes, in the U.S. Congress—at the urging of the Great Lakes delegation—WRDA was amended so that diversions *and* exports of water required the unanimous approval of all eight Great Lakes governors on the U.S. side of the border.

The International Joint Commission was also consulted. The Canadian and American federal governments asked the IJC to draw up a blue-ribbon report about Great Lakes water use, including diversions and exports. That was a brilliant idea. The IJC was formed by the U.S./Canadian Boundary Waters Treaty of 1909 to resolve water disputes along their shared border. After Nova, a lot of alarmist misinformation was flying around, and the public hungered for knowledge and facts that could help put things into perspective. Before the report was released, the IJC held a series of listening sessions on both sides of the border about the Nova proposal, and people turned out in droves to testify against diversions and to pledge their devotion to the lakes. "What struck me," remembers Tom Baldini, who was the U.S. cochair of the IJC during the Nova dispute, "was the number of people who testified, and the amount of written testimony we received, and the numbers of drawings from little kids, and schools, and the people who commented on not diverting water from the Great Lakes."

In February 2000 the IJC released its comprehensive and well-researched report, which reviewed the lakes' diversion history, touched on international trade issues, and included a number of noteworthy conclusions. One crucial finding was that less than 1 percent of the waters of the Great Lakes was renewed every year through precipitation, groundwater recharge, and runoff. What's more, the report said that if all of the Basin's water uses were considered (including hydropower and the environment) there was no "surplus" water in the system.[1] It also declared that the "era of major diversions and water transfers in the United States and Canada has ended," and that in the short run the greatest diversionary pressures would not come from Texas or Atlanta, but from the "growing communities in the United States just outside the Great Lakes Basin divide."[2] The IJC predicted that, due to climate change and population growth, the region was heading into a period of great water uncertainty, and it urged officials to use a "precautionary approach" and "great caution" regarding Great Lakes water policy. The IJC also said that if diversions were approved, diverters should be required to treat and return 95 percent of the diverted water to the Great Lakes. Finally, the commission argued that new "major" consumptive uses should not be permitted unless strict conservation measures were implemented and the cumulative impacts of subsequent copycat projects considered.[3] While the IJC report was not binding, it was highly influential and helped policymakers hone their arguments as they worked to build a new water-management structure for the Basin.

But the IJC report was not the only post-Nova study commissioned in the region. During the summer of 1998 the Council of Great Lakes Governors met in a closed session in Chicago to discuss what should be done to revamp the regional water-management system. The governors dispatched Russ Van Herik, executive director of the Great Lakes Protection Fund, to round up a team of top-notch national and international legal experts. These lawyers would be asked to pore over state, provincial, federal, and international law—and water regulations—to determine where all the potential diversion vulnerabilities in the Great Lakes might be and then to provide "confidential" legal advice about how Great Lakes officials might best go about plugging those holes.

With Canada moving swiftly to pass provincial and federal anti-diversion laws, the north side of the Basin seemed to be adequately battened down. How the south shore of the Basin would respond hinged on what the governors' legal team turned up regarding laws and regulations on the U.S. side of the border. Mr. Van Herik pulled together a team of twelve attorneys, seven from the United States and five from Canada. The group was asked to engage in a sort of war-game exercise, drawing up what a mock legal attack on Great Lakes water might look like, and then to provide counsel on how the governors should erect the necessary defenses to fend off such an attack. "If you're going to try to keep the money in the bank," Mr. Van Herik explains, "you spend a lot of time thinking about 'How do you rob banks?' Or the same thing software developers use: give me the best hackers in the land and start backing into the defenses from there."

Several of the legal team's water experts came from "dry" states such as Colorado and Texas, including James Lochhead, a former executive director of the Colorado Department of Natural Resources who had extensive experience dealing with the Colorado River—one of the most contentious waterways in North America. Why would dry-land lawyers be hired to give legal opinions about such a water-rich region? First, because they are experts on fighting for water, and second, according to one source who asked not to be identified, they were hired "to conflict-out the best in the land." In other words, once they were retained to work for the Great Lakes governors, they couldn't be hired by someone else to file a water lawsuit against the governors.

In April 1999 the team presented the Council of Great Lakes Governors with an extensive confidential legal brief and an options paper that has never been publicly disclosed or discussed, although several people were willing to describe it privately. The document laid out five main points:

1. A "just say no" approach to Great Lakes water diversions was likely to be found unconstitutional and probably violated international trade agreements.
2. Current Great Lakes anti-diversion statutes—specifically WRDA—were unlikely to withstand legal challenges.
3. As alarming as all that might sound, the governors did have options, including the pursuit of a Great Lakes water compact, especially if a compact were to be mirrored by similar legislation on the Canadian side of the border.
4. In-Basin consumptive uses of water could be just as damaging to the Great Lakes ecosystem as diversions and should be dealt with as well.
5. Water applicants inside and outside the Great Lakes Basin should be judged evenhandedly.

The legal report also included an example of what a Great Lakes water compact could look like, and it gave the governors a sense of how a cross-border nontreaty anti-diversion agreement with the Canadian provinces might be crafted. The secret briefing paper gave examples of different kinds of water withdrawal standards and mechanisms, including the benefits and drawbacks of the various options available.

While the brief made for fascinating reading, some officials received it with alarm. Several Great Lakes gubernatorial aides thought that parts of the privileged document read like a top-notch blueprint on how to rob the Great Lakes water bank. "When it came out everyone looked at it and said, 'This is a brief that could be used to challenge the system!'" says one source who asked not to be identified. "It *is* privileged information—but it could get out." In particular, there was confusion about how far the document's attorney-client privilege extended. Technically the governors were the clients, but were governors' aides considered clients as well? What about department heads? The fear was that if this document was disseminated widely enough, the key to the Great Lakes water kingdom might be available to anyone who had the time to file an open-records request. "They're all public agencies, so even though it's stamped 'privileged' if it hits their desk, it's possible people could get it through the Freedom of Information Act," one source said. "There was very real concern about that."

While much of the document needed to remain confidential, there were other parts of it that the governors felt needed to be released to the public, and soon. There was broad consensus in many governors' offices that the public needed to know just how legally inadequate the current anti-diversion system appeared to be, and that the legal team had also determined that a "just say no" approach would be shredded in the courts. Governor John Engler, in particular, was interested in getting that message across, because Michigan voters have been the most vociferously opposed to diversions. If he was being asked to soften his state's longstanding rigid anti-diversion policy, he wanted his voters to know why. By releasing some of the broader themes of the legal team's research, the governors were starting a slow, methodical public-education campaign to help people realize that a more complicated anti-diversion mechanism was going to be necessary to withstand scrutiny in court.

The governors asked the legal team to produce a boiled-down

version of the brief for the public, and James Lochhead, the Denver attorney, was tapped as the lead author. Not only was Mr. Lochhead a former head of the Colorado DNR, and an expert on the Colorado River, he had also represented Denver and New Mexico on water issues and had served as an expert witness in numerous federal and state water-rights cases. The fifty-page background paper that he produced became known throughout the region as the "Lochhead Report," and it did a remarkable job of cutting through the legalese in a way that average citizens could understand. Mr. Lochhead's public report included the same points as the privileged document: WRDA likely would not stand in court; a "just say no" approach was unconstitutional; and he suggested that the best option was to create a regional water compact, with a parallel provincial agreement in Canada. He also argued that both accords should contain a new standard for grading, approving, or rejecting water-withdrawal applications.[4] And Mr. Lochhead said there was no time to lose. "It has become clear," he wrote, "that there is an immediate need to develop a comprehensive, effective framework among the Great Lakes States and Provinces for regulating future withdrawals of water from the Great Lakes Basin."[5]

The heart of the Lochhead Report highlighted weaknesses in Great Lakes water regulations and then suggested how the governors should go about crafting a new water-management structure. Mr. Lochhead divided the content into several key sections, including federal law, international trade, and WRDA.

Federal law: The report argued that U.S. law, especially the "dormant commerce clause" of the U.S. Constitution, imposes "severe limitations" on individual states that want to ban water diversions on their own. "Some might argue that each Great Lakes State should 'just say no' to the export of water out of the Basin," Mr. Lochhead wrote. "While politically popular, . . . a state law embargo on exports of Great Lakes water would not survive a challenge under the commerce clause."

Among other things, the commerce clause regulates trade among the states, and the basic thrust, Mr. Lochhead said, is that a "state may not discriminate against interstate commerce to advance the economic interest of the state or its citizens." He cited three cases that have resoundingly hammered this point home regarding water: *Sporhase*, *El Paso I*, and *El Paso II*. (*Sporhase*, which involved a Nebraska water statute, was discussed in chapter 4.) "*Sporhase* held that groundwater is an article of commerce, subject to the dormant commerce clause," Mr. Lochhead wrote, adding that the Supreme Court rejected the argument that a state "can discriminate as it wishes between in-state and out-of-state [water] use." However, if a state treats citizens inside and outside its borders "evenhandedly," then impacts on interstate commerce can be tolerated. "Therefore," Mr. Lochhead said, "regulation of water withdrawals by the Great Lakes States must be evenhanded. It must apply equally to in- and out-of-Basin users." The bottom line, he said, is that the commerce clause severely limits an individual state's ability to turn away outsiders seeking Great Lakes water.[6]

International trade: The report's interpretation of international water law was equally disappointing to the governors. Mr. Lochhead argued that international trade agreements (like GATT and the World Trade Organization rules) don't allow the Great Lakes states, the Canadian provinces, or the federal governments of Canada and the United States to "unilaterally" prohibit the export of Great Lakes water. "These international trade agreements, signed by the United States and Canada, severely restrict the ability of the Great Lakes states and Provinces to arbitrarily or unilaterally limit the export of Great Lakes water," he wrote.

The key issue, Mr. Lochhead explained, is whether water—in its natural state—is considered to be a good under international trade agreements or a vital, exhaustible resource held in the public trust. (Preventing exports of a good would be much more difficult under international law.) While acknowledging that this legal issue has been widely debated in academic journals, Mr. Lochhead declared that in his opinion water is a good from an international trade perspective and thus any ban on Great Lakes water diversions would violate international trade agreements. (Many Great Lakes lawyers would adamantly disagree with Mr. Lochhead, arguing that the jury is still out on that question.) Mr. Lochhead pointed out that GATT does allow some exceptions for water-export regulations "relating to the conservation of exhaustible natural resources," as long as those water regulations treat domestic and international consumers by the same rules. Thus, he argued that as long as in-Basin and out-of-Basin users are treated the same way, a system could be developed to regulate Great Lakes water withdrawals.[7]

The situation under NAFTA is different, Mr. Lochhead said. On December 2, 1993, Canada, Mexico, and the United States addressed water in a special declaration, saying that NAFTA "creates no rights to the natural water resources of any Party to the Agreement" as long as the water is in a natural state and hasn't entered commerce by becoming a tradable good or product. The statement continued that the accord doesn't "oblige any NAFTA Party to either exploit its water for commercial use or to begin exporting water in any form." The good news, Mr. Lochhead said, is that the NAFTA declaration protected Great Lakes waters from being exported by Mexico, the United States, and Canada. The bad news is that NAFTA only pertained to those three nations, meaning the lakes are arguably open to exploitation by the rest of the world. "The [NAFTA] statement has no force with respect to other countries under GATT or the WTO," Mr. Lochhead wrote, "any one of which could challenge restrictions on the export of Great Lakes water."[8]

WRDA: Then for the next ten single-spaced pages, Mr. Lochhead picked apart the U.S. Water Resources Development Act, the federal law that the governors have used since 1986 to regulate diversions of Great Lakes water. WRDA requires that all eight Great Lakes governors sign off on any U.S. proposal to divert water out of the Great Lakes Basin. All it takes is one gubernatorial veto to kill a project. But Mr. Lochhead declared WRDA to be a legal paper tiger. If Lowell, Indiana (see chapter 8), or any other spurned water applicant were to contest WRDA in court, it likely would win. "We believe any challenge to a gubernatorial veto of a proposed out-of-Basin diversion of Great Lakes water under this provision as written may likely prevail," Lochhead said. Because

WRDA allowed a governor to dictate water policy to citizens in another jurisdiction, Mr. Lochhead argued that WRDA created "tremendous potential for abuse of power." He continued, "A proposed diverter in one state has absolutely no recourse to the democratic process against the Governor of another state who vetoes the diversion." Not only does such a veto violate the commerce clause, and several other provisions of the U.S. Constitution (including the right to due process), Mr. Lochhead argued, it probably violated international trade laws as well.[9]

∼

AND THAT'S WHERE the bad news side of the Lochhead doctrine ended. Mr. Lochhead spent the next several pages describing what the governors could do to rectify the situation and build a modern, binding, legally sound Great Lakes water-management system. He started by reviewing some basic water-law principles in the Great Lakes region, including the public trust doctrine and the riparian reasonable use doctrine.

"As a general proposition, the beds of the Great Lakes and all navigable tributary waters are owned by the contiguous Great Lakes states . . . and are held in trust for the benefit of the public," Mr. Lochhead wrote. "The states may adopt regulations to advance substantial public interests, even if such regulations restrict the rights of its citizens." In other words, under the public trust doctrine the rights of individuals don't trump the broader public interest in Great Lakes water.

Second, all Great Lakes states follow riparian law, which generally holds that each shoreline property owner has a right to "reasonable" water use as long as it doesn't negatively affect other riparian users (see chapter 10 for more on riparian reasonable use). Mr. Lochhead said that while Congress and the courts have repeatedly reaffirmed state authority to regulate water, this kind of jurisdiction is a subauthority often subject to federal oversight. For example, the federal government has primary authority over navigation, and Congress can supersede state law in allocating water between states in order to "serve the national interest."[10]

But there are ways around these obstacles, Mr. Lochhead said. Specifically, he zeroed in on a regional water compact as the ideal model for the Great Lakes governors to pursue. Compacts are cumbersome—because they must be passed by every signatory state's legislature *and* by the U.S. Congress—but the compact model has been used widely throughout the United States. What's more, two Great Lakes states (Pennsylvania and New York) were already parties to other water-use compacts and were intimately familiar with the system. Best of all, Mr. Lochhead noted, once a Great Lakes water compact was adopted by Congress, the compact would be protected against challenges under the commerce clause. Though the states were prevented from signing an international water treaty with the Canadian provinces, the provinces could adopt similar statutes on their side of the border, thereby surrounding the lakes with a parallel water-management structure. The only issue, Mr. Lochhead said, would be international trade agreements—a compact would be vulnerable to a legal attack if it discriminated between domestic and foreign users.[11]

How did Mr. Lochhead suggest the Great Lakes governors make their compact immune to international challenge? By adopting a standard that judged all potential Great Lakes water users—both inside and outside the Basin—evenhandedly. In other words, a proposed consumptive water use within the Great Lakes Basin should be judged by the same standard as a diversion proposal outside the Basin. Both in-Basin and out-of-Basin water withdrawals, Mr. Lochhead argued, result in a loss to the ecosystem and hence should be regulated similarly. "A decision over whether or under what conditions to allow an out-of-Basin use of Great Lakes water must be based on a standard closely related to the conservation of the resource, and should apply to both in- and out-of-basin uses," he wrote. "An out-of-basin use may be more or less disruptive than an in-basin use."[12]

What should that water-regulation standard look like? The governors had three choices according to Mr. Lochhead:

1. A standard that allowed some degradation of the resource—rules so permissive that water withdrawals would slowly

deplete the Great Lakes over time (presumably backed by the argument that the social and economic benefits derived from the water use would justify such resource depletion).

2. A standard of "no net loss" that required diverters, for example, to return their treated wastewater after it was used (a standard similar to the 95 percent return-flow recommended by the IJC in its 2000 report).

3. A standard that would break new legal ground by requiring water users to improve or provide a "benefit" to the Great Lakes ecosystem in exchange for the water that was withdrawn.

Though Mr. Lochhead was remarkably vague about what he meant by a "benefit," he implied that the governors could require restoration work as a way to pay back the ecosystem for water withdrawals. Regardless, it was obvious that this third option was Mr. Lochhead's first choice. "A benefit standard clearly advances the legitimate state interest of protecting the Great Lakes, an interest compelled by each State's duty to protect the resource pursuant to the public trust doctrine," he wrote. "The most compelling position is one that urges the States, Provinces and national governments to set a global example of cooperative governance of a shared critical resource. Adopting a standard based on benefit would set this example."[13]

Of everything Mr. Lochhead mentioned in his report, his remarks about the benefit standard were the most newsworthy. His comments about WRDA possibly being unconstitutional and a violation of international trade agreements were serious, but the governors had heard murmurs about that sort of thing for some time. The question was what could they do about it? The compact model certainly sounded promising, and the benefit standard was an intriguing idea—a whole new way of looking at environmental regulation. The governors were interested; but they weren't quite sure how it would work, so they asked for more detail.

On September 1, 1999, Mr. Lochhead submitted a follow-up memo entirely devoted to the benefit standard. "The new standard ensures that no state or province will approve a new water withdrawal unless there is established benefit to the waters and water dependent resources of the Great Lakes Basin," Mr. Lochhead wrote. "'Benefit' means incrementally improving upon the present state of impaired ecological health of the Great Lakes."[14] In other words, if a community or business wanted to withdraw water, it would have to compensate for the withdrawal through Great Lakes restoration, or cleanup, to "more than offset the unavoidable damages of the new [water withdrawal]." To Mr. Lochhead, using the benefit standard in a regional water compact was a magic blend of policy that would treat all water users even-handedly, would withstand legal challenge, and that—in his view—would leave the Great Lakes better off than they were before the water was withdrawn. "A benefit standard means simply this," Mr. Lochhead wrote, "bring me a project with more good stuff than bad stuff."[15]

~

IT WAS AN ENGAGING CONCEPT, and several gubernatorial aides—especially in Michigan—embraced the idea immediately. "We were worried that [if WRDA were challenged] we would lose our tenuous authority to say no," says Dennis Schornack, former top aide to Michigan governor John Engler. "[The benefit standard] had kind of a visionary aspect—we're drawing a line in the sand here and from this day forward we are only going to act to improve this resource . . . It gave Michigan sufficient justification to back off of the no-diversions stance." But Mr. Schornack says many U.S. environmentalists were skeptical, at least at first. If a conservative Republican governor like John Engler liked it, how could it be good for the environment? "It took some time," Mr. Schornack says, "for the environmental groups to adopt it as an acceptable or reasonable way to settle these constant disputes over diversions."

Great Lakes environmental groups eventually warmed to the idea, at least on the U.S. side of the border. If the Lochhead doctrine was right, and diversions couldn't be prevented, at least under the benefit standard the diverters could be forced to pay an ecological tax that compensated the regional ecosystem. "This is definitely very forward-thinking," said Cheryl Mendoza later, in a newsletter to her members at the Alliance for the Great Lakes. "This means we will manage our water in a sustainable *and* restorative way so that 50 to 100 years from now not only will the Lakes still be here for us—they'll be even better."[16]

The Lochhead doctrine certainly generated a lot of chatter in the Basin—and while Mr. Lochhead had his fans, there were also plenty of critics. Many Great Lakes water lawyers viewed his report as a western water-law interpretation of an eastern water-law issue. Some thought that the public trust and riparian reasonable use doctrines were treated in a cursory manner, and not everyone agreed with some of his statements of fact—like the idea that water in its natural state is definitely a good under international trade agreements. "This was very much taking the view of western water-law guys and didn't represent the riparian tradition that we have in this part of the country," says one Great Lakes official who asked not to be identified. Several gubernatorial officials believed that if more Great Lakes Basin attorneys had been included on the legal team the report's conclusions and recommendations might have been broader. "There's always been debate about the Lochhead legal study," says David de Launay, assistant deputy minister with the Ontario Ministry of Natural Resources. "It was one point of view. Whether, at the end of the day, that should be the final policy was a debate right from the beginning."

Despite that healthy discussion, Mr. Lochhead's report helped spur the governors to act. While officials remained years away from releasing a binding regional water-management agreement, there was growing consensus with Mr. Lochhead that a compact was the way to go. But some regional water regulators were having a hard time grasping how the benefit standard would work. And there were other divisions that kept popping up around the negotiating table (such as whether in-Basin consumptive uses should be judged by the same standards as diversions). With many kinks needing to be worked out, gubernatorial aides decided that pushing hard for a compact right away would be unwise. A slower, more methodical approach would have a greater likelihood of success. Under the leadership of governors Tom Ridge of Pennsylvania and John Engler of Michigan (both Republicans), Great Lakes officials went to work on drafting a new document that would serve as a plan of action, rather than anything binding on the governors and premiers. It became known as the Great Lakes Charter Annex, or simply Annex 2001, and it was packaged as an amendment to the Great Lakes Charter.[17]

Annex 2001 was remarkably short, sleek, and concise—notably devoid of the obfuscating bureaucratic language that is often stuffed into such documents. Just four single-spaced pages, it wasn't water policy per se, but rather a series of directives that told the public where the governors and premiers were headed and hinted at what the ultimate new water-management system would look like. It committed the governors and premiers to developing "an enhanced water management system that is simple, durable, efficient, retains and respects authority within the Basin, and, most importantly, protects, conserves, restores, and improves the Waters and Water-Dependent Natural Resources of the Great Lakes Basin."

Of the six directives in the document, two were definitely the most important. One commanded the governors and premiers to "immediately" prepare a "binding" Basin-wide agreement "such as an interstate compact," and it gave the governors three years to get the job done. The other key directive committed the governors to establishing a new water-withdrawal "decision making standard" based on the following principles: (1) that withdrawn water be returned after use and conservation practices be adopted to prevent waste; (2) that a water withdrawal create no significant adverse impacts on the Great Lakes, either individually or cumulatively when considered with other withdrawals; (3) that the withdrawal comply with existing laws and treaties; and (4) that the water applicant conduct an "Improvement to the Waters and Water-Dependent Natural Resources of the Great Lakes Basin" (the benefit standard had officially become an "improvement" standard).

Because it wasn't a binding agreement, compromises over things like the improvement standard were easier to reach. Some people continued to have their doubts, but they didn't mind signing a nonbinding document that kept the momentum going. "Everybody got their piece, and these were—after all—just principles," Dennis Schornack says. "Michigan got the benefit standard, Ohio got the no significant adverse impact, and Ontario got the return-flow." The benefit or "improvement" standard was cutting-edge policy, but the return-flow requirement was extremely important as well. It was seen as *the* greatest deterrent to large-scale, long-range diversions. "It certainly put the kibosh on diversions to the Southwest," Mr. Schornack says. The Annex was signed with much fanfare at Niagara Falls on June 18, 2001, where Republican governor George Pataki of New York played host to several of his peers. "The Annex we signed today is a roadmap for ensuring the continued protection of the Great Lakes," Governor Pataki said. "We want to make sure that . . . our water is used wisely and effectively to the benefit of all our citizens."[18]

It had been three years since the Nova Group's proposal sank in Sault Ste. Marie, spurring an unprecedented movement to revamp the regional water-management system. During that time, the IJC had spoken. The U.S. Congress had amended WRDA. The province of Ontario had banned Great Lakes diversions and so had the federal government of Canada. And Québec had banned diversions outside provincial boundaries. The governors, meanwhile had merely released their battle plans. The Annex 2001 signing ceremony was marked by a sense of optimism and accomplishment, but in reality it was just the first step toward a solution. Like the Charter to which it was attached, the Annex was not binding. It was a commitment to act, but a document with no real power. As Governor Pataki said, it was a roadmap to a solution, but far from the final answer that the Basin was looking for. More than thirty-six months had passed, yet the Great Lakes' south shore was no safer than it had been before word of the Nova proposal first spread. So despite all the backslapping and handshakes at Niagara Falls, the signing of the Annex was not the end, but a new beginning. And the real work of crafting a binding agreement was yet to come.

Chapter 12

Marching toward a Compact

AFTER THE ANNEX 2001 signing ceremony at Niagara Falls, the governors and premiers dispatched a team of aides to carry Great Lakes water-management negotiations into the next stage. This "working group" of lawyers, policy specialists, and water managers was responsible for turning the Annex principles into comprehensive policy. The team included a few representatives from each jurisdiction—the eight Great Lakes states and two provinces. Some members were fairly new to the water-policy arena, but most had been dealing with Great Lakes water issues for years—some even helped draft the Great Lakes Charter back in 1985. After the Annex 2001 signing, the governors and premiers promised the public that a final Great Lakes water-management system would be crafted in thirty-six months. The working group would end up needing all that time—and then some—to get the job done.

The next three years were a grind—marked by an endless string of laborious conference calls and face-to-face negotiations where bureaucrats haggled over enormously important legal language as well as minutiae. In short order, the working group decided to craft two water-management accords, not one. The first was the *Great Lakes–St. Lawrence River Basin Sustainable Water Resources Agreement*, sort of an updated version of the nonbinding Great Lakes Charter. It detailed the promises made between the governors and premiers to implement policies to protect regional waters for the foreseeable future. Federal law may have forbidden the states and provinces from signing a water treaty, but nothing prevented them from adopting parallel water regulations on either side of the international border. The second document was the *Great Lakes–St. Lawrence River Basin Water Resources Compact.* It was designed to be a binding agreement among the eight Great Lakes states, and it codified precisely how the governors would uphold their side of the International Agreement. The catch was that, in order to be binding, the Compact would eventually need to be adopted by all eight Great Lakes legislatures as well as by the U.S. Congress. Together, the International Agreement and the Compact came to be called the Annex Implementing Agreements.

From the start, the working group grasped the ambitious nature of its task. If the Lochhead Report represented the initial research phase, and Annex 2001 was the road map, the implementing agreements were the final product. While the International Agreement was the driver during the negotiations, the Compact was arguably the more important of the two documents—not because the United States was more important than Canada, but because the Compact was binding. The Compact was designed as an Iron Curtain of sorts along the U.S. side of the watershed, where everyone agreed the primary problems lay.[1]

More than once the talks teetered on the edge of failure. Crafting a new water-management paradigm among ten jurisdictions, across an international boundary, in the absence of a crisis was not going to be easy. "What we are trying to do is create a system that says people who use water in Milwaukee have an impact on the people who live in Québec City—and that the people in Québec City ought to have a say in that. That's a huge concept," declares Todd Ambs, head of the Water Division at the Wisconsin Department of Natural Resources. "Of all the things that I do in my job, this is the only thing that people will still be talking about fifty years from now. It's about the future. It's about having a system in place to deal with problems that we don't have today."

A core group—one or two people from each jurisdiction—kept

the process on track through regular conference calls and frequent in-person negotiating sessions. The in-person meetings were chaired by Sam Speck, director of the Ohio DNR, the "elder statesman" who was instrumental in crafting compromises and bridging philosophical divides. "He would always be able to pull it back from the brink when one of us was ready to slit the throat of somebody else," says one negotiator. To break up the tension of these two- to three-day gatherings, a healthy amount of social time was also regularly scheduled into the mix, like long cocktail hours and relaxed group dinners.

As previous chapters have shown, each state and province has its own "water personality." Michigan is adamantly opposed to diversions, but balks at limitations on its own in-Basin consumptive use. New York has major hydropower considerations. Illinois is worried about maintaining its U.S. Supreme Court–mandated water allocation that keeps metropolitan Chicago alive. Ontario shares many of Michigan's anti-diversion sentiments, and Québec, at the tail end of the system, is concerned about what everyone else does upstream. Minnesota has been the most progressive water jurisdiction in the Basin—Indiana decidedly less so—with Wisconsin, Ohio, and Pennsylvania somewhere in between.

These different water personalities loomed large in the backroom negotiations, but partisanship did not. The diversion debate has always been an extraordinarily bipartisan issue. For example, when the Great Lakes Charter was signed back in 1985, the governorships were dominated by Democrats. When Annex 2001 was signed, Republicans controlled the Basin. As the negotiations dragged on, the gubernatorial offices in the Basin would eventually end up being evenly split between Democrats and Republicans (the premiers were both provincial liberals). Throughout the region's water-management history, it has never been about party; it has always been about place. And as the implementing agreements were being finalized, geographic loyalties were pushed to the test as the different stakeholders figuratively circled one another in the negotiating room. "As someone who has done public policy work for twenty-five years," Mr. Ambs says, "I'm fascinated by this issue because it has nothing to do with partisan politics and it has every-thing to do with geography."

~

MICHIGAN, AS USUAL, was in the thick of things. Its negotia-tors spent a lot of time living down the baggage of past Great Lakes water controversies, such as vetoing Lowell, Indiana's, water-diversion application while approving Mud Creek's consumptive-use proposal despite regional objections (see chapters 8 and 9). "Michigan has always been different in how the two [state political] parties try to beat each other up for not doing enough to protect Great Lakes water," says one high-level Compact negotiator. "They have been the toughest state when it comes to diversions, [but] the other states feel like they've been burned by Michigan in the past . . . On the other hand, it's been very difficult for Michigan. They don't see why they should agree to any diversions." All negotiators realized, however—including those from Michigan—that on the final day, when officials exited the negotiating room for the last time, everyone would have to leave a little bit of their own blood on the floor. "Nobody," Sam Speck said, "is going to get everything they want."[2]

There were issues between Canadian and U.S. negotiators as well. The commerce clause was one definite sticking point that frustrated the Canadian delegation. They had no similar constitu-tional headache on their side of the border. And many Canadian negotiators thought that James Lochhead's concerns about interna-tional trade agreements were exaggerated.

More than once, emotions ran high behind closed doors. Some of the most contentious debates—which included raised voices, heated words, and accusatory finger-pointing—often were between just a couple of jurisdictions. In some cases, a few negotiators were asked to remove themselves to a separate room until they ironed out their differences and were in a position to present their negoti-ated subsettlement to the rest of the group. To add transparency to the process, the negotiators met regularly with an advisory committee, or stakeholder group, made up of industry, agriculture, environmental, and other organizations that were given face-to-face briefings and status reports on where the documents were heading. These gatherings were much more than courtesy briefings, negotiators say, arguing that valuable feedback was received from the advisory committee throughout the process.

One of the most emotionally charged issues revolved around how the Compact should treat the Illinois diversion (see chapter 5). At one point it appeared that the debate over the diversion might torpedo the entire process. For years the topic had been avoided in the negotiating room, but during one late session, just before the first draft of the Compact was released, Pennsylvania suggested that the Illinois diversion be covered under the Compact just like other water withdrawals. Ontario quickly backed up Pennsylvania, and then "it was like a forest fire that starts with a spark," one negotiator says. Several states and provinces—though not all—insisted that if Illinois ever wanted to ask for an increase in its diversion, it should be required to come before the Compact Council for approval—just like any other jurisdiction. Illinois adamantly objected, arguing that the U.S. Supreme Court had ruled over the diversion for more than 70 years, and the state had no interest whatsoever in seeing that change (Illinois would likely get a more impartial hearing from the Court than from its neighbors in the Great Lakes Basin). "There definitely was a desire that there would be more controls over the Illinois diversion through this agreement," says one senior negotiator. "There is absolutely no question that the whole Illinois diversion became a big issue that almost derailed things."

But Illinois held firm in the face of stiff opposition, refusing to sign any agreement that changed the way the Illinois diversion was regulated. When the rest of the jurisdictions were faced with no deal, or a special deal for Chicago, they backed down. "Where we've ended up," says one negotiator, "is that essentially the Illinois diversion is governed by the Supreme Court decree." That was a key moment, according to those who have followed Great Lakes water politics for years. "The real fascinating thing," says one observer, "is what Illinois extracted for its signature, which was saying that the Supreme Court's jurisdiction trumps the Annex Compact." This was a sensitive issue because Illinois had tried to increase its diversion three times in the last half century—once in the 1950s, again in the 1960s, and finally in the 1980s. Because the Court actually granted Illinois' request in the 1950s (albeit temporarily) and permanently increased the diversion in 1967, there remained an ever-present concern among other jurisdictions that sometime in the future Illinois would return to the trough.

~

WITH THE ILLINOIS DIVERSION debate behind them, on July 19, 2004, the first drafts of the Annex Implementing Agreements were released to the public. Six years after the Nova proposal had shocked the Basin, and three years after the governors and premiers met at Niagara Falls, the public finally got a glimpse of what a new water-management system might look like. In an unusual move, the draft agreements weren't consensus documents. Negotiators remained at odds on some key issues, but they had gotten as far as they were going to get for the moment, so they were genuinely interested in the public's feedback. "For all the criticism that the government officials take for being just a bunch of faceless bureaucrats not accountable to the public," one senior negotiator says, "there sure is a lot of time given in these [negotiations] to what the public thinks." In many ways, the documents resembled what James Lochhead had recommended. They were definitely not a "just say no" policy on diversions, but what might best be described as "occasionally saying yes—as long as there's improvement to the Great Lakes ecosystem."

While the documents followed Mr. Lochhead's advice by regulating both diversions and in-Basin consumptive uses of water, they ignored his advice by holding diversions to a tougher review process. That meant that regional review of diversions would kick in much sooner than the regional review of in-Basin consumptive uses—and that was not quite as "evenhanded" as Mr. Lochhead had promoted in his report. The 2004 draft of the Compact included the following key proposals.[3]

Diversions: A new diversion (or an increased diversion) that was 1 million gallons per day (mgd) or larger required regional review by the Great Lakes governors—one gubernatorial veto could kill a proposal. In addition, a diversion proposal would only be approved if the following conditions were met: (1) there was no other water alternative; (2) the quantity requested was "reasonable"; (3) water withdrawn would be returned, minus an "allowance" for consumptive use; (4) the diversion caused no significant individual or cumulative adverse impacts; (5) an "environmentally sound and economically feasible" conservation plan was adopted; (6) in exchange for the water, the applicant agreed to do an "improvement" to the Great Lakes ecosystem; and (7) that the diversion proposal didn't violate any other laws or agreements.[4]

In-Basin withdrawals: A new or increased consumptive use of water inside the Great Lakes Basin of 5 mgd or higher had to be reviewed by the governors as well, but three gubernatorial "no" votes would be required to kill a proposal, not just one. These withdrawals would only be approved if (1) all or part of the proposed withdrawal could not be avoided through conservation; and (2) all the other stipulations listed above for a diversion were met (except the alternative water-supply requirement).[5]

Improvement: The document also defined "improvement," which it said included but was not limited to "mitigating adverse effects of existing water withdrawals, restoring environmentally sensitive areas, or implementing . . . conservation measures in areas or facilities that are not part of the specific proposal undertaken by or on behalf of the withdrawer."[6]

The 2004 draft Compact contained other details as well. It delegated approval of smaller diversions to the individual states where the diversions took place. It said that a diversion of less than 1 mgd did not require a regional review but still needed to meet all the other diversion requirements listed above. The draft also required each state to regulate all water withdrawals in excess of 100,000 gallons per day, but it gave the states ten years to implement a regulatory and management system for those withdrawals. And finally, the draft made clear that the Illinois diversion was not subject to the Compact, but would be ruled over as usual by the Supreme Court decree.

~

DURING THE SUMMER OF 2004 the Annex Implementing Agreements were opened up to a ninety-day public comment period. Dozens of hearings were held throughout the Great Lakes region and people turned out in large numbers. More than ten thousand comments poured in to the Council of Great Lakes Governors that summer, ranging from one-line citizen e-mails to polished policy papers submitted by industry groups and environmental organizations. Individual states and provinces received thousands more comments.

The agreements were highly unpopular among industry and agriculture groups, who equated them with a regulatory lovefest and a threat to jobs. "We must be careful not to make this a jobs diversion plan," said Michael Johnston, director of regulatory affairs for the Michigan Manufacturers Association, in a comment representative of the time.[7] U.S. environmentalists were more welcoming, but were also critical of several key elements. Many environmentalists argued that all water withdrawals—consumptive uses and diversions—should be judged by the same rules and that the agreements should put a greater emphasis on water conservation.

The response in Canada, however, was much more critical—even shrill in its condemnation of the documents. Ironically, on the U.S. side of the border, it was industrial and agricultural interests that emerged as the chief critics of the documents, while in Canada much of the opposition came from environmentalists and even Canadian nationalists. The Toronto Star ran a number of editorials and news stories that excoriated the Compact as an American pro-diversion Trojan horse. One editorial said the agreements would give states "the power to siphon off the waters of these lakes." A news story contained the headline, "Plan for Great Lakes may kill them, critics say."[8] The Council of Canadians, a nationalistic advocacy organization, was particularly harsh in its criticism of the

2004 drafts and was successful in convincing its members to attend the public hearings.

Canadian concern about the Annex Implementing Agreements had been mounting long before the documents were released. Adèle Hurley, director of the Program on Water Issues at the University of Toronto's Munk Centre was skeptical about the Annex from the start, and her program funded a highly critical position paper on the agreements. The twenty-two-page document was published one month before the draft Compact came out and was written by Andrew Nikiforuk, a Canadian journalist. Mr. Nikiforuk argued that the motive behind the Annex Implementing Agreements was "to supply water to thirsty communities outside of the Basin and [governors] want to do so without being vetoed by a neighbor such as Michigan, a key anti-diverter state."[9]

He drew a bead on Waukesha, Wisconsin, a water-troubled community on the outskirts of Milwaukee that lies just beyond the Basin boundary (see chapter 13). Waukesha sits atop declining contaminated water wells and would love to tap into Lake Michigan just fifteen miles down the road to the east. According to Mr. Nikiforuk, the Annex Implementing Agreements were an ingenious and disingenuous scheme designed to get Great Lakes water to Great Lakes communities just beyond the Basin line without creating a precedent that might make more far-flung diversions possible. "Annex 2001," he wrote, "is all about saying 'yes' to communities such as Waukesha without saying 'yes' to Phoenix, Arizona, Singapore or global water bottlers."

Mr. Nikiforuk euphemistically referred to his report as a "critical assessment," and he expressed deep reservations about the motivations behind the Annex process, arguing that it wasn't designed to protect the lakes, but to exploit them. "Annex 2001 appears to be a regional compact dedicated to protecting the Great Lakes Basin," he wrote. "Yet in real terms it is a water taking permit system designed to minimize conflict among potential water takers." This paper circulated widely on both sides of the border. While many Americans dismissed it as a one-sided anti-Annex editorial, many Canadians embraced it as a muckraking call to action.

As the summer of 2004 passed, Canadian opposition to the agreements mounted, culminating at a public hearing held in Toronto on September 20, 2004. Speaker after speaker rose to lambaste the agreements. "The Annex 2001 agreement is nothing more than a unilateral U.S. water grab," complained Sarah Ehrhardt, with the Council of Canadians. "By putting no limitations on the amount of water that can be withdrawn from the lakes by the U.S. states . . . the Annex 2001 is, simply put, a U.S. permit to drain the Great Lakes dry."

At first blush the Canadian critics seemed to be strafing the draft Annex agreements, but in truth they were attacking the Lochhead doctrine. What these opponents hated most was that the agreements didn't ban diversions—something Lochhead told the governors they couldn't do. By contrast, in the wake of the Nova proposal, Canadian officials had moved swiftly to ban Great Lakes diversions under provincial and federal law. Now the Canadian public was asking, Why should their officials sign international agreements that pledged to do anything less? Canadian critics couldn't have cared less about the U.S. commerce clause or alleged vulnerabilities from complex international trade agreements—what they wanted was a ban on diversions. Any agreement that waffled on that point had to be a complicated American pro-diversion ploy to trick the Canadian public out of Great Lakes water.

Canadians were particularly concerned about the improvement standard, which they interpreted as a materialistic bartering system that turned their waters into an international commodity. And they weren't comfortable with the apples-and-oranges trade-offs that the improvement standard implied. They didn't see how exchanging water for ecological cleanup would necessarily leave the lakes better off. "Let's not waste the time and energies of the region's best water and environmental experts trying to equate buckets of water with dozens of ducks," complained Ralph Pentland, a former Canadian environmental official and critic of the improvement standard. What bothered Mr. Pentland, and many of his compatriots, about the improvement standard was that if a diverter withdrew 50 mgd and then cleaned up tons of contaminated sediment as payback, that would create a water-for-restoration bartering system. That, they argued, ran the risk of turning water "in its natural state" into a commodity.

The Canadian criticism was heavily influenced by the broader geopolitical climate as well. Anti-Americanism was running high throughout the world at the time the Compact hearings were held, and Canada was no exception. The Iraq war was notably unpopular north of the border, but more important, the United States and Canada were engaged in a number of cross-border disputes—from softwood lumber exports to North Dakota's plans to divert tainted, unwanted water from Devil's Lake into Canada's Hudson Bay watershed. And while most Americans were blissfully unaware of these issues, the topics were perennial front-page stories in Canada, which helped to whip up anti-American fervor.

While Canada is not known for being shy about extracting its natural resources, many Great Lakes Canadians look at water exploitation differently—particularly if that water might be headed to the United States. "A reflexive 'aqua-nationalism,' clothed in environmental righteousness, is hostile to any suggestion that Canada's water could ever become a tradable commodity," wrote Chris Wood in *The Walrus*, a Canadian magazine. "The animus is all the more implacable if the discussion involves trading water with Americans—an idea close to treason in some eyes."[10] Canadian opponents to the Annex may have seen themselves as upholding "aqua-nationalism" but for many U.S. residents in the Great Lakes region—including environmentalists—the more emotional Canadian objections seemed more like anti-Americanism wrapped in an environmental banner.

As the debate raged in Canada during the summer of 2004, a few Canadian advocates began arguing against regional control of the resource. They didn't trust provincial leaders—and particularly the Great Lakes governors—to be responsible stewards of Great Lakes water, and they argued for federalization of the issue. Such voices, however, were in the minority and were perceived by officials throughout the Basin as being out of touch with internal population-driven political trends in the United States. What trends were these? Population in much of the Great Lakes region was continuing to grow, but it wasn't growing as fast as the Sunbelt. As more and more Americans migrated to that water-starved region, they were taking northern seats from the U.S. House of Representatives with them. That resulted in a loss of congressional power in regions like the Great Lakes and an enormous gain in places like the American South and the Southwest. After the 2000 census, for example, the eight Great Lakes states lost nine congressional seats. Minnesota was the only Great Lakes state not to loose a seat, but New York and Pennsylvania each lost two. Where did those lost seats end up? In water-troubled states like Arizona, Texas, California, Colorado, Georgia, and Nevada.[11] You didn't have to be a political scientist to realize that federalization of Great Lakes water issues—at least on the U.S. side of the border—would put control of the lakes into the hands of states whose familiarity with the region was lacking and whose motivations could be suspect.

During the fall of 2004, Canadian criticism over the Annex Implementing Agreements reached such a fevered pitch that Ontario premier Dalton McGuinty had no choice but to distance himself from the documents. On November 15, 2004, the Ontario Ministry of Natural Resources released a statement saying that the citizens of Ontario had spoken and there was no way Mr. McGuinty was signing the latest draft documents until significant changes were made. "Ontarians, and the McGuinty government, clearly want a 'no diversions' agreement, or the position of 'no net loss' as proposed by the International Joint Commission," the statement read. "Ontario is not prepared to ratify the agreement in its current form." But the statement also sent a message to those arguing for federalization of the process. "If the [Canadian] federal government were to direct the negotiations, it would have to deal directly with the U.S. federal government, which would have to represent the interests of water users across the continental United States, not just the Great Lakes states," the communiqué said. "We are concerned that other U.S. states may have an interest in accessing Great Lakes waters that will conflict with our desire to prevent diversions from the Basin."[12]

A few weeks later, the Canadian edition of *Time* magazine ran a cover story titled, "Are the Great Lakes for sale? An inside look at the controversial proposal to export water from our precious resource."[13] The key words there were "proposal to export water." The Annex Implementing Agreements that had started out as a well-meaning effort to prevent or severely minimize diversions had now been labeled—in Canada at least—as a pro-export initiative. As a result, the Council of Great Lakes Governors was in the middle of an international public-relations nightmare. It had completely lost control of its message and the Lochhead doctrine was the primary casualty.

~

THE GOVERNORS HAD TWO OPTIONS: drop Canada from the picture, or head back to the negotiating table with some major revisions in mind. Few of the negotiators had expected the comment period to go the way it did. The strong Canadian reaction to the documents caught many off guard, and the negotiation-room mood cooled for a time. Low morale became an issue for some. But that stage was short-lived. "The group settled down and they have really been working well together," said one negotiator in late 2004. "[We're] trying to come up with an agreement we all can acquiesce to." Group chemistry helped overcome the setback as the negotiations continued. After years of drafting the agreements, many of the negotiators had become friends. "As much yelling as there has been, we always find a way to come back and laugh about it after the twelve-hour negotiations," a senior water official says. He adds that after one marathon session in 2005, "we drank American *and* Canadian beer well into the night and played some music."

The Great Lakes environmental community had some fence mending to tend to as well. The U.S./Canada split over the first draft agreements—particularly the improvement standard—created a very tense moment for Great Lakes environmentalists. As greens on the south side of the border trumpeted the improvement standard, Canadian advocates tore it apart, which sent mixed messages to the public *and* the Annex negotiating team. Given that environmentalists on both sides of the border have a long tradition of working closely together, the divergent cross-border Annex debate was creating a rare example of international tension among regional interest groups. This was not only upsetting the advocates themselves, it was also disappointing the large influential foundations in the Great Lakes Basin that pour millions of dollars annually into environmental programming.

In February 2005 the foundations organized a private meeting for Great Lakes environmentalists from both countries. Many leading regional foundations sent representatives for a short portion of the meeting, including the Joyce Foundation, the Walter and Duncan Gordon Foundation, the Charles Stewart Mott Foundation, and the George Gund Foundation. The session was well attended by regional environmental advocates, who were obviously the target audience. The purpose of the strategy meeting was to reach agreement on fundamental principles regarding the Annex that everyone could support without discord. For two days they engaged in a series of frank, private strategy sessions that became very heated at times. The workshop was held at the Johnson Foundation's famous Wingspread Conference Center near Racine, Wisconsin, and the ultimate goal was to craft a joint statement to the Council of Great Lakes Governors's negotiating team. While the group discussed an array of Annex-related issues, Canadian concern about the improvement standard was a key topic. In the end, however, the advocates could only go so far in bridging the U.S./Canada divide. In the postworkshop memo that was eventually forwarded to the negotiators, the environmentalists said that the Annex should "require" that future water use include an associated "restoration action," but it also added an italicized qualifier: "*Participants agreed that more discussion was needed on this point.*"[14] The environmentalists had sent a signal to negotiators that while the days of cross-border bickering were over, complete agreement on the improvement standard remained elusive in the advocacy community.

As the negotiations dragged on in 2005, Wisconsin and Ontario exerted themselves behind the scenes. Wisconsin had its Waukesha problem—a rapidly growing water-troubled suburb just outside the Basin boundary. But several other states, including Ohio and Indiana, had Waukesha-like communities (large and small) that needed an alternative water source as well. Ontario, meanwhile, had always shared Michigan's anti-diversion stance, and after the 2004 public hearings it pushed hard to shunt aside much of the Lochhead doctrine, arguing that what the Basin needed was an anti-diversion agreement with exceptions, as opposed to the other way around. Ontario, and others, argued that if the Compact were to be adopted by the U.S. Congress, the commerce clause problem would be nullified (even James Lochhead agreed with that). And there was a growing consensus among working-group negotiators that the only major argument against a no-diversions policy came from the international trade accords—the idea that a foreign entity could argue it was being discriminated against. But Ontario felt that was far too gray a legal area to warrant curbing its anti-diversion stance, and it was gaining converts around the room.

Meanwhile, the improvement standard had become an orphan on the negotiating table. As the months passed, it slowly faded deeper and deeper into the margins. There's no question that Canadian opposition put a dagger in the back of the improvement standard, but American industrialists helped twist the knife. Ultimately, however, the improvement standard died under the weight of its own complexity. "It exceeded the sophistication of the general public," says Dennis Schornack, U.S. cochair of the International Joint Commission. "'Just say no,'" he adds, "is sort of a nonthinking way" to deal with the diversion issue. The improvement standard was definitely a profound, new, and optimistic way of pursuing environmental regulation. But even some of the improvement standard's most passionate defenders had a hard time explaining how it would work in practice. "When you say, 'Improve the water and water-dependent natural resources,' everyone kind of nods and says, 'Yeah, that's a good idea. We're for that," says Jeff Edstrom, a former official with the Council of Great Lakes Governors and a fan of the improvement standard. "But when it comes down to what you actually have to do [to improve the ecosystem], then it becomes a little bit more difficult to deal with." By early 2005 most of the negotiators were ready to let the improvement standard go. "Even if you still liked the idea," says David de Launay from the Ontario Ministry of Natural Resources. "No regulator had figured out how you did it."

~

IN JUNE 2005, new drafts of the Annex Implementing Agreements were released for another round of public hearings. While much of the boilerplate remained the same, the new compromise created some markedly different documents at the core. While the 2004 drafts permitted diversions as long as there were improvements, the 2005 documents banned diversions with limited exceptions. Those limited exceptions fell into three distinct categories: "straddling communities," "straddling counties," and "intra-Basin transfers."

Under the straddling community exception, if a town or city overlapped the Great Lakes Basin boundary (like Pleasant Prairie, Wisconsin, for example), under the 2005 agreements it was considered to be completely within the Basin line. As long as its diversion request was for the public water supply, its water withdrawal wouldn't be treated as a diversion at all, but as an in-Basin consumptive use—assuming the water was returned to the Basin. The natural Great Lakes watershed was no longer the legal dividing line—it had been replaced by man-made city boundaries instead. What's more, under the 2005 drafts, local governors could approve diversions to straddling communities without the hassle of a regional review.

The same was not true for straddling counties, however. If an applicant inside a straddling county wanted to divert Great Lakes water, it would have to submit its diversion request to all eight Great Lakes governors—and meet the long list of requirements that were left over from the 2004 draft agreements. Those requirements included adopting a conservation plan, proving there was no alternate water source, and—most important—treating the diverted water and returning it to the Basin after it was used. The one thing these various diversion applicants would *not* have to do, however, was some kind of ecological improvement project. The improvement standard was dead (nominal references to the ethic of improvement were spliced into the Compact's language, but that was it).

And what about the intra-Basin diversion exception? That exception covered diversions that transferred water from one Great Lake watershed to another without the water ever leaving the Great Lakes Basin—for example, a pipeline that withdraws water from the Lake Huron basin and transports it into the Lake Erie basin. Like other diversions, intra-Basin water transfers would have to prove there was no reasonable water-supply alternative, including conservation. If the diversion resulted in a consumptive water loss of less than 5 mgd, then the diverter wouldn't have to return the water to the original watershed—as long as the water ended up somewhere in the Great Lakes Basin.[15] Other governors wouldn't have the option of vetoing these smaller intra-Basin diversions. But if an intra-Basin diversion resulted in a consumptive water loss greater than 5 mgd, the diverter *would* be required to return the water to the original watershed—and the diversion would need the approval of all eight Great Lakes governors, with one no vote being enough to kill a project.

In the negotiating room, consensus over the 2005 draft agreements remained elusive, but the group was getting closer to a final accord. Wisconsin—with the support of Ohio in particular—had successfully obtained its Waukesha clause in the form of the straddling counties exception. And Ontario, to the glee of Michigan and Québec, had come pretty close to obtaining a document that "just said no." Illinois, for its part, managed to grandfather the U.S. Supreme Court's governance of the Illinois diversion. But after years of heated debate, the vast majority of the Lochhead doctrine ended up on the cutting-room floor.[16]

During the 2005 public hearings, the Council of Great Lakes Governors received three thousand comments and, as in 2004, individual states received thousands more. But the total number was less than half of what had been experienced in the prior round.[17] As a rule, the comments were less combative and more accepting, but there continued to be complaints—and the straddling counties/cities proposal was the most obvious target. "That's been one of our big concerns about the second round of the Great Lakes Annex," says Susan Howatt, national water campaigner with the Council of Canadians. "That is really kind of troubling—when we start using political boundaries rather than environmental boundaries." Even some former governors found the straddling counties clause to be a sellout. "Counties are political institutions . . . watersheds on the other hand are natural jurisdictions," complains Tony Earl, former governor of Wisconsin. "The straddling counties concept [is] really the steep, slippery slope."

But there was also a feeling—particularly in Canada—that things had improved. After years of sifting and winnowing, the right document was beginning to emerge. It was a compromise document that no one was embracing with resounding enthusiasm, but it didn't suffer from the fervent criticism of the year before. "There was a big breakthrough between the 2004 version and the 2005 version," Ralph Pentland says. "[Public reaction] went from almost total condemnation . . . to a fairly broad consensus beginning to form." Industry on the U.S. side of the border, however, remained concerned. Jon Allan, an executive with Consumers Energy, a power company in Michigan, declared that the draft didn't have "a chance in hell" of passing the eight state legislatures.[18] And yet, despite the griping from industrialists, negotiators believed that a final agreement might be within reach.

"Annex fatigue" had also started to become a real factor in the negotiating room. Dozens of high-ranking regional water officials had devoted a large part of their careers to crafting these agreements. Now they wanted the process to come to an end. A goal had been set to release the final drafts of the Annex Implementing Agreements by the end of 2005, and there was an anxious, cautiously optimistic feeling that closure might finally be at hand. "You really have to make a decision," one key negotiator says. "How far do we think we can push other sovereign entities? And we think in six years we've pushed everybody about as far as we can."

~

THEN IN THE MONTHS surrounding the 2005 comment period, Indiana began to assert itself in the discussions. After all these years, the Hoosiers weren't sure they liked the agreements after all. To be fair, a new regime had taken over in the state. Republican Mitch Daniels, a former top budget official to President George W. Bush, became governor of Indiana in January 2005, and his staffers were still getting up to speed on the Compact while the second public-comment period was underway. By the fall of 2005, as the rest of the fatigued, battle-scared negotiators looked forward to releasing a final agreement by year's end, they had to spend an increasing amount of time with Governor Daniels's new negotiators. Thanks to political turnover in the Basin, this had been done before, of course. Of the ten governors and premiers who had signed Annex 2001, only two—governors Pataki of New York and Taft of Ohio—remained in office as the Compact headed for completion.

But the more the other negotiators worked with Indiana, the more worried people became. Mr. Daniels was the first Republican governor the state had seen in sixteen years, and he made it abundantly clear that all his predecessor's projects would be heavily scrutinized. "My feeling is that every garden needs weeding every sixteen years or so, and it's time for Indiana to weed the garden," he said in a newspaper interview shortly after taking office.[19] The Annex Implementing Agreements were being heavily vetted just like everything else, even if it rubbed some of Governor Daniels's Great Lakes Republican peers the wrong way. The governor was a strong free-market, antiregulation politician with no notable connections to environmental policy or the Great Lakes—his official biography mentions neither.[20] To the casual observer—in Indiana or anywhere else—the Annex Implementing Agreements looked like one giant piece of regulation.

Compact negotiators from other jurisdictions started to worry that Indiana might weed six years of hard-fought regional collaboration right out of existence. A special delegation from Ohio, New York, and Wisconsin traveled to Indianapolis to meet with Governor Daniels's representatives. Ohio governor Bob Taft— a fellow Republican—also did some crucial lobbying with

Governor Daniels by phone. The Council of Great Lakes Industries played an important role as well, arguing that while the documents needed changing, the overall goals were quite worthy.

As things bogged down, people began to suspect Indiana's motives, and rumors flew that the state might scotch the whole process. "They didn't have the ownership," complains one long-time Compact negotiator from a Republican administration. "There was a very big concern that Indiana was just going to walk away." People started using words like "fragile" in reference to the negotiations, and there was a tangible fear that the entire process was about to implode. "It's just incredibly difficult to predict where it's going to go," said one senior negotiator late in 2005. "On one level, it's pretty solid, because what keeps us together is a common interest to protect the resource and manage it within the region. And then, after that, everything else just complicates it—different histories, different traditions, different politics, different needs, et cetera." To some members of the negotiating team, Indiana's last-minute machinations were bringing to life a scenario that many had worried about since the beginning: that at the eleventh hour, after years of painful negotiations and with a compromise document possibly within reach, a new governor would enter the mix and derail the process. At one point, things became so tense that there was serious talk about drafting a compact for just seven states—and then trying to embarrass Indiana into signing on.

For students of Great Lakes water history, it was a particular irony that Indiana—of all states—was the one to throw a last-minute wrench into the water works. In many respects Indiana had been out of step with its peers in the Basin for nearly a century. When Wisconsin filed suit in federal court in the 1920s to challenge the Illinois diversion, Indiana was notably absent from the list of states that ended up joining with Wisconsin in the litigation. When the Council of Great Lakes Governors was founded in the early 1980s to form an anti-diversion strategy, all the other states paid their nominal dues to get the organization off the ground except one—Indiana.[21] When regional officials gathered in 1985 to sign the Great Lakes Charter in Milwaukee, Indiana was one of two states that failed to send its governor to the signing ceremony. When the governors took the progressive step in 1989 to create the Great Lakes Protection Fund—a $100 million endowment dedicated to protecting and enhancing the Great Lakes Basin—only one state balked at paying its share—Indiana (it never has). And when Annex 2001 was signed at Niagara Falls, Indiana's governor was one of only three who couldn't fit the signing ceremony into his schedule.

Whether a Republican or a Democrat was in charge, Indiana regularly came off as the laggard in the Great Lakes Basin. "Indiana's always been the odd man out," complains Tony Earl, the former Wisconsin governor. "Mitch Daniels has appointed people who not only represent Indiana's intransigence, but want to undo what other people are doing." What Indiana wanted was simple: a compact with less regulation and oversight of its in-Basin water use. In many ways the state parroted the concerns of Great Lakes industries, which was not all that surprising given that Indiana's slice of Lake Michigan waterfront is comparatively minute and much of it is heavily industrialized.

∼

TWICE DURING THE FALL of 2005 the negotiators gathered at a hotel in Skokie, Illinois, for what they hoped would be the final negotiating sessions on the Annex Implementing Agreements. The meetings, one of which became known as the "Scuffle in Skokie," devoted many hours to dealing with Indiana's concerns. A key moment came when Kyle Hupfer, Governor Daniels's young and controversial director of the Indiana DNR, showed up to deliver Indiana's position. His state wouldn't sign agreements that gave other jurisdictions control over Indiana's internal consumptive water use. It was fine if the Compact dealt with diversions, Mr. Hupfer said, but Governor Daniels wasn't going to sign anything that unduly infringed upon Indiana's Great Lakes water withdrawals.

"We did take a fairly strong position that we were not comfortable moving forward with the way [the Compact] was," Mr. Hupfer says. "The biggest [concern] was the concept of giving up sovereignty in the area of in-Basin usage." The tone of his presentation, others say, was "take it or leave it." Many of the other negotiators were stunned. "Here's people who have spent literally years, and in some cases decades, on these issues," complains one insulted negotiator. "Everybody around the table was like, 'Who the hell is this guy?! You've got to be kidding me!'" Then Michigan, seeing an opportunity to relax controls on consumptive use, started wondering aloud whether Indiana was right. Ontario, Québec, Pennsylvania, and Wisconsin pushed back, arguing that an agreement that was too soft on consumptive use would be seen by the public as hypocritical. Cracks were beginning to form in the coalition.

When Mr. Hupfer left Skokie, Governor Daniels's environmental policy director, Kari Evans, stayed behind to mop up. If Mr. Hupfer was the bad cop, Ms. Evans was the good cop, and other negotiators credit her with rescuing the talks from failure. She listened to the reasoning behind the agreement and was open to hearing other people out, and she spent a lot of time reiterating the reasoning behind Indiana's position as well. "She basically said exactly the same thing as Kyle," says one negotiator. "But to her credit, her whole tone was completely different." Over time, her actions convinced the rest of the team that Indiana was not interested in trashing the agreements, but was chiefly concerned about signing off on a document that stood a chance of passage in the Indiana legislature. "I don't think it would be fair to say Indiana was holding this hostage," Ms. Evans says. "This administration has taken this issue very seriously . . . We wanted to make sure that we had a package that had a reasonable hope of making it through our general assembly."

Then bottled water—which had repeatedly been on the negotiators' agenda over the years—emerged as an emotional last-minute issue as well, particularly for Michigan. In recent years, bottled water had become controversial in much of the Great Lakes region, and it peaked as an issue in Michigan during 2005 (see chapter 14). Some environmentalists argued that shipping water out of the Great Lakes Basin in bottles was no different than the Nova Group's proposal to export bulk water in tankers. Other constituencies argued that if restraints were placed on bottled water, similar limits would be required for other water-based products like beer or fruit juice. No one was interested in that.

The negotiators had widely varying interpretations about how the Annex Implementing Agreements should deal with the bottled-water controversy. "We have some questions about what bottled water means as it relates to the question of diversion," says Ken DeBeaussaert, director of Michigan's Office of the Great Lakes. But other states didn't see the need to even mention bottled water in the agreements. "[Michigan was] so worried about bottled water," complains Kent Lokkesmoe, head of the water division at the Minnesota DNR. "It's their political world and I don't understand it all . . . To me that's a nonissue." For its part, Ontario had already passed a law, in the wake of Nova, that banned bulk water exports but permitted shipments of water out of the Basin in containers of 20 liters or less (which is just over 5 gallons). That meant shipping a tanker of bulk water out of the Basin was illegal, but shipping a tanker of bottled water wasn't. The Canadians weren't interested in signing international agreements that weakened those regulations, despite pressure from states to do so. Meanwhile, bottled-water opponents in the United States thought the 20-liter limit went too far.

Interest groups played a key role during the final stretch of the negotiations as well—particularly the National Wildlife Federation (NWF) and the Council of Great Lakes Industries (CGLI). Sensing that key polarizing issues remained unresolved in the negotiating room, NWF and CGLI made a controversial move during 2005: they spent hours and hours secretly working together to forge their own compromises on key points, and then they quietly forwarded their compromise language to the negotiating team. Some of their most noteworthy findings: because the U.S. federal government considered bottled water to be a product, NWF and CGLI didn't think bottled water should be considered a diversion under the Compact, but recommended that states be allowed to impose their own more restrictive bottled-water rules. And in an extremely important nod to industry (and to Indiana), the two groups said that large consumptive water uses within an individual state shouldn't be subjected to binding regional review by all the other states, as long as those withdrawals met the standards laid out in the Compact. But in a nod to environmentalists, NWF and CGLI also told negotiators to beef up the conservation wording in the Compact by making water-conservation programs mandatory.

The NWF/CGLI compromise language came at a crucial and insecure time in the drafting process, giving many negotiators the courage to cut deals, knowing that they wouldn't be eviscerated later by two of the most influential advocacy groups in the Basin (or so they hoped). "If they could find common ground with each other," says Kate Bartter, chief policy advisor to Ohio governor Bob Taft, "it showed that we, of course, should be able to find common ground."

While the NWF/CGLI compromise helped facilitate discussions in the negotiating room, it brought criticism from other interests groups around the Basin who accused both organizations of consorting with the enemy. "We've got enviro groups that are pissed off at NWF, and industry groups that say CGLI doesn't speak for them," said one negotiator during the fall of 2005. Many environmental advocates felt betrayed. "I think it was pretty presumptuous for those organizations to assume that they had the authority to do what they did," says Jim Olson, an environmental attorney in Michigan. "What they did was sell out." Others say the final agreements would have included stronger protections for the environment if NWF had spent more time working with other environmental groups than with industry. "I was disappointed that—without consulting with very many, if any, other environmental groups—that NWF went off and cut a deal that I think undermined the position that we could have achieved with more unity," complains Dave Dempsey, Great Lakes policy advisor with Clean Water Action. "Some environmental groups were so desperate for any agreement that they were willing to settle for what I think is pretty much an adulterated agreement."

Many saw the hand of industry in several of the last-minute changes. "It's not the hand of industry," counters George Kuper, president of the CGLI. "It's the hand of common sense!" Despite the criticism from some environmentalists, negotiators say that NWF provided an important service by showing the team just how far they could push the document while still avoiding fervent industry opposition as the Compact moved through regional legislatures. Many team members also reminded themselves that the Compact was the minimum standard that the states would be required to adopt. While the Compact itself could not be amended, individual legislatures had the option of passing even more stringent water rules in their respective jurisdictions. That, negotiators say, helped them forge an ultimate agreement.

~

IN EARLY NOVEMBER 2005, a final-final compromise was reached. From an overview perspective, the Annex Implementing Agreements remained documents that banned diversions with limited exceptions. But in the last several months the fine print had changed in several key areas. Regarding bottled water, the Compact ended up following Ontario's lead, banning sales in containers larger than 5.7 gallons, though the Compact made clear that individual governments were welcome to make those rules even more restrictive. More importantly, everyone in the negotiating room agreed to give Indiana the sovereignty flexibility it had requested regarding in-Basin consumptive uses—as long as those in-Basin water withdrawals followed the standards listed in the Compact.

Under the prior version of the Compact, states were required to regulate all in-Basin water withdrawals larger than 100,000 gallons per day (gpd). In the final compromise document, at the insistence of Indiana (and eventually backed up by some other states), that 100,000 gpd threshold was removed, and individual states were allowed to set their own regulatory benchmarks. If after ten years a state failed to set a trigger level, the Compact would do it for them—the Compact included a default threshold of 100,000 gpd.[22] And while a state would be required to inform other states about a large consumptive-use proposal greater than 5 mgd—and while those other states could comment on that water use—the other states could not vote it down. That meant after years of negotiations not much had changed regarding in-Basin consumptive use since the days of Mud Creek in Michigan, with one notable exception: if a state was believed to be approving large consumptive uses that were in violation of the Compact's standard, the state could be taken to court.

So while the final version of the Compact took a big step forward by banning diversions except for limited exceptions, it was notably weaker when it came to in-Basin consumptive water use. Other sections of the document attracted less attention, but were likely to influence regional water policy in coming years. For example, the Compact defined the waters of the Great Lakes Basin very broadly, not just including the lakes themselves, but also their tributary waters—and most notably of all—groundwater that is hydrologically connected to the Great Lakes.[23] In addition, the Compact required the states to monitor their water use for the first time. While a similar pledge had been made in the Great Lakes Charter, and some states—Minnesota in particular—did an exemplary job of monitoring their water use, others did not. If and when the Compact becomes binding, skipping out on that duty will no longer be an option. Every state will be required to monitor water withdrawals above 100,000 gpd. This would give everyone in the Basin a better idea of how much water was cycling through—or being consumed—by the various jurisdictions, providing important information to Basin water officials about the so-called cumulative impacts of regional water use.

The Compact also required each state to create and follow a water-conservation plan. While the specific details of a conservation plan were left up to each state, their plans would have to be submitted to and reviewed by a Compact-created committee on a regular basis.[24] The idea was to keep close track of the conservation leaders and the conservation laggards, using peer pressure to bring the lax into line. Making conservation programs mandatory was a "huge leap," says negotiator Cathy Curran Myers, deputy secretary of the Pennsylvania Office of Water Management and a key negotiator from that state. "It means we will come up with a whole

suite of conservation practices . . . It may be one of the more important things that comes out of [the Compact]."

Perhaps most noteworthy of all was that a new mechanism had
been set up, committing the states to work together as a region to
manage the Great Lakes resource through a binding compact. Assuming the Compact is adopted by all the Great Lakes legislatures
and by the U.S. Congress, a state that violates the rules could be
taken to court—not just by other states, but even by citizens or advocacy groups—and a judge would level the final penalty. "A compact is essentially a contract," says one Great Lakes official. "If
someone doesn't fulfill the contract, that's a breach and they can be
sued."

The provinces weren't legally bound by the Compact, but the
nonbinding International Agreement that mirrored the Compact
ensured that the states and provinces would heavily coordinate

---

Compact Highlights

The final version of the Compact included the following key
provisions:

- A ban on new water diversions, with limited exceptions.
- A requirement that states regulate in-Basin water uses.
- The creation of a uniform regional standard for evaluat-
  ing proposed water withdrawals.
- A requirement that states each adopt a water-conserva-
  tion plan.
- Water shipped out of the Basin in bottles smaller than
  5.7 gallons was not classified as a diversion.
- The waters of the Great Lakes were defined as including
  rivers *and* groundwater within the Basin.
- The Illinois diversion at Chicago was specifically ex-
  empted.
- The Compact language mirrored that of the nonbinding
  International Agreement signed with Ontario and
  Québec.

---

their water activities with one another. While the provinces wouldn't have the power to veto diversion proposals on the U.S. side of the border, they would have a voice. That drew criticism from some Canadian constituencies, but it was the best arrangement the negotiators were able to come up with, given that the federal governments on both sides of the border wouldn't allow the states and provinces to draw up a binding international treaty with one another.

~

THE FINAL DOCUMENTS were released at a ceremony in Milwaukee, Wisconsin, on December 13, 2005. While the event was billed as a signing ceremony for the Great Lakes governors and premiers, there was a shockingly low turnout—only three governors and premiers showed up: Bob Taft of Ohio, Dalton McGuinty of Ontario, and Jim Doyle of Wisconsin.[25] The no-shows did send stand-ins, and hundreds of other officials, businessmen, and environmentalists attended the ceremony, but it was an embarrassingly low chief-executive turnout for what had been touted as such a major event. Many more governors and premiers had shown up for the signing ceremonies of the Great Lakes Charter in 1985 and of Annex 2001, raising questions about just how much political support there really was behind the Annex Implementing Agreements.

"This is a proud and historic day for the people of the Great Lakes and the St. Lawrence Basin," Governor Taft said after the final documents were released. "These waters are a global treasure that we hold in trust for future generations."[26] Governor Taft was correct. It was a proud moment, particularly for the negotiators who managed to forge a deal despite enormous adversity. Releasing comprehensive agreements to manage one of the largest reservoirs of fresh surface water on the planet was definitely a momentous occasion. But was it really historic? If so, why did so many governors and premiers fail to show up?

In truth, history was still waiting—waiting for a binding compact on the U.S. side of the border—home to the largest population in the Great Lakes Basin, and where the greatest increase in water demand would likely be found. The agreements released in Milwaukee, while impressive, were nonbinding. Would the governors really be able to make the Compact law by pushing it through all eight of their legislatures and the U.S. Congress? Now *that* would be historic. But the low turnout at the signing ceremony wasn't reassuring. Maybe more governors and premiers would show up for the final Compact's signing ceremony—assuming, of course, that they ever provided themselves with such an opportunity.

Chapter 13

Waukesha Worries

JUST BEFORE MIDNIGHT on May 7, 1892, the town fire bell rang out in Waukesha, Wisconsin. But the citizens knew that this time the alarm wasn't heralding a fire. They grabbed shotguns, pistols, and clubs and headed for the railroad tracks. Rumors had been swirling that a secret train loaded with workmen would arrive from Chicago to steal some of Waukesha's internationally acclaimed spring water. The thieves' plan—under cover of darkness—was to lay a pipeline from Waukesha's Hygeia Spring to some unknown destination outside town. From there, the water would ultimately be delivered to the Windy City to be served to thirsty sightseers at the upcoming world's fair.[1]

Chicago's water was notoriously bad at the time. One Chicago mayor was even accused of stashing Waukesha water at city hall to avoid the local tap water.[2] By contrast, dozens of gurgling Waukesha springs had become premier tourist destinations for moneyed travelers from throughout North America. Some springs were even said to have healing powers, including Hygeia, which was owned by Chicago entrepreneur James McElroy—the man behind the secret train. With cachet like that, Waukesha water was the ideal world's fair beverage, and Mr. McElroy was desperate to serve it to fairgoers.

Initially Mr. McElroy had formally asked Waukesha for permission to send spring water south, but he met stiff resistance. Locals worried that piping water to Illinois would curtail Waukesha's prized tourist traffic. If people could get Waukesha water in Chicago, why would they travel to "Spring City"? It was only after being spurned that Mr. McElroy resorted to the midnight train full of workmen. But rumors arrived long before the locomotive departed Chicago, and when that unscheduled train reached the outskirts of town, the fire bell sounded, and the community was roused from slumber.

Upon arrival, the surprised workmen were met by hundreds of armed, angry Waukesha citizens who yelled, "Throw them into the river!" After a tense, extended showdown, the work train headed back to Chicago as dry as it had arrived.[3] Waukesha had valiantly defended its famous springs in a standoff that received wide publicity. The *Milwaukee Record* ran an editorial cartoon showing an enormous hog named "Chicago" wallowing in Mr. McElroy's spring, surrounded by armed, stern-faced residents—including one with a revolver trained directly at the pig's head (fig. 13.1).[4] That kind of media coverage only bolstered Waukesha's national water reputation, cementing its place as a tourist destination for many years to come.

~

MY, HOW THE WATER fortunes have fallen in old Spring City. Most of Waukesha's historic springs have been obliterated or abandoned, covered by gas stations, apartment buildings and parking lots. The last local bottler from the springs era closed shop in 1997.[5] Waukesha (pronounced WAU-ka-shaw)[6] has since become a Milwaukee suburb of seventy thousand people, and its water has become famous for entirely different reasons. Water levels have plummeted by more than five hundred feet in municipal wells, and the more deep groundwater the city pumps, the more salts and contaminants emerge. The chief concern is radium, a naturally occurring radioactive element that—after years of exposure—is believed to cause cancer. It exists in Waukesha's wells at twice the federal limit.[7]

After decades of ominous test results and no corrective action by Waukesha officials, Wisconsin authorities formally pressured the community to take action. In late 2003, Waukesha signed a consent order with the state forcing the suburb to resolve the radium

WAUKESHA FRIGHTENING AWAY THE CHICAGO HOG.

(Printed by courtesy of the Milwaukee Record.)

Fig. 13.1. *Waukesha once defended its water from outsiders, now it wants to divert water from the Great Lakes. (From the collection of John M. Schoenknecht)*

issue by December 8, 2006. The city would either have to use expensive treatment methods to extract the radium from its water or find a cleaner, safer alternative water supply. The suburb, which lies just beyond the edge of the Great Lakes Basin, had made no secret of its interest in diverting 20 million gallons of water per day from Lake Michigan, a stance that put Waukesha on the frontline in the Great Lakes water war. More importantly, it also meant that Waukesha was poised to become one of the first Great Lakes diversion applicants to step forward since the Annex Implementing Agreements were signed in Milwaukee in December 2005.

~

BY THE TIME WAUKESHA signed its 2003 consent decree with the state it had already hired consultants to help survey the landscape for water alternatives. The city quickly focused in on two main options: spending $77 million to sink new wells in aquifers west of town, or looking east and spending $42 million to pump water from Lake Michigan, just fifteen miles away. The western aquifer option had drawbacks beyond the cost; there were concerns that drawing down those aquifers eventually would lower water levels in nearby streams and lakes. The problem with option two—tapping the Great Lakes—was that because Waukesha lies outside the Great Lakes Basin, under the Water Resources Development Act of 1986 and the Great Lakes Compact of 2005, a diversion to Waukesha required the unanimous approval from all eight Great Lakes governors (Waukesha fell under the Compact's "straddling counties" exception; see chapter 12). And though the Compact had been released, it hadn't been enacted into law by any of the Great Lakes state legislatures. So Waukesha's application would be received under WRDA, where it was believed that the governors would use the new standards enumerated in the Compact to evaluate Waukesha's diversion application.

But there was another problem with the Lake Michigan option: the issue of return-flow. Since 1986 no U.S. community had been allowed to divert water outside the Great Lakes Basin without agreeing to return the water to the lakes after it was used. The Compact reiterated the return-flow principle as well. The idea behind that standard was simple: in the rare instances when diversions from the Basin are permitted, the water should be returned (after being treated, of course) to minimize water lost to the Great Lakes system. That's why any Great Lakes diversion application—under WRDA or the Compact—that didn't include return-flow would likely be considered dead on arrival.

This posed a serious problem for Waukesha, which was

adamantly opposed to return-flow—primarily because of cost. For decades the city's treated wastewater has discharged into the Fox River, a tributary in the Mississippi watershed. That meant a return-flow requirement would force Waukesha to retrofit its urban water-treatment system to send its wastewater back to Lake Michigan. But the city said the return-flow requirement made Great Lakes water outlandishly expensive. While the Compact was still being negotiated, city officials made it clear that, while they were very interested in diverting Lake Michigan water, they had no interest in returning that water to the lake after it was used.

That rankled environmentalists from throughout the region, and they attacked Waukesha from all sides. As usual, the critics' chief concern was not the effect that Waukesha's diversion would have on Lake Michigan water levels (hydrologists said the effect would be imperceptible). As with prior diversion controversies, what Waukesha's critics worried about was precedent. The effect of one Waukesha-like diversion without return-flow would be hard to measure, but a hundred Waukesha diversions would not. (In fact, a hundred Waukeshas would nearly equal the Illinois diversion.) Critics worried that a Waukesha return-flow exemption could be replicated over time to a damaging degree by communities large and small that lay beyond the Basin line. (A lot of Waukesha's critics also worried about using Great Lakes water to support sprawl, and the drain that would have on urban Milwaukee.)

Despite fierce environmental opposition, Waukesha refused to budge on the return-flow issue. As the months passed, positions hardened, and as the criticism mounted, Waukesha started acting like a spurned suitor even before submitting a formal request for Great Lakes water. Waukesha's attitude didn't play well in newspapers around the Great Lakes Basin, and overnight, it seemed, the suburb became the latest polarizing figure in the anti-diversion movement. "They have been quite successful in keeping themselves in the paper to the extent that they showed up in *The New York Times*," remarks Chuck Ledin, chief of the Great Lakes office at the Wisconsin Department of Natural Resources. "Every characterization of their posture was one of aggressiveness, and how they had the 'right' to [Great Lakes] water."

Waukesha's rigid attitude made it an unsympathetic water applicant in many people's eyes. No other regional community evoked more visceral reactions among the Great Lakes anti-diversion crowd. Unlike Akron, Lowell, or Pleasant Prairie, Waukesha became an anti-diversion focal point before even submitting a water-diversion application.[8] With each passing decade, it seemed, the Great Lakes water-diversion debate was growing hotter and hotter. "Waukesha is a poster child," admits Dan Duchniak, the embattled head of the Waukesha Water Utility, adding that the debate over Waukesha is "almost like a cyst that has grown into a cancerous tumor, and we need to figure out a way to treat it."

∼

IN MANY WAYS, Waukesha brought this image problem upon itself. The city regularly appeared pugnacious, irascible, and unreasonable—particularly in the early years of the debate. When the U.S. Environmental Protection Agency pressured Waukesha to find a safer water source, Waukesha took the EPA to court (and lost). When environmentalists suggested that local leaders adopt water conservation measures, they refused (at least at first). When people mentioned that the Great Lakes governors were unlikely to approve a Waukesha diversion without return-flow, Waukesha threatened to sue. Throughout the debate, there was an arrogant undertone from Waukesha's leaders that *they* weren't the ones at fault, *others* were to blame. Hovering in the background was an almost ever-present hint from Waukesha officials that they would resort to litigation if they didn't get Great Lakes water on their own terms.

But Waukesha was also a victim of historical circumstance. It wanted to apply for Great Lakes water while the Annex Implementing Agreements were still being drafted. Yet Great Lakes negotiators had no interest in entertaining a new, highly charged diversion application while the final wording of the agreements remained unresolved. Behind the scenes, Waukesha was told to wait until final drafts of the agreements were released. So all Waukesha could do was sit back and dream about the day it could finally apply for Great Lakes water. Even so, while Waukesha hung in an awkward limbo its name kept coming up in public hearings and news stories about the agreements—often in a critical light. City officials defended their community vociferously. But the more defensive Waukesha became, the more isolated it appeared.

Eventually Waukesha softened its hardball strategy, admitting that it didn't work. "There was a recognition," Dan Duchniak says, "that if we're looking for future water supply options we need to be making friends, not foes . . . There was a change of tone." There was also a change of strategy. Waukesha started spending $100,000 per year on public relations and water consultants to help the city make its case, burnish its image, and increase the sophistication of its message.[9] The consultants reminded the city that lawsuits aren't cheap and that the governors and premiers—the officials behind the diversion rules that Waukesha often criticized—were the ones who held the controls to the Great Lakes tap.

One of the first things the consultants homed in on was Waukesha's underwhelming water-conservation record. Waukesha residents paid notoriously low water rates—some of the lowest in all of Wisconsin—and the city had policies that encouraged lawn watering by giving customers a sewer credit for water applied to their grass. "The utility had always prided itself on never having a sprinkling ban," Mr. Duchniak admits, adding that the attitude had always been, "If this was a service that [residents] were requiring, 'Gosh darn it, we're gonna provide it.'"

With encouragement from its consultants, however, and to make its eventual Great Lakes diversion application more politically palatable, in 2005 Waukesha embarked on a new conservation strategy designed to raise rates, rein in water use, and—ideally— turn Waukesha into a leading example of water conservation, instead of water waste. Mr. Duchniak says his community has gotten the conservation message, and things are going to change. "I think Waukesha could be a role model that could set a good precedent for everyone to follow in the Great Lakes when it comes to conservation," he says. Maybe so, but is a Johnny-come-lately water conservationist a viable candidate for a Great Lakes diversion? The city would have to file an application to find out.

The consultants not only helped soften Waukesha's image, they increased the sophistication of the city's message. Waukesha spent a lot of time arguing that it really was *inside* the Great Lakes Basin, not outside as people had claimed. Waukesha does sit in a hydrologically unique geographic position. Yes, it's outside the Great Lakes surface-water divide—rain that falls on Waukesha and runs off into nearby streams eventually finds its way to the Mississippi River. But independent research also showed that Waukesha is inside the presettlement Great Lakes deep *groundwater* divide (fig. 13.2).[10] That means water in the deep aquifer underneath Waukesha eventually discharges into Lake Michigan, because the aquifer is connected to the lake bottom. Waukesha is quite literally in a hydrogeologic gray area. And as the Great Lakes water Compact was being negotiated, Mr. Duchniak argued that Waukesha's unique position made it deserving of special consideration.

While that may have helped Waukesha's image, there was still the lingering issue of return-flow. How did Waukesha plan to resolve that issue? By claiming it deserved special treatment because it was already pulling water away from Lake Michigan underground. The reasoning behind this complex argument emanated directly from the hydrogeologic uniqueness of Waukesha's location. Before European settlement, the deep aquifer under Waukesha fed groundwater into Lake Michigan. But because of excessive pumping in the region—by Waukesha and others—that groundwater flow had been reversed and water was instead being pulled from Lake Michigan into the aquifer rather than the other way around. You would think this news might hurt Waukesha's case, but Dan Duchniak says it helps. Since Waukesha was already pulling water away from Lake Michigan underground all it wanted to do, he says, was move that subterranean "diversion" to the surface—and keep its Mississippi River discharge system the same. In other words, his argument goes, because Waukesha's groundwater pumping was already "diverting" water by pulling it away from Lake Michigan beneath the surface,

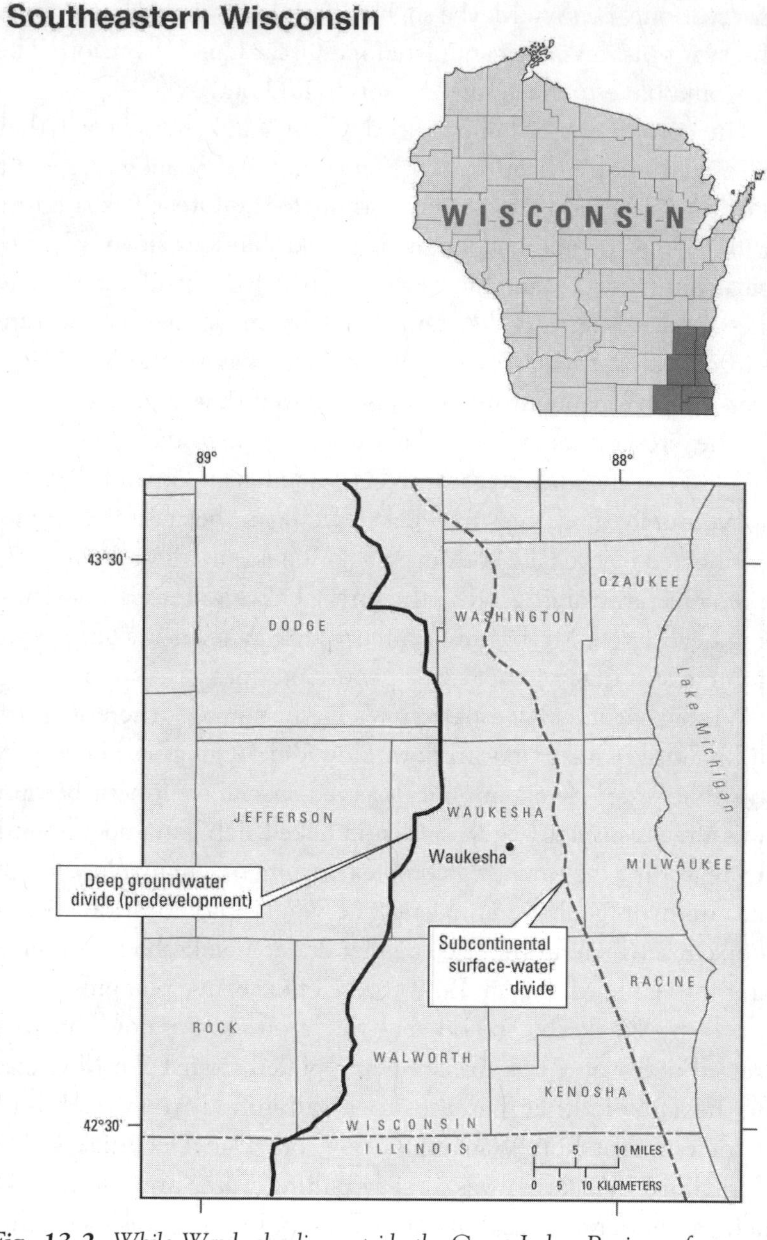

Southeastern Wisconsin

Fig. 13.2. *While Waukesha lies outside the Great Lakes Basin surface-water divide, it is actually inside the Great Lakes groundwater divide. (Courtesy of the U.S. Geological Survey, modified from D. T. Feinstein et al.,* Simulation of Regional Groundwater Flow in Southeastern Wisconsin, *Wisconsin Geological and Natural History Survey Open-File Report 2004-01 [2004])*

why should it have to do return-flow if it diverts water from Lake Michigan on the surface?

~

THAT KIND OF REASONING infuriates Great Lakes environmentalists, who see Waukesha finagling for an undeserved special exception. First, they argue, Waukesha is misrepresenting what's happening underground. Yes, the groundwater flow has been reversed, but because the aquifer is so huge—and the water moves through it so slowly—Lake Michigan water hasn't yet reached Waukesha's wells. Hence, Waukesha can't claim that it's already diverting Great Lakes water below the ground. Second, environmentalists say, communities that divert water from the Great Lakes have to send it back—period—no matter what kind of convoluted groundwater situation they might have. Advocates charge that Waukesha is asking for special treatment without precedent in modern times. Every community that has diverted water from the Great Lakes since 1986 has had to return the water to the Basin—a principle that is also strongly reiterated in the 2005 Compact. Advocates are particularly adamant that exceptions shouldn't be made for sprawling suburban communities that have grown beyond their ecological means. The Great Lakes, they say, shouldn't be used as a water subsidy for urban sprawl outside the Basin. If Waukesha residents want Great Lakes water, they should move to the water, rather than moving the water to them. (Many Milwaukee residents couldn't agree more.)

The main point, environmentalists say, is that it's time for people to think about water before they decide where to live—something that they argue people moving to Waukesha have failed to do. Environmental advocates argue that if a community has a water problem, people shouldn't just continue moving there and assume the government is going to bail them out. "We're concerned that Waukesha is the shape of things to come," complains Susan Howatt, national water campaigner for the Council of Canadians. "We can't get into these situations where we make it okay for urban sprawl to [receive] water diversions that aren't sustainable." While many environmentalists are opposed to Waukesha getting water, most can't imagine that a diversion application—without return-flow—would get the green light from regional officials. "If [Waukesha] doesn't meet the return-flow requirement, it won't be approved," predicts Cheryl Mendoza, water-conservation manager at the Alliance for the Great Lakes. "Under the Compact you'd basically need unanimous approval and I can't see Michigan, in particular, approving that."

Great Lakes business leaders also find it hard to give Waukesha a sympathetic ear. "I don't see any reason why Waukesha should be exempted from the requirements that any other municipality located outside the Great Lakes Basin watershed would have to face," says George Kuper, president of the Council of Great Lakes Industries. "I don't see the arguments that Waukesha is making . . . to be particularly commanding."

But under WRDA and the Great Lakes Compact, businessmen and environmentalists don't have a vote. That responsibility is reserved for the Great Lakes governors. How do the governors in other parts of the Basin feel about Waukesha's claim to a return-flow exemption? According to one gubernatorial confidante intimately involved in drafting the Great Lakes Compact, Waukesha does garner sympathy for many of its claims—but there's zero tolerance for the city's stance regarding return-flow. "There is no sympathy for Waukesha," this person says, "when they say they should be allowed to divert water outside the Basin and then dump it in the Mississippi River watershed—none."

∼

CITY OFFICIALS MAINTAIN they have looked into the return-flow option and there's just no way they can afford it. Dan Duchniak says he has even explored cheaper return-flow alternatives, such as sending Waukesha's wastewater back to Lake Michigan via Milwaukee's sewer system, which serves a number of suburbs including segments of Waukesha County that are just a few miles from his office. But Mr. Duchniak says that when he informally approached Milwaukee with that idea, he was rebuffed. "We've been told by the Milwaukee Metropolitan Sewerage District that they cannot accept our wastewater, and they have reasons for that," he says. "They have commitments that they made to other communities with regard to their capacities so they can't accept any more [effluent]." Milwaukee *has* experienced a number of widely publicized and highly embarrassing sewer overflows into Lake Michigan in recent years, raising questions about the capacity of its sewer system. Consequently, Mr. Duchniak claims, any return-flow option would require Waukesha to build a pipe all the way back to Lake Michigan, and that pipe would have to be buried two hundred or three hundred feet underground to avoid Milwaukee's urban infrastructure. "The return-flow piping [would] be in the hundreds of millions of dollars," he says. "And that makes it cost prohibitive."

But officials in Milwaukee have a notably different interpretation of the situation. They admit that informal conversations did indeed take place between Waukesha and the Milwaukee Metropolitan Sewerage District (MMSD), but they deny that Waukesha was turned away. In fact, Kevin Shafer, executive director at MMSD, says that while the ultimate decision would be up to the district's commissioners, in his opinion capacity isn't really an issue for Waukesha. "Flows at our treatment plants have dropped over the years, because we lost all the breweries except for Miller [and] we've lost tanneries—a lot of tanneries—which use a lot of water. So our average daily flow has been getting smaller and smaller over the last ten, twenty years," he says. "MMSD would have capacity for [Waukesha's] flow."

The two treatment plants at MMSD have a cumulative capacity of 630 million gallons per day (mgd), but only run a combined 150 mgd during dry weather. Mr. Shafer says MMSD has undertaken a major planning effort regarding future capacity, and some people have encouraged the district to factor Waukesha's 20 mgd of return-flow into future plans. But Mr. Shafer says that because Waukesha hasn't formally asked to be considered, so far the suburb is out of the planning process. In addition, he says, MMSD is already servicing six communities in Waukesha County, so its pipelines are in Waukesha's neighborhood already. Waukesha may have issues with return-flow, but according to Mr. Shafer, capacity in the MMSD isn't one of them. "They need to ask us first," he says, "before they say that we've turned them down."

~

DAN DUCHNIAK ARGUES that there are other reasons why Waukesha shouldn't send its wastewater back to Lake Michigan. As odd as it may seem, he argues that the Fox River (where Waukesha currently discharges its wastewater) needs the city's effluent. If Waukesha were forced to send its treated wastewater back to Lake Michigan, Mr. Duchniak maintains, it would hurt the regional environment—not help it. During droughts, 35 percent of the Fox River's flow is actually Waukesha sewer discharge, which is why Mr. Duchniak says the Fox River needs the city's effluent more than Lake Michigan does. He is particularly concerned about the Vernon Marsh, a wetland downstream. Mr. Duchniak's pleas on behalf of the marsh resonate with a few environmental advocates and particularly those people who live near the wetland. But most environmentalists argue that the Vernon Marsh doesn't make a sympathetic case, particularly because the Fox River is a waterway that has already been highly altered by man.

What's more, critics add, the farther you get away from Wisconsin, the less sympathy that argument will attract. "The idea behind the Compact is that the Great Lakes Basin is connected, and therefore folks in Ontario, and Ohio, and New York have some reason to comment on a Great Lakes withdrawal or diversion proposal in Wisconsin," says Derek Scheer, the former water-policy director for Clean Wisconsin, an environmental group. "Why would folks in Ohio, New York, or Ontario be concerned about a dammed-up, unhealthy river ecosystem that is based on effluent?" After requiring return-flow in Pleasant Prairie and Akron, and spending years drafting a compact that emphasizes the importance of return-flow as well, it seems highly unlikely that Great Lakes officials will approve a diversion that doesn't send treated wastewater back to the Great Lakes system. "If return-flow were on the table for Waukesha, I think they'd have a much better argument for gaining Great Lakes water," Mr. Scheer says.

Waukesha has other obstacles to overcome as well. Its main argument against return-flow is cost. Yet, according to figures from the Wisconsin Department of Administration (DOA), Waukesha County has the highest median household income in the state and the second-lowest percentage of people below the poverty line. Dan Duchniak argues that those are county figures, not city data, and that the numbers are skewed by wealthy people who live outside of town. While that may technically be true, it still makes it hard for Waukesha to cry poor. In addition, Waukesha County's growth statistics are even more problematic. According to estimates supplied by the DOA, between 2000 and 2005 Waukesha County received the second-largest influx of new residents in the state. An estimated 16,581 people moved to Waukesha County during that five-year period, which suggests that Waukesha's water woes are not yet influencing where people choose to live.

Complicating matters even more for Waukesha is the fact that it *does* have an alternate water option—the aquifers west of town. Lowell, Indiana's, water application was rejected under WRDA, in part, because Michigan governor John Engler was convinced the village had other water options (see chapter 8). And the Great Lakes Compact strongly suggests that diversion applicants that haven't exhausted all their water options will be denied. Despite that clause, Mr. Duchniak says his city is exploring a two-pronged water approach—the western aquifer option and the Lake Michigan option. If one option falls through, the other will remain on track. But because the Lake Michigan option is $35 million cheaper (not counting the cost of return-flow), that option is by far Waukesha's top choice.

There's another reason for Waukesha to lean toward Lake Michigan. Mr. Duchniak says the aquifers bordering Waukesha have become mired in controversy too. Conflicts have flared, and lawsuits have been filed by property owners alleging that regional groundwater levels have already been affected by overpumping. "We continue to investigate the western well supply," Mr.

Duchniak says. "[But] there's going to be conflicts if we go there [too] . . . we're surrounded by water conflict." What if Waukesha can't find an alternate long-term water supply before the 2006 state-mandated deadline? The city will have to depend on a combination of water blending and expensive treatment methods to bring its water into regulatory compliance for the short and medium term.

That's why Waukesha (or one of its water-troubled neighbors) is expected to be one of the first water-diversion applicants to step forward since the release of the Annex Implementing Agreements. "We would probably make an application that would not include return-flow," Mr. Duchniak says, "and see what happens." But Waukesha can't file a water-diversion application under the Compact until the Compact is adopted by all eight Great Lakes legislatures and the U.S. Congress. That will take years—if it happens at all—and Waukesha can't wait that long. Until the Compact is passed, WRDA will remain the primary regulator of Great Lakes water diversions in the United States. What will Waukesha do if its water application is rejected? Possibly sue—either by challenging WRDA or the Compact in court. "I would say the legal option is something that is not off the table," Mr. Duchniak says. History will show whether Waukesha's threat of litigation is just saber rattling by an anxious water applicant or if it represents a new paradigm in how water disputes will be handled in the Great Lakes region.

～

THE TALK ABOUT LITIGATION confounds Doug Cherkauer, a hydrogeologist at the University of Wisconsin–Milwaukee. He is an expert on groundwater issues in southeastern Wisconsin and is a regular panelist and commentator on the Waukesha issue at regional conferences and on talk shows. He would like to see people spend less time battling in the courts and more time sitting around the table thinking about new ways to better utilize the water resources that are available within a watershed. "As a society, the U.S. has historically treated water as a really cheap commodity and as something that is there for the convenience of people. And if we have to move it from one location to another to satisfy the demands of people, so be it—we don't care what happens to the place we took it from," he says. "That worked in the eighteenth century, and it worked in the nineteenth century, and it started to fall apart in the twentieth century, and we ended up with Las Vegas, and Phoenix, and Los Angeles—and places that just shouldn't exist. But now we're seeing that same sort of problem move into the so-called water-rich areas."

Mr. Cherkauer says it's time to move on to a more sustainable way of managing our water. Specifically, he would like to see groundwater-dependent communities like Waukesha take their wastewater, treat it extensively, and then apply it to the ground's surface in ways that allow it to soak into the soil and recharge the regional aquifers, where it can then be withdrawn again and again. It's time to stop the "pump and dump" systems of old that send groundwater wastefully rushing downstream, he says, adding that society needs to start thinking more seriously about water recycling—not just in Waukesha but in all sorts of places.

Whether Waukesha follows his counsel is not the point, he says. What matters is that the city spend more time looking beyond the business-as-usual approach and less time drawing up legal strategies with attorneys. "Southeastern Wisconsin is at a crossroads right now," Mr. Cherkauer says. "We have the opportunity to move forward into the twenty-first century and look for sustainable options, or we have the alternative approach of continuing to do things the way we've always done them—and impacts be damned. I would like to think that we would take this opportunity to sit back and reflect a little bit and do it right, rather than charging off down a path because it's easy."

Chapter 14

Who Will Win the War?

WATER IS THE FOUNDATION of life. It is a key driver of ecosystems and economic development. From remote wetlands to Wall Street, water availability is often the determining factor between prosperity and deprivation. Citizens in the Great Lakes Basin—who have traditionally taken water for granted—learned that lesson late, but just as bitterly as anywhere else. Since the mid-twentieth century, water quality and the introduction of exotic species have been the chief ecological concerns in the Great Lakes Basin. But in recent years water *quantity* has emerged as an important environmental worry as well. Prior chapters in this book have shown that the Great Lakes region is blessed with abundant water resources, but cursed by an era of water conflict. That era began in 1900 with the reversal of the Chicago River, and it reached a new and contentious stage as the twentieth century came to a close.

Most experts believe that water conflict has become a permanent fixture of life in the Great Lakes region. Polluted tributaries that once caught fire now host water battles resembling those of drier climes. Along the southern rim of the Great Lakes Basin, water skirmishes will be a regular feature of the future—and that will be particularly true in places like the southwest shore of Lake Michigan where the edge of the Basin lies so close to the water's edge. What's more, the effects of climate change on the Great Lakes could dwarf the impacts of human water withdrawals, raising regional water tensions to unprecedented heights. That people are fighting over water in one of the wettest regions on earth is an ironic sign of just how precious potable freshwater has become.

"If the Great Lakes are going through this struggle, imagine what more arid parts of the world are going through," says Cameron Davis, executive director at the Alliance for the Great Lakes in Chicago. "Nobody's immune from this tension. The entire world is struggling with it."

Are the Great Lakes ready for their acrimonious water future? Not yet. The release of the Annex Implementing Agreements in December 2005 was just one stage in the process of creating a modern water-management system in the Great Lakes Basin. Negotiators of the agreements persevered despite a merry-go-round of governors and premiers, divisive regional differences, conflicting water philosophies, and merciless mission fatigue. They survived battles over the Illinois diversion, the improvement standard, and the last-minute protestations from Indiana. Completing the process was an impressive collaborative feat that bound together ten different jurisdictions that cross an international boundary and stretch from the Iron Range of northern Minnesota to the rushing waters of the St. Lawrence in Québec.

While the accomplishment was notable, it was only the halfway mark. The documents, while extensive, remain toothless—lacking the force of law. Technically speaking, the Great Lakes remain as legally vulnerable as before. "The question," says Professor Dan Tarlock at the Chicago-Kent College of Law, "is whether there is sufficient pressure from the governors or [environmental groups] to take the next step and turn this into a compact." Mr. Tarlock's point is that for the Great Lakes Compact to be binding it still has to be adopted by all eight Great Lakes legislatures *and* the U.S. Congress—a task that makes the drafting process look easy. *The Great Lakes–St. Lawrence River Basin Water Resources Compact* was designed to help officials manage regional waters in an era of heightened tension, but they'll never get to use it if the legislatures fail to act. "It will be very challenging to get the Compact ratified by each of the eight state legislatures, and also consented to by Congress," warns David Naftzger, executive director at the Council of Great Lakes Governors. "[But] there is momentum. It's building and our hope is certainly to see quick action."

The Compact was finalized seven years after the Nova Group's controversial water-diversion proposal roused the region to action. Following the Milwaukee signing ceremony, many were predicting that it could take at least that long to move the Compact through all the various assemblies required to make it law. "There's a fair amount of enthusiasm for [the Compact]," says George Kuper, president of the Council of Great Lakes Industries, the Basin's leading corporate lobby. "It will be interesting to see how long that can be sustained, and how it translates into support in the legislatures. It's going to be tough. There's nothing easy about what has to happen."

As the document transitions from the negotiating room to the floor of the legislature, skeptics and special interests are bound to pick at it from all sides. No doubt, a key goal of the critics will be to stall, and stall, and stall—until the momentum wanes—with the hope that the Compact will slip into the graveyard of untested ideas. Mr. Kuper's organization is one that has already begun to question sections of the Compact—the infamous compromise he forged with the National Wildlife Federation notwithstanding. His concerns? That seemingly obscure language in the document could possibly leave regional industries vulnerable to harassing antibusiness litigation because the Compact allows citizen lawsuits to challenge water applications. And because the Compact is designed to allow regional water-management policy to evolve over time, Mr. Kuper worries that it could give the Compact Council unchecked power at some undetermined point in the future.

Mr. Kuper also says that despite the bottled-water exemption in the Compact, even water bottlers are worried that the document doesn't go far enough in protecting their industry. "We support the direction—the fundamental underpinnings of the document," he says. "But there are some things here that [legislators] have to pay attention to because they are going to have a long-term effect on the economy and the stability of sustainable development." But opponents of the bottled-water industry are unhappy with the Compact as well, arguing that the document doesn't go far enough in protecting the waters of the Great Lakes region. "This whole thing began with the Nova Group and the concern was about tankers of water going to Asia and then you end up with an agreement that allows the same or greater amounts of water to go anywhere in the world in bottles? It just doesn't make sense to me," says Dave Dempsey, Great Lakes policy advisor for Clean Water Action. "[That] is essentially conceding that the waters of the Great Lakes can be turned into a product . . . We may well look back on this Compact as having been the white flag that surrendered the Great Lakes."

Others argue that the Compact, as well as its companion International Agreement, lost their way once they veered from the Lochhead doctrine (see chapter 11). Yes, banning diversions was politically popular, these critics argue, but they find it particularly ironic that after all these years of research and negotiations, Basin water policy pretty much returned to where it started before the Nova proposal—a ban on diversions with limited exceptions. "What it did is come full circle. I'm extremely disappointed with what they've come up with," says Dennis Schornack, U.S. cochair of the International Joint Commission and a former aide to Michigan governor John Engler. "What the hell have we been doing for six years? We said we had a weak policy, a flawed policy, one that was risky because Congress could overturn it with a majority vote, and the courts could overturn it if a case ever came before them. So we spent six years grinding paper and giving speeches and in the end we're not going to change anything? Give me a break."

What recourse do these Compact critics have? Those that want to weaken the agreement are in a tight spot because the Compact represents the minimum standard that each state legislature must pass. But environmentalists who would like to see the rules strengthened have the option of lobbying legislators to pass water regulations that are even more restrictive than those stipulated in the Compact. There is nothing in the Compact language that prevents politicians from doing that, which is why lobbyists from both sides of the aisle are going to be following the Compact legislation intimately as it passes through various regional legislatures in coming years. Then the package needs to clear Congress.

Others have tried to remind the public that the Compact will not be the last chapter in Great Lakes water policy. It has been crafted in a way that, drafters hope, will allow it to evolve over time. "I don't think this is a perfect document," says Cameron Davis, who nevertheless supports the Compact's passage. "I think it's a strong first step to have all the states on the same page. That in itself is an achievement. And there are some good provisions to this. But we still have some work to do in the future to make sure that the document is truly protective of the Great Lakes." Several Compact negotiators agree. "Personally it's not everything I hoped it would be," says Cathy Curran Myers, deputy secretary of the Pennsylvania Office of Water Management. "[But] having this framework is a start, and even if it isn't perfect . . . the Compact will grow and evolve to fit the needs of the Basin."

Few if any observers see a return to the negotiating room as an option. "The reason it's taken so long, and been so difficult to get here, is the [talks] have been much more on the order of UN negotiations," says Andy Buchsbaum, head of the National Wildlife Federation's Great Lakes office. Mr. Buchsbaum worries that if the Compact fails to pass, the U.S. federal government will exert itself over Great Lakes water-management policy like never before. "The stakes are incredibly high. It's not just the diversions aspect, [but] whether the *region* will retain control over the *region's* water—which also happens to be 20 percent of the world's fresh surface water," he says. "And if we can't jointly agree on how to manage it ourselves, then we don't deserve that control." Others worry that if the momentum falters—particularly if many of the signatory governors leave office before the Compact passes—that the document runs the risk of sliding onto a slow track in regional legislatures that could lead to a fatal stall in the process. "Some of these compacts have dragged on for decades," warns Professor Tarlock. "It would only take one spoiler state to put a damper on things."

~

WHAT ARE THE COMPACT'S CHANCES? In the weeks and months that followed the release of the Annex Implementing Agreements, key water officials from all eight Great Lakes states were contacted for their prognostications. Time will tell how accurate their predictions will be. The results of that reporting—working from west to east in the Great Lakes Basin—were as follows.

Minnesota

After the Great Lakes Charter was signed in 1985, Minnesota officials promptly passed the legislation necessary to ensconce the Charter's principles in state statutes. Then they watched in frustration as several other Basin states (especially Michigan) moved at a slower pace. Kent Lokkesmoe, director of the water division at the Minnesota Department of Natural Resources, has been working at the DNR for thirty years and says his state learned its lesson from the Charter experience. This time around he plans to let other states go first. "My recommendation to our legislature is to wait for Michigan," he says. "We aren't going to be the first ones to pass it." Another reason for his lack of urgency: some of Minnesota's progressive water policies already exceed the Compact's statutory requirements.

Wisconsin

Even before the Annex Implementing Agreements were released in Milwaukee in December 2005, a bipartisan group of Wisconsin legislators pledged their support for the Compact's rapid approval. At a press conference following the Compact's release, Governor Doyle was equally bullish. "I think this is a very, very good thing for Wisconsin," he said, "and I would expect that it would find very, very strong support from both parties." Despite this bipartisan support, a Compact bill was not even introduced during Wisconsin's 2006 legislative session.

Illinois

Because Illinois is exempted from most of the Compact's key provisions—deferring instead to the U.S. Supreme Court decree regarding the Illinois diversion—that state is in a unique position when considering the document for adoption. "In Illinois' case it's a little strange in the sense that we would be asking our legislature to pass legislation that . . . sort of exempts us out of most of the operative requirements of the agreement," says Dan Injerd of the Illinois DNR. Because the Compact affects Illinois the least, presumably the state's legislature would be the least resistant to passage. As it happens, Illinois was the first Great Lake state to introduce Compact legislation, doing so in January 2006. Whether or not Illinois ends up being the first state to actually adopt the Compact, it will always be known as the first state out of the gate . . . and as the jurisdiction that has the least to lose by passing the Compact's implementing legislation.

Indiana

Many of Indiana's peers in the Great Lakes Basin are assuming the state will be one of the last to adopt the Compact—if it ever does so at all. Kyle Hupfer, director of the Indiana DNR sees the situation very differently. While he doesn't anticipate that Indiana will adopt the Compact first, he doesn't think the state will be last either. "I would put us in the middle," he says. By late 2005, discussions in Indiana had already begun on when it would be best for the state to introduce the Compact in the legislature. Mr. Hupfer said legislators will ultimately decide "whether '07 or '08 is better."

Michigan

Despite doubts from Minnesota—and perhaps other states and provinces—Michigan officials say they don't plan to be the last state to pass the Compact either. Ken DeBeaussaert, director of Michigan's Office of the Great Lakes, says that after the final draft of the Compact was released in Milwaukee, Michigan's congressional delegation began pressuring state officials to adopt the document as quickly as possible. Michigan passed a new comprehensive state water management law just months after the Compact was signed, which should make it less intimidating for state officials to consider the slightly more ambitious language found in the Compact. "It's important that we act on this sooner rather than later," Mr. DeBeaussaert says. "This is something that should not just be allowed to gather dust."

Ohio

Republican governor Bob Taft's family has been involved in Great Lakes water policy as long as any family in the Basin. His great grandfather, President William Howard Taft, signed the Boundary Waters Treaty of 1909 that created the International Joint Commission. Later, when President Taft was appointed chief justice of the Supreme Court, he authored the Court's primary decision in the first round of the Illinois diversion case.[1] In the modern era, Governor Taft was the only Great Lakes leader to attend the signing of the Great Lakes Charter Annex in 2001, as well as the release of the Annex Implementing Agreements in 2005. In an interview after the 2005 signing ceremony, he made it clear that he hoped to get the Compact passed in Ohio before he left office at the end of 2006. "I'm very optimistic that we can get this done," he said.

Pennsylvania

With some of the shortest Great Lakes shoreline of any state in the Basin, Pennsylvania has rarely taken the lead in setting Great Lakes water policy (the administration of former Republican governor Tom Ridge—who was raised in Erie, Pennsylvania—being a notable exception). But Pennsylvania is no stranger to water compacts and may hold the record in the Great Lakes region by being a party to five. Unlike many other Basin states, Pennsylvania's legislature is very familiar with water-management compacts, which is why members of the state's Compact negotiating team anticipate that Pennsylvania will adopt the necessary implementing legislation before most other Great Lakes states. "From the beginning the concept of a compact was near and dear to Pennsylvania," says Pam Bishop, assistant counsel at the state Department of Environmental Protection. Cathy Curran Myers, from the state Water Management Office says, "I think 2006 or 2007 is realistic and we're hopeful that that will happen."

New York

It's the most populous state in the Great Lakes region, but because most New Yorkers live in the Atlantic watershed they don't often perceive themselves as members of the Great Lakes community. Republican governor George Pataki is leaving office at the end of 2006. Will he get the Compact adopted in New York before he goes? The governor declined to be interviewed for this book, but a key staffer was optimistic about the Compact's chances—in part because of a fear that Governor Pataki's successor may not follow through. "I'm very hopeful that we'll be able to get the Compact passed [in 2006]," says Mike Elmendorf, director of intergovernmental affairs for Governor Pataki. "We definitely want to get this done while we're still here. Folks have put a lot of effort into it; the governor has been involved from the beginning. . . . Hopefully we'll be able to get it done."

Ontario and Québec

While Ontario and Québec are not parties to the Compact, they have signed the companion International Agreement, which commits them to implementing the same regulations on their side of the border. How much work do they have to do in order to meet the terms of the agreement? In Ontario, not much at all. As has been mentioned in prior chapters, Ontario already bans diversions from one major watershed to another, and the International Agreement virtually mirrors Ontario's statutes with regard to bottled water. The only rules that Ontario needs to buttress, officials say, are in the area of intra-Basin diversions—from one Great Lakes watershed to another. And Ontario officials predicted that those rule changes could be done relatively easily, without actually passing legislation.

As for Québec, when the International Agreement was adopted in December 2005, the province already banned diversions outside its borders. According to Louise Lapierre, counselor at Québec's Ministry of Sustainable Development, Environment and Parks, that language will need some "tweaking" to make it clear that water can't be diverted outside the Great Lakes–St. Lawrence Basin as well. Ms. Lapierre says that while her province has had solid regulations on groundwater withdrawals since the late 1990s, surface-water statutes have been weaker by comparison, and so those regulations will likely see the biggest changes when Québec adopts the International Agreement. "We have many steps to take before complete implementation," she says. "[But] we want to implement it as soon as possible"—a process that she said realistically could take "a few years."

~

UNTIL THE COMPACT IS PASSED, the Water Resources Development Act of 1986—with all its faults and vulnerabilities—will continue to serve as the key, binding anti-diversion backstop on the U.S. side of the border. But many legal experts agree with James Lochhead that WRDA is so flawed that it will only serve as a legal barrier to diversions until it is challenged in court, where most expect it to fall. There are some commerce clause concerns (see chapters 4 and 11), but most experts agree that WRDA is most vulnerable to allegations that it is arbitrary and capricious. Because the thin two-page statute contains no rules or standards by which governors are to judge diversion applicants, state officials have been forced to make up the rules as they go along. In addition, the law provides no means for due process; diversion applicants have no rights under the statute to plead their case—or even appeal—and that, many legal experts say, is the statute's greatest weakness. "What is the basis for a decision under WRDA?" asks one Great Lakes official rhetorically. "It's a fundamental right under the American jurisprudence system that people have an opportunity for due process and appeal and there's no guidelines or process for that under WRDA, which is where the concern lies."

In fact, the legal challenges to WRDA have already begun. During the summer of 2005 Nestlé Waters North America Inc., one of the largest water-bottling firms in the country, filed a federal water lawsuit in Michigan that challenged WRDA on a wide variety of grounds. Bottled water is controversial in much of the Great Lakes region, and Nestlé has been besieged by opponents for years. The controversy started back in the late 1990s, when Nestlé's Perrier division planned to mine spring water in a rural area of central Wisconsin. Citizen opposition—fueled by concerns that groundwater pumping would harm a local trout stream—eventually chased Nestlé out of the state. The company shifted its focus to Michigan, where Nestlé built a plant and began bottling spring water under the Ice Mountain brand name—only to be served with a citizen lawsuit in that state. The lawsuit argued Nestlé's groundwater pumping was negatively affecting area lakes, rivers, and springs. While key parts of that suit have been settled, the case continues to work its way through the courts.

While that Nestlé suit was underway, company opponents began arguing that sending bottled water out of state was actually a diversion, and they pressured Michigan governor Jennifer Granholm (elected in 2002) to ban bottled water sales outside the Great Lakes Basin. These critics argued that if Nova's proposal to ship drinking water by tanker was a diversion, so was the export of bottled water. In response, Nestlé—and others—argued that bottling and selling water was not a diversion but was rather a "consumptive use" that turned water into a product. They said that if states prevent the sale of bottled water they would have to include other water-based items in the ban as well, such as beer, soda—or even potatoes (because agricultural crops consume water too). But water-bottling opponents like Jim Olson, an environmental attorney who has been battling Nestlé for years, argue that water belongs in a special category all its own and should not be mixed together with value-added goods like fruit juice or a can of cherries. Society has long recognized water's special status, he argues, which is why there are so many laws devoted to it. "There is no potato law, or Coca-Cola law," he says, "[but] there is water law."

In May 2005, Governor Granholm took action in the debate. She ordered a temporary moratorium on new or expanded water-bottling operations in Michigan unless those operations certified that their product would only be sold to customers inside the Great Lakes Basin. In her directive the governor complained that Michigan law "lacks clarity" on how the state should regulate water bottlers, so she imposed the temporary moratorium until the legislature enacted more comprehensive water laws. "Despite on-going debate over whether or not bottled water for sale represents a diversion of

Great Lakes water," her directive said, "the Michigan legislature has failed to seriously debate and act on this issue. Based upon this and the recommendations of the Department of Environmental Quality, I have determined that the imposition of a moratorium on the permitting or approval of new or increased bottled water plants, processors, or operations is the appropriate course of action for state government."[2]

Nestlé responded to the moratorium by suing the governor in federal court. While Governor Granholm didn't invoke WRDA once in her directive—concentrating her authority on state statutes instead—Nestlé focused on WRDA heavily in its legal challenge. Of the twenty-two pages in the suit, ten were devoted to an attack on WRDA. Not surprisingly, among Nestlé's chief criticisms were the allegations that WRDA was arbitrary and that it violated Nestlé's right to due process. The suit immediately attracted the attention of water managers and environmentalists around the Basin, who wondered whether it was the long-anticipated beginning of WRDA's end. The concern, of course, was that if a federal judge agreed with Nestlé and found WRDA to be unconstitutional, the Great Lakes would become vulnerable to unregulated diversions.

The lawsuit created an odd dynamic in the Great Lakes region. While the governors were pursuing a compact to replace WRDA, Nestlé was pursuing a lawsuit to have WRDA thrown out. The question everyone wanted to know? Who would get there first? "If [the Compact] doesn't pass," said Andy Buchsbaum in late 2005, "then the backstop against diversions is essentially WRDA, and our protection against diversions is only as strong as WRDA is legally—and WRDA's being challenged now." Business leaders who sympathize with Nestlé's position worry that if WRDA falls before the Compact is enacted, regulatory chaos will ensue in the Great Lake Basin, creating an insecure climate for regional industry and capital investment. "[If] WRDA is determined to be unconstitutional, we'll be naked and the resource is there for the taking," says George Kuper at the Council of Great Lakes Industries. "That, to me, would be terrible."

Those concerns have been appeased however—at least for the

time being. When Michigan adopted its new water management law on February 28, 2006, the state set off a series of events that ultimately took pressure off of WRDA. Not only did Michigan's law finally follow through on commitments that the state made when it signed the Great Lakes Charter twenty years before, but it also permitted the export of bottled water as long as the water was in containers smaller than 5.7 gallons. So when Governor Granholm signed Michigan's water law, she also withdrew her ban on the export of bottled water. Nestlé, in turn, withdrew its federal lawsuit against the governor and suddenly the assault on WRDA evaporated.

Fine. But the point is that sooner or later *someone* is going to challenge WRDA—or so many Great Lakes water managers believe. If not Nestlé, then perhaps Waukesha. If not Waukesha, then some other spurned water applicant—unless, of course, the Compact is adopted before that day comes and WRDA becomes superfluous. But what if the Compact never makes it through all eight legislatures and Congress? If the Great Lake states can't prove themselves worthy stewards of this globally significant resource then the U.S. federal government is likely to step in and do it for them. "If they don't adopt it, then what's at stake is what's always been at stake," warns Kate Bartter, chief policy advisor to Ohio governor Bob Taft. "You will see action in Congress to do something in this area . . . we are more at risk for that than we've ever been if we don't go through with this. We'll lose control of the resource."

Others argue that the situation just isn't that dire. James Lochhead got it all wrong on WRDA, they say. While the federal law isn't model legislation, these observers argue that because Congress adopted WRDA and specifically delegated water-management authority to the Great Lakes states, the law is not as vulnerable as Mr. Lochhead and other Great Lakes legal experts have led regional decision makers to believe. "I'm guilty along with other people of trashing the Lochhead Report," confesses Professor Tarlock, who thinks WRDA should be able to withstand a legal challenge whether it be from Nestlé, Waukesha, or whomever. "Congress has said, 'This is for the Basin states to decide.'" Some environmental advocates don't find the arguments about WRDA's vulnerabilities to be all that convincing either. "I really strongly object to the whole Lochhead analysis because I think it was deeply flawed, but it seems to have been effective in suckering a lot of people into believing that WRDA is vulnerable," says Dave Dempsey at Clean Water Action. "The legal experts that I've talked to . . . really believe that Congress was well within its powers to delegate that decision-making authority to the states and that there is enough of a narrative history of WRDA, as amended in 2000, that it would stand up in court." The problem with that analysis, counters Cameron Davis at the Alliance for the Great Lakes, is that it ignores the political realities that lie behind the debate. "Nothing prevents Congress from changing its mind on WRDA," he warns. "What was given by Congress can also be taken away—especially if the Great Lakes states keep losing congressional seats."

~

WITH WRDA, or the Compact (or without either of them), the Great Lakes Basin has entered a period of accelerating water conflict that will change the face of regional water relations forever. "There's no doubt about it, there will be increasing water tension in the region and it's not going away," predicts Andy Buchsbaum. "The earlier we put in place good protective standards and good protective laws, the better, because if you wait for the water tensions to worsen before you try to address them, then it's much more difficult to put a rational system in place." While many experts see an era of increased conflict on the horizon, there is debate about how those water tensions will be borne out. "There are a lot of people who feel that once you fire one shot it will be all out war—it will be scorched earth," Professor Tarlock says. "I'm in the camp that believes there will be an endless series of small guerilla acts . . . There are going to be more conflicts. They just aren't going to be big ones."

Large or small, most of those battles will be fought in the courts. Many observers believe that if and when a minutiae-laden

Compact is passed, water law will be a budding new profession in the Great Lakes region as attorneys set upon the Compact to test its weaknesses. That's a scenario that regional water managers have been expecting from the beginning. "Everything gets refined by litigation," says Chuck Ledin, chief of the Great Lakes office at the Wisconsin DNR. "That's just the way the system works. So I'd say somewhere along the line it will happen [to the Compact]."

As regional leaders consider the future of water policy in the Great Lakes Basin, they need to remind themselves that they are heading off into the great unknown. Think back to the time of the Illinois diversion for a moment (chapter 5) and the mindset of city leaders more than a century ago. At the time the diversion was launched, its primary purpose was to solve Chicago's abysmal sewage-disposal problem. Local officials never imagined that, decades later, the Illinois diversion would be transformed into a water crutch for one of the world's greatest metropolitan areas. They never imagined that fears would one day arise that the waters of the Great Lakes might be siphoned off to the Ogallala or Las Vegas. They never imagined that communities like Pleasant Prairie, Lowell, Akron, or Waukesha would become the front lines in the Great Lakes water war. They never imagined that the negative effects of the Illinois diversion would be more than offset by a much larger pair of diversions on the north side of Lake Superior. They never imagined that half a world away in Central Asia, an inland sea would be ruined by ignorant water policies. And they certainly never imagined that a phenomenon like global warming would one day emerge to potentially transform the Great Lakes more than anything has since the last ice age.

This long view raises an obvious question for regional leaders in the twenty-first century: What's out there in the Great Lakes' water future that we are not imagining today? What unknown water crises—local, regional, national, international, or climatological—lie ahead? What undiscovered technologies might make large-scale, long-range water diversions more cost-effective—or even obsolete? Predicting the future is not an option. All one can do is implement the most comprehensive, adaptable, binding water-management system imaginable and hope it helps navigate the region through the insecurities of an unpredictable world. Regional leaders have spent years crafting such a mechanism. As imperfect as it may be, it's the best they have been able to put forth. That may, or may not, end up being enough. Regardless, something must be done in order to preserve one of the world's great treasures. The Great Lakes belong to everyone, and to no one. And as other experts have already pointed out, if the region can't figure out a way to protect and manage the waters of the Great Lakes Basin, someone else will step in to do it for them. Rightly so. The Great Lakes are far too precious to be left in the hands of the incompetent and incapable.

Time and again throughout Great Lakes history the people of the region have risen to ensure that the lakes are protected. During the heavy pollution years of the early and mid-1900s, the public roused late, but brought about historically significant changes in water policy that—generations later—have made the lakes a cleaner, healthier ecosystem (though more work definitely needs to be done). Once again the Great Lakes find themselves at a pivotal moment in history. This time policymakers are attempting to resolve an issue *before* it becomes a crisis. Will regional residents rise to the occasion and make sure that modern, binding water policies are implemented? Or will they turn their attention elsewhere?

On December 13, 2005, when the Annex Implementing Agreements were released in Milwaukee, and regional officials gathered at a press conference afterward, the most eloquent remarks came from Premier Dalton McGuinty of Ontario. In essence, he was saying that the governors and premiers had done the best they could to create a plan for protecting the waters of the Great Lakes Basin. Now it was up to the people of the region to help complete the task. Speaking to the press corps that day, Premier McGuinty said, "You have raised legitimate questions about the what-ifs . . . [but] you know there's a way that we can all take out a little insurance against those things, and that is quite simply to enlist the people to our cause," he said. "If the forty-three million who are the immediate beneficiaries of the Great Lakes waters don't understand how important it is for us to assume our responsibility—if we can't protect this water, not only for ourselves but for future genera-tions—who else will? So it's now up to all of us [to] drive this in our own respective jurisdictions and make it a reality . . . If we don't protect this water, we're going to compromise our quality of life, and we're going to compromise our ability to generate prosperity. That's what it's all about . . . It's [up to] the forty-three million. It's their water. It's their future. It's their quality of life that is at stake here . . . It's a matter of the forty-three million people saying, 'This is important to us, we want it done, and we won't suffer any opposition.'"

Times change. Circumstances evolve. Compact or not, the job of protecting and managing the Great lakes will never be complete—it will always be a work in progress. And what about failure? What if adequate protections for the lakes do not evolve? Who will be the winners and losers then? As of this writing the winners are impossible to predict. The losers, however, are not. There are five of them, and they have been around for ten thousand years. Who among us wants to be associated with their demise?

Epilogue

WHAT ABOUT WATER conservation? Until recently, the Great Lakes region rarely emphasized conserving water—mainly because it never had too. The Basin's world-renowned water abundance created a lack of appreciation for the global preciousness of potable freshwater, leading to a regional culture of misuse and neglect. Water utilities in the Basin have traditionally looked at conservation as a tool to combat drought, rather than as a standard operating procedure.[1] For years the City of Chicago was well known for charging residential customers a flat rate for water, no matter how much they used. Numerous Great Lakes industries were attracted to the Basin because of the region's water abundance, and many made a habit of using that water without regard to waste. Residential customers were equally dismissive of the need to conserve water.

In the Great Lakes region that regressive view of water is changing, and the attitude adjustment is part of an international trend. Citizens the world over are showing a greater appreciation for the global scarcity of clean, reliable drinking water—call it a "water awakening." By declaring 2003 the International Year of Freshwater, the United Nations globalized the movement toward greater water awareness and conservation. And in North America—one of the most wasteful water regions on the planet—that water awakening is long overdue.

Anecdotal signs of the awakening abound. Every year large numbers of North Americans flock to water conferences as the continent's water intelligentsia meet to share strategies on how to prevent future crises. Between 1995 and 2000 per capita water use in the United States *declined* by 4 percent, while the economy and the population grew.[2] Industries in the Great Lakes region and elsewhere are discovering that water conservation and recycling are good for the environment and the bottom line. Numerous magazine cover stories, front-page news articles, and books are being written about water, or the lack of it. And a simple Internet search for "water conservation" turns up a seemingly endless list of outstanding suggestions for average citizens to follow. On many college campuses bottled water has fallen out of vogue—in a statement of sustainability students are using trendy refillable backpacking water bottles instead. The City of Chicago, once a symbol of water waste, has embarked on an ambitious conservation program, including mandatory water meters on residential properties. Even Las Vegas—everyone's favorite water whipping boy—now offers $1-per-square-foot rebates to residents who replace grass with native desert plants or other water-friendly landscaping.[3]

There is a growing appreciation, in the Great Lakes and elsewhere, that communities need to find a way to live within the water budgets of their drainage basins. Perhaps green lawns and opulent golf courses don't belong in places that receive less than twelve inches of rainfall per year. "I think that the 'awakening' has already started," says Cameron Davis, executive director at the Alliance for the Great Lakes in Chicago. "We have to live within our means . . . There's no new magic [water] supply that's miraculously going to appear once we run out." Others argue that conservation—squeezing more mileage out of the water we have—is the only new water-supply option that's left. "When we needed more water in the past, we built a dam, dug a canal, or drilled a well. With some exceptions, these options are no longer viable due to a paucity of sites, dwindling supplies, escalating costs, and environmental objections," writes Robert Glennon, a law professor at the University of Arizona and an expert on groundwater. "Instead, we are entering an era in which demand for new water will be satisfied by reallocating and conserving existing sources."[4]

It is particularly important that this conservation ethic take hold in the Great Lakes region. The Basin will not remain credible in the eyes of the world if it denies water to outsiders and then continues to waste it with reckless abandon at home. That is precisely why the Annex Implementing Agreements emphasized the importance of water conservation much more than the prior regional water accords. There is a growing realization that living amid water wealth is not a license for waste.

The time has come for the Great Lakes region to become a global leader in water conservation. In that regard it has a lot to learn from the more arid regions of the continent that were forced to embark on serious water restrictions decades ago. It's time for the people of the Basin to lead by example and stop taking the region's most important economic and ecological resource for granted. Conserving water because they want to—not because they have to—is the only way that the Great Lakes states and provinces can credibly claim their mantle as stewards of one of the most abundant freshwater ecosystems on the face of the earth.

www.greatlakeswaterwars.com

W HICH STATE WILL BE THE FIRST to pass the Compact? Which will be the last? For details and the latest news regarding the Great Lakes Water Resources Compact, the International Agreement, or other information regarding the Great Lakes water diversion issue, logon to www.greatlakeswaterwars.com. This website will serve as a key source of information about the Compact as the accord moves through the various Great Lakes legislatures on its way toward Congress. In addition, the website features numerous photos, graphics, and other primary documents referenced in this book, including the complete texts of the 1909 Boundary Waters Treaty, the Great Lakes Charter of 1985 and the Water Resources Development Act of 1986. The site also includes copies of the Great Lakes Charter Annex of 2001, drafts of the Compact and International Agreement as they transitioned through the public hearing process, as well as the final versions of the Annex Implementing Agreements that were released in Milwaukee on December 13, 2005.

Notes

Chapter 1. To Have and Have Not

1. Shawn Tully, "Water, Water Everywhere," *Fortune*, May 15, 2000.

2. Fen Montaigne, "Water Pressure," *National Geographic*, September 2002, 9.

3. Peter Gleick, *The World's Water: 2004–2005* (Washington, DC: Island Press, 2004), 13.

4. For these water use and populations statistics, see University of Wisconsin Aquatic Sciences Center, *Liquid Assets: Wisconsin's Water Wealth* (Madison: University of Wisconsin Aquatic Sciences Center, 2003), 26.

5. United Nations World Water Assessment Programme, "Executive Summary," of *1st UN World Water Development Report: Water for People, Water for Life* (Paris: UNESCO and Berghahn Books, 2003), 4.

6. Throughout, quotations that appear without text or endnote citations are from interviews conducted by the author.

7. Gleick, *The World's Water: 2004–2005*, 236–52.

8. Interview with Sandra Postel, director, Global Water Policy Project, February 2005.

9. "Update on China's South-North Water Transfer Project," U.S. Embassy, Beijing, June 2003, http://www.usembassy-china.org.cn/sandt/ptr/SNWT-East-Route-prt.htm

10. Mark Clayton, "Forget OPEC, the next cartel may export drinking water," *Christian Science Monitor*, December 30, 2004.

11. John Driscoll, "More caution flags hoisted on Mad River bag proposal," *Eureka (CA) Times-Standard*, January 18, 2003.

12. Gleick, *The World's Water: 2004–2005*, 17.

13. International Joint Commission (IJC), *Protection of the Waters of the Great Lakes: Final Report to the Governments of Canada and the United States* (February 22, 2000), 15.

14. Gleick, *The World's Water: 2004–2005*, 18.

15. Juan Forero, "Latin America fails to deliver on basic needs," *The New York Times*, February 22, 2005.

277

16. United Water is a subsidiary of the French conglomerate Suez.

17. Douglas Jehl, "As cities move to privatize water, Atlanta steps back," *The New York Times*, February 10, 2003.

18. John Cramer, "A chronology of the Klamath Basin water conflict," *The* [Bend, OR] *Bulletin*, May 14, 2001.

19. Dean Murphy, "Pact in West will send farms' water to cities," *The New York Times*, October 17, 2003.

20. Interview and field visit with Michael Carpenter, research hydrologist, U.S. Geological Survey, Tucson, AZ, April 2004.

21. Paul Krza, "Texas water case is 'takings' on steroids; farmers want $500 million in damages from Mexico, but critics say the water wasn't theirs in the first place," *High Country News*, February 21, 2005.

22. Stacy Shelton, "Water: States scramble to reach accord on usage," *The Atlanta Journal-Constitution*, July 25, 2004.

23. Linda Greenhouse, "Justices to take up interstate water fight," *The New York Times*, April 29, 2003.

24. Robert Glennon, *Water Follies: Groundwater Pumping and the Fate of America's Fresh Waters* (Washington, DC: Island Press, 2002), 99–111.

25. Robert Glennon, "Water Scarcity, Marketing, and Privatization," *Texas Law Review* 83, no. 7 (June 2005): 1873.

26. Montaigne, "Water Pressure," 26.

27. Report by Peter Jennings in "Las Vegas Shows Strains of Population Boom, Learning Lessons from One of the Country's Fastest-Growing Cities," *ABC World News Tonight*, November 30, 2004. Information about the Las Vegas boom is also from this ABC News report.

28. Ibid.

29. Marc Reisner, *Cadillac Desert: The American West and Its Disappearing Water* (New York: Viking Press, 1986), 121.

30. IJC, *Protection of the Waters of the Great Lakes*, 16.

31. "Great Lakes Factsheet No. 1," in *The Great Lakes: An Environmental Atlas and Resource Book*, 3rd ed., ed. Kent Fuller and Harvey Sheer (Chicago and Toronto: U.S. Environmental Protection Agency Great Lakes National Program Office and the Government of Canada, 1995), http://www.epa.gov/glnpo/atlas/gl-fact1.html.

32. IJC, *Protection of the Waters of the Great Lakes*, 6, 43.

33. Kent Fuller and Harvey Sheer, eds., *The Great Lakes: An Environmental Atlas and Resource Book*, 3rd ed. (Chicago and Toronto:

U.S. Environmental Protection Agency Great Lakes National Program Office and the Government of Canada, 1995), 3.

34. Great Lakes statistics are from ibid., 3, 4.

35. IJC, *Protection of the Waters of the Great Lakes*, 10.

Chapter 2. The Aral Experiment

1. Interview with Professor Nikolay Aladin, Laboratory of Brackish Water Hydrobiology, Zoological Institute, Russian Academy of Sciences, September 2004.

2. Clean Wisconsin, "Clean Wisconsin works with Council of Great Lakes Governors to develop comprehensive water management system for Great Lakes Basin," press release, June 1, 2004.

3. Médecins Sans Frontières, *Karakalpakstan: A Population in Danger* (Tashkent, Uzbekistan, 2002), 3.

4. Quoted in ibid., 6.

5. Ibid., 14.

6. Quoted in John Flesher, "Gingrich says Michigan regulators out of touch," Associated Press, September 17, 2005.

Chapter 3. Rising Temperatures, Falling Water?

1. Peter J. Sousounis and Jeanne M. Bisanz, eds., *Preparing for a Changing Climate: The Potential Consequences of Climate Variability and Change, Great Lakes Overview*, a report for the U.S. Global Change Research Program (Ann Arbor, MI: Great Lakes Regional Assessment Group, October 2000), 2.

2. Intergovernmental Panel on Climate Change (IPCC), "Summary for Policymakers," in *Climate Change 2001: Synthesis Report* (2001), 8. 5. The collection of reports that make up the 2001 climate-change assessment is known as the Third Assessment Report.

3. Sousounis and Bisanz, *Preparing for a Changing Climate*, 2.

4. George Kling et al., *Confronting Climate Change in the Great Lakes Region: Impacts on Our Communities and Ecosystems* (Union of Concerned Scientists and the Ecological Society of America, April 2003), 24.

5. For background on the IPCC, see the organization's Web site, especially the "About IPCC" page, http://www.IPCC.ch/about/about. htm.

6. Elizabeth Kolbert, "The Climate of Man—I," *The New Yorker*, April 25, 2005 (accessed online May 2005).

7. "2005 Warmest Year in Over a Century, NASA, January 24,

2006, http://www.nasa.gov/vision/earth/environment/2005_warmest.html.

8. IPCC, "Summary for Policymakers," 4, 5.

9. Ibid., 6, 8.

10. Ibid., 9, 12.

11. Sousounis and Bisanz, *Preparing for a Changing Climate*, 2, 30.

12. Ibid., 55–62.

13. Ibid., 3 (quote), 65.

14. Ibid., 4.

15. Ibid., 31.

16. Ibid., 30.

17. Ibid., 33.

18. Ibid., 17.

19. International Joint Commission (IJC), *Protection of the Waters of the Great Lakes, Final Report to the Governments of Canada and the United States* (February 22, 2000), 24.

20. Sousounis and Bisanz, *Preparing for a Changing Climate*, 2, 3, 4, 24.

21. The UCS report's executive summary was updated in late 2005 and can be found at Union of Concerned Scientists, http://www.ucsusa.org/assets/documents/global_warming/GL-Exec-Summary-Update-05-doc.pdf.

22. Kling et al., *Confronting Climate Change in the Great Lakes Region*, 1.

23. Ibid., 24.

24. Ibid., 2, 4.

25. Ibid., 18.

26. Ibid., 18.

27. Ibid., 19.

28. More information on a prior example of abrupt climate change can be found by conducting an Internet search for the "Younger Dryas period."

29. This Frank Quinn is not the same person as the Canadian Frank Quinn, formerly of Environment Canada, in chapter 6.

30. Kling et al., *Confronting Climate Change in the Great Lakes Region*, 14.

31. Ibid., 23.

32. Ibid., 34.

33. IJC, *Protection of the Waters of the Great Lakes*, 25, 22.

34. The channel was dredged again in 1930 and 1962, resulting in a maximum depth in dredged areas of thirty feet.

35. IJC, *Protection of the Waters of the Great Lakes*, 18. By comparison, the Lake Michigan diversion at Chicago (see chapter 5)—the largest diversion of water outside the Basin—dropped Lakes Michigan and Huron by a mere 2.5 inches. See International Joint Commission (IJC), *Great Lakes Diversions and Consumptive Uses* (January 1985), 15.

36. Georgian Bay Association. "Large permanent drop discovered in Huron and Michigan lake levels," press release, January 24, 2005.

37. Georgian Bay Association, "Large permanent drop discovered."

38. U.S. Army Corps of Engineers, "Corps responds to recent lake level study," press release, February 4, 2005.

Chapter 4. Aversion to Diversion

1. Marc Reisner, *Cadillac Desert: The American West and Its Disappearing Water* (New York: Viking, 1986), 487–88.

2. Ralph M. Parsons Co., *North American Water and Power Alliance: NAWAPA*, undated promotional video circa early 1960s.

3. Ibid. An acre foot equals 325,851 gallons.

4. Reisner, *Cadillac Desert*, 488.

5. Ibid., 487. Parsons video.

6. "A Question of Birthright," *Time*, October 1, 1965, Parsons video.

7. Reisner, *Cadillac Desert*, 489.

8. Interview with Tom Kierans, creator of the GRAND Canal proposal, March 2005.

9. The Dutch did successfully complete a project similar to the GRAND canal on the IJsselmeer, which Kierans holds up as a model.

10. Reisner, *Cadillac Desert*, 495.

11. Robert Bourassa, *Power from the North*, 146–55.

12. "The Erie Canal: A Brief History," New York State Canal System, http://www.canals.state.ny.us/cculture/history/index.html.

13. One map of the pipeline was printed on the cover of *The Proposed Powder River–Midwest Coal Slurry Pipeline*, transcript of an October 27, 1982, meeting between William Westhoff, Powder River Pipeline Inc., and representatives of Wisconsin state agencies (Wisconsin Coastal Management Program, February 1983). The second map was printed in the *Oil & Gas Journal*, January 19, 1981, 41.

14. *Proposed Powder River–Midwest Coal Slurry Pipeline*, 1, 2, 6.

15. Ibid., 6, 7.

16. Ibid., 7.

17. Wisconsin Coastal Management Council, *The Interbasin Transfer of Water . . . The Great Lakes Connection* (May 1982), 53.

18. U.S. Army Corps of Engineers, *Six-State High Plains Ogallala Aquifer Regional Resources Study, Summary Report* (1982), 3.

19. Ibid., 1.

20. Ibid., 4.

21. Ibid., 20.

22. Ibid., 61, 90–94.

23. Interview with Peter Gleick, president, Pacific Institute, May 2005.

24. Interestingly, the Corps' findings on cost mirrored those of a similar study conducted by the U.S. Bureau of Reclamation in 1973. The West Texas and Eastern New Mexico Import Project envisioned diverting water from the Mississippi River via a canal stretching from Louisiana to the High Plains. But after studying the idea, the Bureau declared the plan "economically infeasible." See "Not a Drop to Drink," *The Wisconsin Magazine*, Wisconsin Educational Television Network, March 1, 1985.

25. *Sporhase v. Nebraska*, 458 U.S. 941 (1982).

26. *Final Report and Recommendations: Great Lakes Governors Task Force on Water Diversions and Great Lakes Institutions; A Report to the Governors and Premiers of the Great Lakes States and Provinces Prepared at the Request of the Council of Great Lakes Governors* (January 1985), 15.

27. Ibid., 4.

28. The idea of excluding Lake Michigan from the Boundary Waters Treaty seems particularly outdated given that scientists have pointed out that, hydrologically speaking, lakes Michigan and Huron are considered to be one lake, thanks to their massive connecting channel at the Straits of Mackinac.

29. When the council was originally formed in January 1982 it was called the Council of North Central Governors Inc. and only included the states of Wisconsin, Minnesota, and Michigan. Eventually all eight Great Lakes governors joined the organization and its name was changed to the Council of Great Lakes Governors in March 1984.

30. Information in this paragraph on the council and its resolutions is from *Water Diversion and Great Lakes Institutions*, 4, 5.

31. "The public trust doctrine is a common-law doctrine. The essence of the doctrine is the legal right of the public to use certain

lands and waters. The right may be concurrent with private ownership. The legal interest of the public isn't absolute; it's determined by a balancing of interests," University of Toledo College of Law website. For more information, see http://www.utlaw.edu.

32. Council of Great Lakes Governors, *The Great Lakes Charter* (February 11, 1985), 1–6. All quotations from the Charter are from this source.

33. Pennsylvania and Indiana were the only states not to send a governor to the Charter's signing ceremony, although Indiana sent an official to sign on the governor's behalf. Neither provincial premier was in attendance, but representatives did serve as stand-ins.

34. Quoted in Paul MacClennan, "State to weigh using Great Lakes to ease N.Y. city water crisis," *The Buffalo News*, September 12, 1985.

35. Paul MacClennon, *The Buffalo News*, September 8, 1985.

Chapter 5. Reversing a River

1. Donald L. Miller, *City of the Century: The Epic of Chicago and the Making of America* (New York: Simon and Schuster, 1996), 218–19 (the quote is from p. 219).

2. Ibid., 123.

3. Erik Larson, *The Devil in the White City: Murder, Magic and Madness at the Fair That Changed America* (New York: Vintage Books, 2004), 138, 175.

4. A long-held Chicago legend says that thousands of city residents died in a cholera and typhoid epidemic after a massive rainstorm in 1885. Though many people, including public officials, regularly repeat the story, Libby Hill debunked the myth with her well-researched book, *The Chicago River: A Natural and Unnatural History* (Chicago: Lake Claremont Press, 2000). See p. 117.

5. Hill, *Chicago River*, 119.

6. Miller, *City of the Century*, 130–31.

7. Hill, *Chicago River*, 122–127.

8. Miller, *City of the Century*, 131.

9. See Hill, *Chicago River*, 128–130.

10. Quoted in Stanley A. Chagnon, ed. *The Lake Michigan Diversion at Chicago and Urban Drought: Past, Present and Future Regional Impacts and Responses to Global Climate Change*, final report to the Great Lakes Environmental Research Laboratory (Ann Arbor, MI, November 1994), 21.

11. Hill, *Chicago River*, 132. Although the canal was capable of

handling up to 10,000 cubic feet of water per second, the diversion flowed at less than half that rate during the early years because of a concern that the current would be too strong. Chagnon, *Lake Michigan Diversion at Chicago*, diversion history timeline, 3.

12. Hill, *Chicago River*, 132. Chagnon, Lake Michigan Diversion at Chicago, timeline, p. 3.

13. Quoted in Chagnon, *Lake Michigan Diversion at Chicago*, 22.

14. Hill, *Chicago River*, 139, 184.

15. Unless otherwise cited, information about the diversion's flows and the associated history of suits and countersuits is from Stanley Chagnon's *Lake Michigan Diversion at Chicago*. See especially pp. 23, 26, 28, 30–31 and the diversion history timeline toward the end of the report.

16. Chagnon, *Lake Michigan Diversion at Chicago*, 29.

17. Ibid., 31. Research would later show that by the late 1970s water levels in deep aquifer wells in northeastern Illinois had plummeted by a jaw-dropping nine hundred feet, revealing one of the worst examples of groundwater overuse in the nation. See International Joint Commission (IJC), *"Protection of the Waters of the Great Lakes: Final Report to the Governments of Canada and the United States,"* (February 22, 2000), 27.

18. Just as in the 1922 lawsuit charging illegal expansion of the Illinois diversion, Wisconsin was later joined in this 1957–1958 suit by other Great Lakes states.

19. The Corps' study was titled, *Increased Lake Michigan Diversion at Chicago: Demonstration and Study Program Information Report to the Congress*, and helped influence the adoption of the Great Lakes Charter, discussed in chapter 4. The study and its initial ramifications are covered in "Not a Drop to Drink," *The Wisconsin Magazine*, Wisconsin Educational Television Network, March 1, 1985.

20. Douglas Turner, "Battle looms as Reagan gets plea to OK diversion of lakes water," *Buffalo News*, July 9, 1988.

21. International Joint Commission (IJC), *Great Lakes Diversions and Consumptive Uses* (January 1985), 15.

22. The Army Corps of Engineers is responsible for monitoring the diversion, but it can take years for the agency to produce certified results, which helps explain why it took other states so long to discover that Illinois was so far out of compliance.

23. Office of Governor Rod Blagojevich, "Governor Blagojevich orders statewide water supply study," press release, January 9, 2006.

24. Gary Washburn and Rudolph Bush, "Drink up, city, but meter will be running; Chicago will measure all water use, drop flat fee charge," *Chicago Tribune*, April 9, 2003.

25. Rebecca Lameka, *Regional Case Studies: Best Practices for Water Conservation in the Great Lakes–St. Lawrence Region* (Great Lakes Commission, June 18, 2004), 13.

26. David Pementel et al., "Environmental and Economic costs of Nonindigenous Species in the United States." *BioScience*, (January 2000). 50.

27. Gregory M. Ruiz et al., "Global Invasions of Marine and Estuarine Habitats by Non-Indigenous Species," *American Zoologist*, (1997) vol. 37, no. 6, 626.

Chapter 6. Long Lac and Ogoki

1. Unless otherwise cited, specifications of the Waboose Dam and the associated Ogoki Reservoir are from Keith Charles Bridger, "The Ogoki River Diversion: Reservoir, Downstream, Diversion Channel and Receiving Water-Body Effects" (master's thesis, University of Waterloo, Ontario, 1978), especially pp. 11, 12. The crest length on Hoover Dam is 1,244 feet according to the U.S. Bureau of Reclamation; see http://www.usbr.gov/lc/region/pao/hoover.html.

2. According to the International Joint Commission, the largest diversion in the Great Lakes Basin is at the Welland Canal, which bypasses Niagara Falls. At 9,200 cfs it greatly exceeds the Ogoki diversion in size. However, because the Welland Canal transfers water from one Great Lake to another, it is considered an *intra-Basin* diversion within the Great Lakes watershed. The Long Lac and Ogoki diversions are *inter-Basin* water transfers, withdrawing water from the Albany River drainage basin in the Hudson Bay watershed and sending it to the Great Lakes.

3. According to officials at Ontario Power Generation, which owns and operates the Long Lac diversion, "Long Lake" is the name of the diversion (and the lake), while "Longlac" (one word) is the name of the town nearest the diversion. However, the diplomatic notes exchanged between the United States and Canada refer to the diversion as "Long Lac." All official references by the International Joint Commission also use the name "Long Lac." Consequently Long Lake and Long Lac are used interchangeably by officials when referring to this diversion. The names are used interchangeably in this chapter as well.

4. International Joint Commission (IJC), *Protection of the Waters of*

the *Great Lakes: Final Report to the Governments of Canada and the United States* (February 22, 2000), 12.

5. The history of the Long Lac diversion is told in Simon Edward Peet, "The Long Lake Diversion: An Environmental Evaluation" (master's thesis, University of Waterloo, Ontario, 1978). Unless otherwise cited, details about the diversion's impetus, negotiations surrounding implementation, hydro rights, and construction logistics are from this source, especially pp. 18, 22, 24–29.

6. This Frank Quinn is not the same person as the American Frank Quinn, formerly of the U.S. National Oceanic and Atmospheric Administration, in chapter 3.

7. Ogoki construction details, unless otherwise noted, are from Bridger, *Ogoki River Diversion*, 11. As subsequent diplomatic notes would make clear, the Canadians decided to build a new generating plant on the Welland Canal to capture the Long Lac and Ogoki waters, rather than capturing the waters at Niagara Falls. See Glenys Biggar, *Ontario Hydro's History and Description of Hydro-Electric Generating Stations* (Ontario Hydro, 1991), 84. Also see International Joint Commission (IJC) Great Lakes Diversions and Consumptive uses (January 1985) 78.

8. According to Chief Veronica Waboose of Long Lake No. 58 First Nation, "Waboose" is the local Ojibwa term for "rapids." Interview with Chief Waboose, October 2005.

9. Quoted in IJC, *Great Lakes Diversions*, 77.

10. Ibid., 78. For more information on the Niagara Treaty see the International Joint Commission's International Niagara Board of Control Web site, http://www.ijc.org/conseil_board/niagara/en/niagara_home_accueil.htm.

11. International Joint Commission, International Lake Superior Board of Control, minutes of the September 22, 2004 meeting, http://www.ijc.org/php/publications/html/September222004-e.htm.

12. Canada agreed to have the diversions "reduced or stopped" in 1952 and 1973. See IJC, *Great Lakes Diversions*, 13.

13. Mr. Pentland is referring to the IJC study, *Great Lakes Diversions*. See p. 23.

14. J. C. [Chad] Day and Frank Quinn, *Water Diversion and Export: Learning from Canadian Experience* (Waterloo, ON: University of Waterloo Press, 1992), 78.

15. See Bridger, *Ogoki River Diversion*, 136.

16. See Peet, *Long Lake Diversion*, 58.

Chapter 7. Pleasing Pleasant Prairie

1. Copies of all of the letters quoted from or referred to in this chapter were provided upon request by the agencies or people involved.

2. Letter from J. D. Snyder, director, Michigan's Office of the Great Lakes, to Bruce Baker, Wisconsin Department of Natural Resources, August 10, 1989.

3. Letter from J. D. Snyder, director, Michigan's Office of the Great Lakes, to Bruce Baker, Wisconsin Department of Natural Resources, September 7, 1989.

4. Memorandum from consultant George Loomis to Michael Pollocoff, Pleasant Prairie village administrator, September 29, 1989.

5. Letter from Bruce Baker, Wisconsin Department of Natural Resources, to J. D. Snyder, director, Michigan's Office of the Great Lakes, October 9, 1989.

6. Letter from David Hales, director, Michigan Department of Natural Resources, to Wisconsin governor Tommy Thompson, December 12, 1989.

Chapter 8. Sacrificing Lowell

1. Kevin Voigt, "The larvae are back in Lowell's water," *Northwest Indiana Times*, September 14, 1990.

2. Letter from U.S. Environmental Protection Agency, Region 5, to Lowell Water Department, December 30, 1987, provided upon request by the EPA.

3. Ibid.

4. Melanie Csepiga, "Water woes put Lowell in scramble," *Northwest Indiana Times*, March 15, 1990.

5. Melanie Csepiga, "Lowell opts for Lake Michigan water," *Northwest Indiana Times*, April 3, 1990.

6. Ibid.

7. Melanie Csepiga, "Michigan governor may leave Lowell thirsting for water," *Northwest Indiana Times*, April 26, 1991.

8. All information about this initial meeting concerning Lowell's diversion request is from State of New York, Department of Environmental Conservation, Hearing Report and Interviews. January 10, 1992. Appendix B, *Summary, June 7, 1991, Indiana Consultation Meeting Regarding the Lowell Water Diversion Project*, especially pp. B-35–B-38.

9. Letter from Patrick R. Ralston, director, Indiana Department of Natural Resources, to Thomas C. Jorling, commissioner, New York

Department of Environmental Conservation, March 4, 1992, provided by John Hughes, Lowell's attorney.

10. Letter from Michigan governor John Engler to Indiana governor Evan Bayh, May 8, 1992, provided by John Hughes, Lowell's attorney, and other sources.

11. Ibid.

12. "Lowell optimistic about chances for lake water, officials believe town should qualify under new guidelines for tapping into Great Lakes," *Northwest Indiana Times*, June 19, 2001.

Chapter 9. Tapping Mud Creek

1. The two volumes of research were *The Saginaw Bay, Michigan Subirrigation/Drainage Project: 1987–1988*, and *The Saginaw Bay, Michigan Subirrigation/Drainage Project: 1989–1990*. Both were are edited by Frank M. D'Itri and Jody A. Kubitz and were published by the Institute of Water Research at Michigan State University.

2. Williams, Ominski and Associates, and Fishbeck, Thompson, Carr and Huber Inc., *Public Information Document, Great Lakes Water Use Proposal, Mud Creek Irrigation District*, presented to the Office of the Governor, State of Michigan, the Natural Resources Commission, and the Michigan Department of Natural Resources (January 1993).

3. International Joint Commission (IJC), *Protection of the Waters of the Great Lakes: Final Report to the Governments of Canada and the United States*, (February 22, 2000). 10.

4. Williams, Ominski and Associates, and Fishbeck, Thompson, Carr, and Huber, Inc., *Public Information Document, Great Lakes Water Use Proposal, Mud Creek Irrigation District*, 26.

5. Letters requesting or supporting a consultation were received from governors in Illinois, Pennsylvania, Minnesota, Ohio, and New York and from the premier of Ontario.

6. The description of the April 28, 1993, Mud Creek consultative hearing is from handwritten notes taken by David Hamilton, then chief of the Water Management Division at the Michigan Department of Natural Resources, and "Charter Consultations: Mud Creek Irrigation District—Summary of Key Issues," both of which are on file at the Michigan Department of Environmental Quality. Several meeting attendees were interviewed as well.

7. As has been pointed out in prior chapters, consumptive use can result in a loss of water to the system through evaporation or

integration into a product. Such losses would occur in Mud Creek, but the water lost would be much less than if Mud Creek were a diversion.

8. Draft of letter from Michigan governor John Engler to the governors of Ohio, Wisconsin, Indiana, Pennsylvania, New York, Minnesota, and the premiers of Ontario and Québec, May 7, 1993, on file at Michigan Department of Environmental Quality.

9. The response letters to Governor Engler's May 7, 1993, letters are all on file at the Michigan Department of Environmental Quality.

10. Michigan Department of Natural Resources, interoffice communication, from G. Tracy Mehan, director, Michigan's Office of the Great Lakes, to Larry DeVuyst, chairman, Natural Resources Commission, June 9, 1993.

11. State of Michigan Irrigation Districts Act, Act No. 205, Public Policy Acts of 1967, as amended by Act No. 221, Public Acts of 1978.

12. David Poulson, "Word about water diversion bottled up Engler staff," *Grand Rapids Press*, July 16, 1993; "Huron irrigation risks too much," *Bay City Times*, July 22, 1993; and Peter Luke, "Irrigation OK hurts Engler," *Kalamazoo Gazette*, July 18, 1993.

13. E-mail response to author from David Hamilton, Michigan Department of Environmental Quality, December 2, 2005.

Chapter 10. Akron Gets the Nod

1. *Portage County Board of Commissioners, et al., v. City of Akron, et al.*, Case No. 98 CV00325, "Akron's Motion for Summary Judgment as to Akron's Rights Under the 1911 Grant" (Portage County [Ohio] Court of Common Pleas, January 31, 2000), 4–5. Much of the information in this chapter concerning Akron's early 1900s water problems and the resulting legislation comes from filings in this court case.

2. City of Akron, *Report of the Board of Control Transmitting to the City Council the Report of the Engineers on an Improved Water Supply for the City of Akron, Ohio, 1911* (August 12, 1911), 14.

3. Ibid., 5–12.

4. Ohio House Bill No. 357, passed May 17, 1911, 1, 2.

5. Letter from David Crandell, manager, Akron Public Utilities Bureau, to Frances Buchholzer, director, Ohio DNR, March 25, 1992, provided upon request by the Ohio DNR Division of Water.

6. Black and Veatch and Public Sector Consultants, *A Report on the Proposed Expansion of the City of Akron Water System*, prepared for the City of Akron (July 1996).

7. City of Akron. "Preserving the Great Lakes through regional cooperation." A proposal by the City of Akron, Ohio (circa 1996).

8. Letter from Governor George Voinovich to all eight Great Lakes governors, September 30, 1996, provided upon request by the Division of Water at the Ohio Department of Natural Resources.

9. Letter from Michele Willis, chief, Division of Water at the Ohio Department of Natural Resources, to Mayor Donald Plusquellic, City of Akron, April 24, 1998.

10. Patrick O'Donnell, "Suit asks court to stop sale of water," [Cleveland] *Plain Dealer*, April 18, 1998.

11. Patrick O'Donnell, "Akron sued over control of river's flow," [Cleveland] *Plain Dealer*, May 11, 1998.

12. Gregory Korte, "1911 deed rejected in court; Akron loses first round in fight for river water," *Akron Beacon Journal*, April 21, 2000.

13. Gregory Korte and Julie Wallace, "Courts to decide who owns Cuyahoga River," *Akron Beacon Journal*, January 8, 2001.

14. John C. Kuehner, "Akron lands in court in fight about water," [Cleveland] *Plain Dealer*, January 9, 2001.

15. *Portage County Board of Commissioners v. Akron*, 156 Ohio App. 3d 657, 2004—Ohio—1665 (11th Dist., Portage). Case No. 98 CV00325, appeals court summary (Ohio Court of Appeals, 11th Dist., March 31, 2004), 667.

16. Korte, "1911 deed rejected in court."

17. Paula Schleis, "Akron case holds water, judge says; city keeps control of Lake Rockwell dam, though recreation will be allowed," *Akron Beacon Journal*, October 10, 2001.

18. *Portage County Board of Commissioners, et al., v. City of Akron, et al.*, Case No. 98 CV 0325, "Findings of Fact and Conclusions of Law" (Judge John A. Enlow, Portage County [Ohio] Court of Common Pleas, October 9, 2001), 17–19.

19. John C. Kuehner, "Court backs Akron claim on river water," [Cleveland] *Plain Dealer*, October 10, 2001.

20. Mike Sever, "Rights to Cuyahoga water argued; Portage County, Ravenna, Akron in appeals court," [Ravenna, OH] *Record-Courier*, December 12, 2003.

21. *Portage County Board of Commissioners v. Akron*, 156 Ohio App. 3d 657, 2004-Ohio-1665 (11th Dist., Portage).

22. Mike Sever, "Court: Set Rockwell flow; deny public access to lake," [Ravenna, OH] *Record-Courier*, April 1, 2004.

23. According to the court, that flow was meant to consist of 5 mgd

that Akron would release from the reservoir daily, as well as an additional amount of leakage (through the dam) and seepage (from the ground underneath the reservoir). Akron shrugged off the 5 mgd release requirement, saying that it had been releasing that much water voluntarily for years.

24. *Portage County Board of Commissioners v. Akron,* _Ohio St. 3d _, 2006-Ohio-954, p. 33. This is the manuscript version of the Ohio Supreme Court's ruling available as of this writing.

25. "Ruling regionally, the Ohio Supreme Court declares an end to the water war. The winners? Akron and its neighbors," *Akron Beacon Journal*, March 8, 2006.

26. Letter from Leonard P. Black, Division of Water, Ohio Department of Natural Resources, to author, February 28, 2005, in response to request for information regarding Akron's diversion.

Chapter 11. The Nova Group and Annex 2001

1. International Joint Commission (IJC), "*Protection of the Waters of the Great Lakes: Final Report to the Governments of Canada and the United States,*" (February 22, 2000), 6, 43.

2. Ibid., 16, 17.

3. Ibid., 22, 46–48.

4. James S. Lochhead et al., *Report to the Council of the Great Lakes Governors, Governing the Withdrawal of Water from the Great Lakes* (May 18, 1999), 44.

5. Ibid., 2.

6. Quotations and arguments from ibid., 15–19.

7. Quotations and arguments from ibid., 19–20.

8. Quotations and arguments from ibid., 20.

9. Quotations and arguments from ibid., 22, 21.

10. For Lochhead's discussion of the public trust and riparian reasonable use doctrines, see ibid., 34, 37.

11. Ibid., 42, 43.

12. Ibid., 44.

13. Ibid., 47–49.

14. James S. Lochhead, "The Benefit Standard," memo to the Council of Great Lakes Governors, September 1, 1999. 1–2.

15. Ibid., 2, 10.

16. Cheryl Mendoza, quoted in Lake Michigan Federation [now called the Alliance for the Great Lakes], "Act Now to Protect Great Lakes Water," *The Lake Effect* (Fall 2004), 1.

17. For all Annex 2001 quotations and directives, see Council of Great Lakes Governors, *The Great Lakes Charter Annex: A Supplementary Agreement to the Great Lakes Charter* (June 18, 2001).

18. Council of Great Lakes Governors, "Great Lakes governors and premiers sign Charter Annex," press release, June 18, 2001.

Chapter 12. Marching toward a Compact

1. By the time of the post–Annex 2001 negotiations, the Canadians had already passed their federal and provincial anti-diversion laws, rendering Great Lakes protections more stringent on the Canadian side of the border.

2. Quoted in Dan Egan, "Diversion rules face rough waters to gain approval, Great Lakes hearing draws 100 in Chicago," *Milwaukee Journal Sentinel*, September 8, 2004.

3. The companion, nonbinding International Agreement was released at the same time.

4. Council of Great Lakes Governors, "Great Lakes Basin Water Resources Compact," draft, July 19, 2004, 7, 14.

5. Ibid., 7, 14, 15.

6. Ibid., 3.

7. "Great Lakes pact opposed," Associated Press, September 15, 2004.

8. "Ominous silence on Great Lakes," *Toronto Star*, October 19, 2004; and Debra Black, "Plan for Great Lakes may kill them, critics say: Bilateral Accord aims to preserve—opponents claim it's a U.S. water grab," *Toronto Star*, September 21, 2004.

9. For quotations from the Munk Centre paper, see Andrew Nikiforuk, "Political Diversions: Annex 2001 and the Future of the Great Lakes" (Munk Centre for International Studies, Program on Water Issues, University of Toronto, June 2004), 3, 4, 6.

10. Chris Wood, "Melting point, how global warming will melt our glaciers, empty the Great Lakes, force Canada to divert rivers, build dams, and, yes, sell water to the United States," *The Walrus*, October 2005, 44.

11. See Genaro C. Armas, "Population: 281,421,906," Associated Press, December 29, 2000.

12. Ontario Ministry of Natural Resources, "Level of protection in draft Great Lakes Charter Annex Agreements not high enough; changes needed before Ontario will sign," press release, November 15, 2004.

13. "Are the Great Lakes for sale? An inside look at the controversial proposal to export water from our precious resource," *Time*, Canadian edition, December 6, 2004.

14. Final proceedings of the Great Lakes Annex 2001 strategy meeting, Wingspread Conference Center, February 22–23, 2005, prepared by Hajo Versteeg (facilitator) and Joanna Kidd (recorder), 11.

15. If a new or increased intra-Basin diversion was less than 100,000 gallons per day, averaged over a ninety-day period, then it was subject to the management and control of the local jurisdiction where the diversion took place.

16. James Lochhead could not be reached for comment.

17. Michigan was a notable exception to this trend, receiving more comments during 2005 than in 2004.

18. Gary Wisby, "Great Lakes states seek lock on water," *Chicago Sun-Times*, November 18, 2005.

19. Rick Lyman, "Focus on Indiana's governor, a tax-cutter who has become a tax-raiser," *The New York Times*, February 20, 2005.

20. See Governor Daniels's biography at the Indiana state government's Web site, http://www.in.gov/gov/bio/index.html.

21. Interview with Tony Earl, former governor of Wisconsin, October 2005.

22. According to law professor Noah Hall, "In the Great Lakes region, 100,000 gallons is enough water to supply approximately 158 typical households." Noah Hall, "Toward a New Horizontal Federalism: Interstate Water Management in the Great Lakes Region," *University of Colorado Law Review* 77 (2006): 440n195.

23. Groundwater is defined as part of the Great Lakes as long as it lies within the boundaries of the surface water watershed.

24. The Compact stipulated the formation of the Compact Council, a committee responsible for reviewing regional water decisions. Technically, the eight Basin governors should sit on the council, but the Compact conceded that governors could assign their seats to staff members or agency officials.

25. Governors Doyle and Taft were cochairs of the Council of Great Lakes Governors at the time and arguably had to be at the signing ceremony, so to his credit Premier McGuinty was the only top official to make a statement through his attendance.

26. Governor Taft, statement read at a press conference following the Annex Implementing Agreements signing ceremony, Milwaukee, Wisconsin, December 13, 2005.

Chapter 13. Waukesha Worries

1. Unless othersise noted, details about Waukesha's midnight stand-off in 1892 are from David P. McDaniel, "Spring City and the Water War of 1892," *Wisconsin Magazine of History*, Autumn 2005, 28–39.

2. Libby Hill, *The Chicago River: A Natural and Unnatural History* (Chicago: Lake Claremont Press, 2000), 116.

3. McDaniel, "Spring City and the Water War of 1892," 28–39. Chicago entrepreneurs did eventually serve "Waukesha water" at the world's fair. It just happened to come from Waukesha County, not the city itself.

4. John M. Schoenknecht, *The Great Waukesha Springs Era, 1868–1918* (Waukesha, WI: John M. Schoenknecht), 156.

5. These details on the downfall of Waukesha's springs are from an interview with John M. Schoenknecht, author of *The Great Waukesha Springs Era*, September 2005.

6. Some Wisconsin residents also pronounce the town's name "WAU-kee-shaw."

7. Radium contamination was also an issue in Pleasant Prairie, Wisconsin; see chapter 7.

8. While Waukesha had not submitted a formal Great Lakes diversion application, Mayor Carol Lombardi did send a letter to Wisconsin governor Jim Doyle on August 18, 2003, saying that the city was "beginning a process to obtain permission to withdraw 20 million gallons of water per day from Lake Michigan."

9. One consultant was a former official with the Council of Great Lakes Governors. Another served as a consultant for the City of Akron on its diversion case.

10. Aquifers have underground watershed divides similar to those on the surface, although, as Waukesha's case shows, the surface-water divide and the groundwater divide don't always line up vertically in the same place. Research has shown that groundwater pumping in Waukesha County and other parts of southeastern Wisconsin has moved the groundwater divide to the west, away from Lake Michigan. However, the city of Waukesha lies between the surface-water divide and the "presettlement" groundwater divide, that is, the groundwater divide before it was affected by excessive pumping. For more information on the groundwater flow system in Waukesha County, see the U.S. Geological Survey, "Water Resources of Wisconsin," http://wi.water.usgs.gov/glpf/.

Chapter 14. Who Will Win the War?

1. Noah Hall, "Toward a New Horizontal Federalism: Interstate Water Management in the Great Lakes Region," *University of Colorado Law Review* 77 (2006): 422.

2. Governor Jennifer Granholm, State of Michigan, Executive Directive No. 2005-5, May 26, 2005.

Epilogue

1. Rebecca Lameka, *Regional Case Studies: Best Practices for Water Conservation in the Great Lakes–St. Lawrence Region* (Great Lakes Commission, June 18, 2004), 4.

2. Pacific Institute, "U.S. Per Capita Water Use Falls to 1950s Levels," http://www.pacinst.org/press_center/usgs/.

3. Las Vegas Valley Water District Web site, http://www.lvvwd.com/html/ws_rebates.html.

4. Robert Glennon, "Water Scarcity, Marketing, and Privatization," *Texas Law Review* 83, no. 7 (June 2005): 1873.

Index

and Nova Group, 193–97, 266; and
Pleasant Prairie (Wis.), 125–38,
142–43, 146–47, 169; threat of, 10–13,
19–21, 38, 78–79; and Waukesha
(Wis.), 242–47, 248, 247–54,
293nn8,9. *See also* Exporting of water;
Illinois diversion; Long Lac diversion;
Ogoki diversion
Downing, Bob, 181
Doyle, Jim, 238, 261, 292n25, 293n8
Dredging, 49, 53-54, 280n34
Duchniak, Dan, 245–47, 250–54

Earl, Tony, 20, 72, 98, 228, 231
Economics of water, 6–7, 12–13, 39; and
Akron (Ohio), 177–78, 180, 190; in
Aral Sea region, 24, 26; and climate
change, 49, 53; and diversions of
water, 68–69, 124, 281n24; and Lowell
(Ind.), 152; and Nova Group, 195;
and Pleasant Prairie (Wis.), 133
Edgar, Jim, 163
Edstrom, Jeff, 150, 194–95, 225–26
Ehrhardt, Sarah, 220
Elmendorf, Mike, 264
Engler, John, 142–44, 148–53, 159,
161–67, 169–71, 200, 207, 209, 253,
259
Enlow, John, 187
Environmental groups: and benefit
standard, 207–8; and bottled water,
266–67; and The Compact, 218, 221,
223–24, 232–35, 238, 258–59; and
Waukesha (Wis.), 244–45, 249–50,
252; and WRDA, 268–69. *See also*
names of environmental groups
Environment Canada, 54, 117, 119
EPA. *See* U.S. Environmental Protection
Agency
Evans, Kari, 232
Exotic species, 106–9, 160–61, 163, 168
Exporting of water, 193–97, 202–3, 223,
233, 258–59, 265–68. *See also*
Diversions of water

Febbraro, John, 193–96
Federalization, 221–22, 268
Federal subsidies, 11, 157, 159, 167, 169
First Nations (Canada), 12, 121–22

Fluoride, 140, 145, 149
Fulton, Neil, 98

Gard, David, 139, 152–53
GATT (General Agreement on Tariffs
and Trade), 195, 202–3
Gilbert, Reg, 58, 60
Gingrich, Newt, 38
Glantz, Michael, 31, 34
Gleick, Peter, 4–5, 13, 58
Glennon, Robert, 8, 274
Global warming. *See* Climate change
Good, water as a, 202–3, 208, 220–21
Governors. *See* Council of Great Lakes
Governors
GRAND (Great Recycling and Northern
Development) Canal, 60–63, 62,
280n9
Granholm, Jennifer, 266–68
Great Lakes Basin: boundary of (*see*
Boundary of Great Lakes Basin);
diversion anxiety in, 10–12, 65–72,
67, 81, 106; geology of, 13–15, 14, 15;
hydrological cycle of, 13, 14; rankings
of, 15–17, 16; water levels in, 41–44,
43, 48–51, 53–55, 92–93, 99–101, 113,
119–21; water use in, 17–19, 17, 38,
51, 73–74, 104–5, 236
Great Lakes Charter (1985), 60, 72–81,
213, 281–82nn31,33, 283n19; and
Akron (Ohio), 179, 182, 189; and
bottled water, 268; and Illinois
diversion, 97–98; and Lowell (Ind.),
141–44, 151; and Mud Creek (Mich.),
157, 161, 163–64, 165, 169–70; and
Nova Group, 195–96; and Pleasant
Prairie (Wis.), 126, 128, 135. *See also*
Annex 2001
Great Lakes Protection Fund, 198, 231
*Great Lakes–St. Lawrence Basin Water
Resources Compact. See* The Compact
*Great Lakes–St. Lawrence River Basin
Sustainable Water Resources Agreement.
See* International Agreement
Great Lakes United, 60, 162, 181
Gregg, Mike, 157

Hadley Centre Model (U.K.), 45, 48
Hales, David, 131, 134

Ogallala Aquifer, 66, 68–69, 281n24; and *Sporhase v. Nebraska*, 70

Jacobs, Leslie, 186, 190
JEDDS (Joint Economic Development Districts), 177
Johnston, John, 13
Johnston, Michael, 218
Joldasova, Ilia, 28–30

Kazakhstan, 5, *26*, 31, 34
Keiper, Chuck, 188
Kenogami Dam (Ont.), *114*, 116, 122–23
Kenosha (Wis.), 126, 130–32, 135
Kent (Ohio), *176*, 182, 184, 186
Khrushchev, Nikita, 29
Kierans, Tom, 60–61, 63, 280n9
Kling, George, 44, 55
Kuper, George, 234–235, 250, 258, 267
Kyoto Protocol, 55

Lake-effect snow/rain, 49-50
Lake Erie, 15, *15*, *16*, 54, 113, 117, 178, 227
Lake Huron, 15–17, *15*, *16*; and Chicago River reversal, 97; and diversions of water, 61, 78, 227, 281n28; and Mud Creek (Mich.), 156, 160, 166; water levels on, 40–42, *43*, 49, 54, 56, 113, 160, 280nn34,35
Lake Michigan, 15, *15*, *16*; and Chicago River reversal, 85–86, 91, 93–101, 107–8; and diversions of water, 65, 71, 281n28; drinking water from, 85–86, 93–97, 101–5; and Indiana, 231; and Lowell (Ind.), 141–44, 146–47, 150–52; and Pleasant Prairie (Wis.), 125–27, 129–31, 136; water levels on, 41, *43*, 49, 54, 99–101, 113, 280n35; and Waukesha (Wis.), 219, 242–44, 247–53, 293–94nn8,10
Lake Ontario, 15, *15*, 17, 78, 113, 117
Lake Rockwell (Ohio), 175, *176*, 178, 182–83, 185, 187–89, 290n23
Lake Superior, 4, 15, *15*, *16*, 57, 113; and diversions of water, 61, 65–66, 69, 71, 270; and Long Lac/Ogoki diversions, 110–24, *112*, *114*, *118*; and Nova Group, 193–95

LakeView Corporate Park, 130–32, 136
Lanyon, Richard, 85, 96
Lapierre, Louise, 264
Las Vegas (Nev.), 9–10, 152, 255, 270, 274
LeCureux, Jim, 155–57, 165–67
Ledin, Chuck, 128, 135, 138, 244–45, 270
Leffler, Mike, 105–6
Legal precedents, 146, 149–50, 160, 181, 190, 195–96, 244
Leipprandt, Phil, 167–69
Liddle, Timothy, 32
Lochhead, James, 198–99, 201–8, 214, 216, 220, 225, 265, 268, 292n16
Lochhead Report, 201–8, 212, 220, 223, 225, 227, 259, 268–69
Lofgren, Brent, 47, 53
Lokkesmoe, Kent, 166, 233, 261
Lombardi, Carol, 293n8
Long Lac diversion, 113–24, *114*, *118*, 284nn2,3, 285nn5,8,13
Loomis, George, 131–33
Lowell (Ind.), 106, 139–53, 159–64, 169–70, 178–79, 184, 189, 253

MacClennan, Paul, 79
McAvoy, Peter, 72–73, 75, 77
McElroy, James, 240–41
McGlinchy, Michael, 177
McGuinty, Dalton, 222, 238, 271–72, 292n25
McNulty, Tim, 144–45, 147–48, 151
Médecins Sans Frontiéres (MSF), 32–33
Mehan, G. Tracy, 165, 169–170
Mendoza, Cheryl, 208, 250
Mercury, 123
Metering of water, 104–5
Michigan: and Akron (Ohio), 183–84, 189; and Annex 2001, 209–10; and benefit standard, 207; and bottled water, 266–68; and The Compact, 213–14, 219, 225, 227, 232–33, 261–62, 292n17; and Great Lakes Charter (1985), 75–78; and Illinois diversion, 99–100, 104–5; and Kenosha (Wis.), 131; and Lochhead Report, 200; and Lowell (Ind.), 142–43, 145–51, 153, 178; Mud

About Island Press

Island Press is the only nonprofit organization in the United States whose principal purpose is the publication of books on environmental issues and natural resource management. We provide solutions-oriented information to professionals, public officials, business and community leaders, and concerned citizens who are shaping responses to environmental problems.

In 2006, Island Press celebrates its twenty-first anniversary as the leading provider of timely and practical books that take a multidisciplinary approach to critical environmental concerns. Our growing list of titles reflects our commitment to bringing the best of an expanding body of literature to the environmental community throughout North America and the world.

Support for Island Press is provided by the Agua Fund, The Geraldine R. Dodge Foundation, Doris Duke Charitable Foundation, The William and Flora Hewlett Foundation, The Joyce Foundation, Kendeda Sustainability Fund of the Tides Foundation, Forrest C. Lattner Foundation, The Henry Luce Foundation, The John D. and Catherine T. MacArthur Foundation, The Marisla Foundation, The Andrew W. Mellon Foundation, Gordon and Betty Moore Foundation, The Curtis and Edith Munson Foundation, Oak Foundation, The Overbrook Foundation, The David and Lucile Packard Foundation, The Winslow Foundation, and other generous donors.

The opinions expressed in this book are those of the author and do not necessarily reflect the views of these foundations.

THE GREAT LAKES Basin is one of the
largest freshwater ecosystems on earth, and it is also
home to forty million people in the United States and
Canada. How that water is used by—or diverted
from—those people is the story of *The Great Lakes
Water Wars*.

These wars are coming. In the years ahead, a
controversial Great Lakes water management compact
will be considered by the eight state legislatures in the
Great Lakes region as well as by Congress. Will we
divert water from the Great Lakes, causing them to
end up like Asia's Aral Sea, which has lost 90 percent
of its surface area and 75 percent of its volume since
1960? Or will we come to see that unregulated water
withdrawals are ultimately catastrophic? Peter Annin
writes a fast-paced account of the people and stories
behind these upcoming battles. Destined to be the
definitive sourcebook for the general public as well as
policy makers, *The Great Lakes Water Wars* is a balanced, comprehensive look behind the scenes at the
conflicts and compromises that are the past—and
future—of this globally significant freshwater
resource.

10386